It's All Good:

A Cookbook for Friends and Family

Gray Scale Edition

It's All Good:
A Cookbook for Friends and Family

Amelia Landi Lednak

"It's All Good"
A Cookbook for Friends and Family
By Amelia Landi Lednak
AdventureTravelPress.com, Lady Lake, FL 32159
Copyright 2014 Amelia Landi Lednak
All rights reserved. Published 2014

Printed in the United States of America
Color Print: ISBN- 978-1-937630-25-6
Grayscale: ISBN-978-1-937630-24-9
E-book: ISBN- 978-1-937630-26-3

Library of Congress Cataloging
Cookbooks
Library of Congress Control Number:

Author's email: riamled@yahoo.com

Author's Thoughts:

Nothing that I have done gave me the pleasure that I get when I cook or when I paint. The cover is my work in acrylic.

The excitement is putting ingredients or colors together and seeing something spectacular emerge.

I believe that if you love to cook, if it is your passion, a recipe will only be a guide.

If you do not love to cook, if it is not a part of you, then no recipe will help you very much.

I wrote this book for my family and friends who all love to cook. Some of these recipes will only be a guide—there are not amounts—you just let it happen and it is yours.

As a word of advice and a little wisdom, "Always wear an apron when you cook."

It says, "I know what I am doing".

It's All Good.

Amelia Landi Lednak

Introduction:

This is my first and last cookbook. It is a collection of recipes handed down from members of my family, from the region that I grew up in and some from my imagination and experimentation. Like the title of the book, "It's All Good." Not all the recipes will be new to you, but most will be worth trying. Some recipes will not have the exact amounts. Some have been simplified. Feel free to make substitutions. That is always a sign of a good cook.

I have tried in this book to cover many methods and courses of cooking, from antipasto to desserts. I hope you find this book helpful, but there is so much more to learn about cooking. That, my dear family and friends, will be up to you to discover.

Amelia Landi Lednak

Su Henry

Acknowledgements:

In addition to my Grandmother, Amelia De Mao, my mother, Jennie Landi, and to members of my family, who gave me much encouragement and raves about my cooking over the years, I would like to acknowledge the valuable assistance I received from the following people.

Gail Benoit, who stepped up and volunteered to type.

Dianne Knight and Carol Basso, who inspired and tweaked my painting for the cover of my book.

Gordon Ralph, dear friend and publisher, who took me from start to finish of my book.

Su Henry, who without her help this book would never have been finished. She flew from Colorado to Florida and spent many long hours over a computer to see it through to completion. My gratitude and thanks to each of you.

Special thanks and appreciation to Dick Lednak, my husband of 60 years who has washed many dishes, pots and pans so I could keep on cooking.

Thanks to all from Amelia (Amy). Fall, 2014

Our children: Melissa, Richard, and Jeannine. Plus Richard and Amelia

Frank "Dutch" and Jennie Landi

TABLE OF CONTENTS

PAGE   RECIPE

1. APPETIZERS

Page	Recipe
2	Antipasto
	Antipasto Rolls
3	Fritto Misto
4	Smoked Fish Dip
5	Tiki Snack Mix
6	Baba Ganooj
	Pizza Fingers
7	Bride's Fingers
8	Hummus / Chickpea Dip
9	Bruschetta
10	Kibbe Nayye (Raw Kibbe)
11	Crostini
12	Polpettes
13	Bagna Càuda
14	Caponata / Quick & Easy Method
15	Hawaiian Meatballs
	Stuffed Pepperoncini
16	Tiropetes
17	Italian Rice Balls
	Rice Balls -- Croquettes
18	Pizza Rustica
19	Swiss Cheese Spread
	Pineapple Cheese Ball
20	Appetizer Holiday Pie
	Hot Jalapeño Pepper Cheese Ball
21	Parmesan Onion Canapes
	Coral Sea Shells
22	Shrimp Stuffed Endive
	Shrimp Toast - Chinese
23	Millionaire Chicken
	Shrimp Appetizers
24	Chocolate Covered Bacon
	Spinach Balls
25	Sauerkraut Balls
	Okeechobee Caviar
26	Blue Cheese Walnut Toast
	Hot Sausage Hors D'oeuvres
	Toasted Sausage & Horseradish
	Two Savory Cheesecakes:
27	Three-Layer Cheesecake

28	Spinach-Herb Cheesecake
29	Stuffed Mushrooms:

                    Crab Stuffing
                    Sausage Stuffing
                    Mushroom Stuffing

- 30 Crispy Parmesan Chickpeas
- 31 French Fried Cheese
- 32 New Potatoes W/Smoked Salmon
      Cherry Tomatoes W/Pesto Tuna
- 33 Fried Calamari
- 34 Caramelized Onions & Apple Cream Cheese Spread
- 35 Pimento Cheese Deviled Eggs
- 36 Bacon-Wrapped Figs
      Cucumber Cups

2. BREADS & BREAKFAST

- 38 The Perfect Fried Egg
- 39 Perfect Hard Boiled Eggs
      Perfect Soft Boiled Eggs
- 40 Perfect Scrambled Eggs
- 41 Scotch Eggs
- 42 Biscuits & Gravy
- 44 Ice Cream Bread
- 45 Gorilla Bread
- 46 Butterscotch Pudding Monkey Bread
- 47 New Orleans Bread Pudding
            With Bourbon Sauce
- 48 Krispy Cream Bread Pudding
- 49 Mexican Cornbread
- 50 Browned Butter & Sour Cream Cornbread
- 51 Artisan Bread
- 52 Tuscan Bread
- 53 Sharon's Pizza Bread
- 54 Old-Fashioned Crackling Bread
- 55 Easy Holiday Breakfast Bake
      Loaf Blintz
- 56 Italian Breakfast Strata
- 57 Peaches & Cream French Toast
- 58 Italian Easter Bread
- 60 Nut Bread
      Lemon Bread
- 61 Breakfast Rolls
      Sausage Hash Browns & Eggs

62	Stuffed Picnic Loaf
63	Cheesy Jalapeño Pull Bread
64	Baked Italian Sandwich Loaf

3. SOUPS, ZUPPA, AND MINESTRONE

67	Bare Butt Skiers Soup
68	Minestrone
69	Italian Wedding Soup
70	Spasatini / Spezzatino / Veal Stew
71	Mexican Alphabet Soup / Sopa de Letras
72	Chicken & Dumplings Soup
73	Cheddar Cheese & Beer Soup
	Italian Sausage Soup
74	Cincinnati Chili
75	Lentil Soup
	Lentil, Potato & Broccoli Soup
76	Mushroom Soup
77	Potato Soup
	Potato Soup – The Way **I** Like It!!
78	Seafood Gumbo
	Stuffed Pepper Soup
	Tangy Beef Stew
79	Texas Chili: Texas Red & a Longneck
80	Pasta E Fagioli (Beans & Macaroni)
81	Hearty Pasta E Fagioli Soup
82	Weight Loss Magic Soup
83	Artichoke Soup
84	Dried Bean Soup
86	Split Pea Soup
87	Black Bean Soup
88	Easy Lentil Chili
89	Barley, Split Pea & Ham Hock Soup

4. SAUCES, PASTA, POLENTA, RICE, and BEANS

92	Pasta
94	The Aunt's Book Of Sauces
104	Hand-Made Pasta
105	My Spaghetti Sauce
106	Rotolo di Pasta
108	Amalfi Calamari Pasta
109	Pasta With Crab
	Pasta With Shrimp Scampi

110	Broccoli & Scallops With Linguine
111	Bucatini With Toasted Bread Crumbs
112	Fettuccine Alfredo
113	Baked Linguine
114	Spaghetti With Haricots Verts, Shrimp & Scallops
115	Pesto
	Mostaccioli With Tomato Pesto
116	Pesto with Potatoes, Pasta, & Green Beans
117	Spaghetti With Tuna & Lemon
	Pasta With Pasta Water Sauce
118	Linguine With Mozzarella, Egg & Capocollo
119	Pasta For A Crowd
120	Spaghetti Alla Carbonara
121	Spaghetti With Anchovies
	Spaghettini Aglio-Olio
122	Lasagna (Meat)
123	Seafood Lasagna
124	Quick & Easy Seafood Lasagna
125	Seafood Fra Diavolo
126	Clam Sauce: White & Red
127	Manicotti
128	1957 Newspaper Article
129	Text From 1957 Newspaper Article:
130	Linguine With Toasted Almonds & Jalapeños
131	Gnocchi: Potato Gnocchi
132	Ricotta Gnocchi
133	Ravioli Dough & Fillings
134	Polenta
135	Risotto
137	Polenta With Game
138	Not Your Every Day Sunday Pasta Sauce
139	Bar-B-Q Baked Beans
140	White Beans With Rosemary & Vinegar
141	Rice With Pork From Puerto Rico
142	Pasta With Sausage & Butternut Squash
143	Pasta With Tomato Cream Sauce
144	Spaghetti With Fresh Clams, Parsley, & Lemon
145	Easy Paella
147	Rice & Lentils
148	Lamb Ragu Sauce

5. MEATS: BEEF, HICKEN, GOAT, PORK, and VEAL

150	Italian Roast Beef

151	Giardiniera For Italian Roast Beef
152	Easy Beef
	Roast Beef Bar-B-Ques
	Beef In Beer
153	Barbecups
154	Sharon's Meatloaf
155	Meatloaf With Mushrooms
156	Coca-Cola Meatloaf
	Coca-Cola Glaze
157	Beef Burgundy
158	Green Chili Burgers
	Beef Alla Certosina
159	The Best Bar-B-Q-Ribs
160	Round Steak Parmesan
161	Chicken Kiev
162	Roasted Italian Chicken
163	Chicken With Potatoes, Sausage & Vinegar
164	Chicken Cacciatore
165	Shredded Bar-B-Q Chicken
	Chinese Chicken Casserole
166	Colonel Sanders Chicken
	Bruschetta Chicken
167	Clark's Barbecued Chicken
168	Oven-Fried Chicken
	Fried & Roasted Chicken
169	Chicken With Rice: "Funeral Chicken"
	Crispy Breaded & Baked Chicken Wings
170	Chicken Wings
	Restaurant-Style Buffalo Chicken Wings
171	Chicken With 40 Cloves Of Garlic
172	Mojo-Marinated Chicken
173	Salsa Couscous Chicken
174	Chicken Casa Amelia
	Pretzel-Crusted Chicken
175	Chicken Liver Pate
	Quick & Easy Pate
177	African Goat Stew – By Way Of Colorado
178	Curried Goat
179	Porchetta
180	City Chicken
181	Pork Chop Casserole
	Italian Sausage & Peppers
182	Ham: Easter, Christmas, or Any Time
	Maple-Bourbon Glazed Ham

183 Scaloppini Saltimbocca Roman Style
184 Stupid-Simple Roast Beef With Horseradish Cream
185 Southern Fried Chicken
186 Standing Rib Roast

6. SEAFOOD & FISH

188 Caledonia Fish
189 Fish Poached In Galliano Butter
      Fish Fillets With Spinach & Mushrooms
190 Fish Chowder
191 Rolled Stuffed Fish
      Baked Salmon With Creole Mustard Sauce
192 Fried Oysters With Panko
      Pan-Fried Oysters
      Crispy Oven-Fried Oysters
193 Jalapeño Mayonnaise
      Fried Calamari
      Mussels & Bread Crumbs
194 Panko-Crusted Crab Cake Bites With Roasted Pepper
195 Grouper With Lemon-Caper Butter
      Shrimp With Anchovy-Caper Butter
196 Fish & Pasta Pinwheels
197 Maryland Crab Cakes
      Remoulade Sauce
198 Shrimp In Ginger Butter Sauce

7. VEGETABLES

200 Eggplant Parmigiana
201 Ratatouille
202 Broccoli Or Squash Casserole
      Broccoli-Corn Bake
203 Broccoli Supreme
      Cauliflower In Vinaigrette
204 Broccoli, With Pine Nuts, Garlic, & Raisins
205 Marinated Carrots
      Creamed Stewed Tomatoes
206 Corn Pudding
207 Clam Stuffed Eggplant
      Eggplant & Oysters
208 Cubanelles Mom's Italian Stuffed Peppers
209 Fried Zucchini Squash
      Green Bean Bake

	Hash Brown Casserole Potatoes
210	Italian Country Beans
	Kluski And Cabbage
211	Mom's Holiday Greens
212	Rosemary's "Streamlined" Greens
213	Stuffed Escarole
214	"Sleek" - Spinach With Burghul
	Tater Tot Casserole
215	Stuffed Artichokes: Carciofi alla Romana
216	Sweet Potato Soufflé
	Veg-All Casserole
217	Italian Potatoes
	Mashed Potato Bake
218	Scalloped Potatoes With Artichokes

8. SALADS

220	Dutch & Jennie's Tomato Salad From The Garden
221	Perfect Pasta Salad Toss
	No-Toss Layered Salad
222	Blueberry Slaw With Raspberry Dressing
223	Cold Asian Noodle Salad
224	Molded Chicken Salad
225	Heavenly Hash Fruit Salad
	Easy Caesar Salad
226	Tabouli Salad
	Panzanella - Italian Bread Salad
227	Sangria Salad
	Aunt Ella's Salad
228	Bean & Little Pea Salad
	Baccala Salad
229	Calico Potato Salad Loaf
	Cauliflower In Vinaigrette
230	Chicken Salads
	Hot Chicken Salad
	Chinese Chicken Salad
231	Cole Slaw With Clear Dressing
	Confetti Sweet & Sour Slaw
232	Special Cole Slaw
	Three Cabbage Salad
233	Cooked Vegetable Salad
	Creamy Waldorf Salad
234	Cucumbers With Oregano, Feta & Pine Nuts
	Cucumber Salad

235	Grilled Romaine
	Insalata Di Potate
236	Macaroni Salads:
	Plain Macaroni Salad
	Macaroni Salad Plus
	Macaroni Salad With Shrimp
237	Pasta, Beans & Vegetable Salad
	Papaya, Jícama & Avocado Salad
238	Scungilli Salad
	Broccoli Salad

9. CANDY, DESSERTS, & PIES

240	Mary Lester's Peach Cobbler
241	Pie Crust
242	Apple Pie
243	Easy Skillet Apple Pie
244	Mock Apple Pie
	Norwegian Pie
245	No-Bake Turtle Pumpkin Pie
	Easy To Make Pie
246	Peaches & Cream Supreme Pie
247	Strawberry Glaze Pie
	Fruit Struesel Pie
248	Easter Rice Pie
250	Delicious Cake Bites
	Birthday Cake Bites
251	Pumpkin Pita (Pumpkin Sheet Pie)
252	Candy Easter Eggs
	Fridge Nut Easter Eggs
253	Quick Bittersweet Chocolate Mousse
	Make Ahead Chocolate Mousse
254	Zeppole St. Joseph's Day Cream Puffs
	Filling #1: Ricotta
	Filling #2: Cream
256	Pine Bark Candy
	Kentucky Kernels
257	Lemon Meringue Pie with Fresh Lemons
258	Banana Split Dessert
	Pretzel Salad Dessert
259	Fresh Fruit Tart Dessert
260	Truffles:
	Chocolate Truffles
	Oreo Truffles

261	Cream Cheese Basic Truffles
	Oreo Cream Cheese Balls*
262	Tequila-Spiked Caramel Corn
263	Melon Carpaccio With Lime
	Fruit With Lime Juice & Rum
264	Richard Iii Homemade Ice Cream

10. CAKES

266	Tiramisu Cake
267	Chocolate Caramel Poke Cake
268	Pineapple Poke Bundt Cake
	Heavenly Pineapple Cake
269	White Texas Cake
	Texas Cake - Chocolate
270	Cookie Sheet Cake With Pie Filling Topping
	Aunt Maddy's Almond Pound Cake
271	Peanut Butter Sheet Cake
272	Fresh Apple Cake With Choice Of 2 Frostings
273	Coconut Cake
274	Icebox Cake With Orange Caramel Cream
275	Oreo Icebox Cake
	Box Cake Delight
276	Layered Chocolate Cake & Peanut Butter Cheesecake
279	Zuppa Inglese
281	Olive Oil Cake
282	Ginger Carrot Cake
283	Pumpkin Surprise Cake
284	Pumpkin Gooey Butter Cake
285	Praline Pumpkin Cheese Cake
286	Black-Bottom Pecan Cheesecake
287	Cheesecake
288	Chocolate Éclair Cake
	Chop Suey Cake
289	Cream Puff Cake
	Creamy Southern Pound Cake
290	Deer Cake: Spicy Raisin Sausage Cake
291	Fruit Cake
	Halloween Cake
292	Italian Love Cake
	Holiday Rum Cake
293	Key Lime Cake
294	Ladies Club Cake
	Lemon Layer Cake

295	Mandarin Orange Cake
	Maple Cheesecake W/Roasted Pears
296	Merk's Coffee Cake
	Neiman Marcus Cake
297	Noodle Cheese Cake
	Orange Coconut Cake
298	Orange Cream Cake
299	Overnight Coffee Cake
300	Pineapple Upside Down Cake
301	Easy Caramel Cake
302	Tres Leches Cake
303	Dulce De Leche Cheesecake
304	Boston Cream Pie
305	Boston Cream Pie: Fast & Easy
306	Dirt Cake
307	Mom's Date & Nut Cake
308	Best Vanilla Frosting
	Chocolate Buttercream

11. COOKIES

310	Large Nut Rolls
311	Kolacky - Rozky: Small Nut Rolls
312	Amy's Traditional Italian Almond Biscotti
313	Mom's Biscotti – Jennie Landi
	Almond Biscotti – Aunt Maddy's
314	Biscotti – Mary Guercione
	Biscotti Ai Cereali: Italian Snowflake Cookies
315	Mocha Cappuccino Butterscotch Biscotti
316	Apricot Horns
317	Beer Cookies
	Pineapple Filled Lemon Cookies
318	Caramel Marshmallow Ball Cookies
	Easy Filled Drop Cookies
319	Knot Cookies
320	Torta Secca Cookies
321	Struffoli - Honey Balls
322	Macaroons:
	Very Light Coconut Macaroons
	Toasted Coconut Macaroons
323	Ricotta Cookies
324	Sesame Cookies
325	Pinwheel Cookies
326	Florentine Lace Cookies

327	Bernadine
	Date Balls
	Double Chocolate Cookies
328	Death By Chocolate Cookie
	Dreamsicle Cookies
329	Fruit Layer Squares
	Flourless Peanut Butter Cookies
330	Fudge Filled Peanut Butter Bars
	Praline Toffee Thins
331	Hungarian Peach Bars
332	Pine Nut Cookies
	Snowballs

12. WITH A LITTLE HELP FROM MY FRIENDS

334	***M.J. Amodeo***
	Oyster Stew
	Scalloped Potatoes
335	***Carol Basso***
	German Meat Balls
	Cucumber Sandwiches
	Carol's Shrimp Dip
	Carol's Potatoes
	Nantucket Cranberry Pie
337	***Joanne Bateman***
	Ohio Bean Casserole
337	***Gail Benoit***
	Gail's Apple Spice Cake
	Caramel Frosting
339	***"Lady Jean" - Jean Blome***
	Velveeta Fudge
340	***Noreen Cherry & Genette Heinz***
	Grandma Nora Regan's Irish Soda Bread
341	***Linda Degood***
	Beef Jerky
342	***Mary Dodsworth***
	Clams Casino Dip

        Mushroom Dip
        Hot Artichoke & Spinach Dip
        Chicken Wing Dip

344   *Jenna Dodsworth*
      Jenna's Cucumber Salad

345   *Emily Emigh*
      Red Candy Cinnamon Apple Slices

345   *Rob Emigh*
      Long Island Iced Tea

346   *Mary Ann Fisher*
      Dream Cheesecake

346   *Doe Pinfold*
      Freezer Pastry

347   *Karen Guarin*
      Beef Bar-B-Q

347   *Kelley Kaufman*
      Honeyed Carrots
      Hot Fruit Casserole
      Apple Glazed Rib Lamb Chops

349   *Dianne Knight*
      Baltimore Crab Cakes
      Cran-Orange Relish
      Million Dollar Pound Cake

350   *Kathy Lyle*
      Pineapple Casserole

350   *Rita Mappin*
      Oven Baked Pecan-Crusted Chicken Fingers

352   *Sheila Mydock*
      Pirogi

353   *Lynn Neeter*
      Better Than Cookies Chocolate Bark
      Pasta To-Go

354 *Linda Paolillo*
Chocolate Bittersweets

355 *Jacquie Ralph*
Brisket

356 *Gordon And "Toby" Ralph*
Cranbery Relish Special

357 *Jill Holland Rustici*
Dates Wrapped In Bacon
Oriental Noodles

358 *Vera Swiergol*
Lasagna Sandwich

359 *Mary Ann Swiergol*
Serbian Torte Cake

360 *Ed Wright*
Trinidadian-Style Chicken
Pickled Topping
Plantain Gratin
Salsa Couscous Chicken
Cabbage Salad

363 *M.J. Wright*
Mandarin Orange Dessert

13. BEVERAGES

366 Argentinean Margarita
Supper Club Bloody Mary Mix
      Bloody Mary Bar Add Ins
Peach Bellini Punch

APPETIZERS

Hors d'oeuvres - French
Pronounced "or dervs" in English
Antipasto - Italian

Antipasto means "before the pasta". At daily meals antipasti are simple. A slice of salami served with ripe fruit, such as cantaloupe, figs, or grapes. When entertaining or dining out, they become more complex but never overpowering.

Antipasto

Fritto Misto

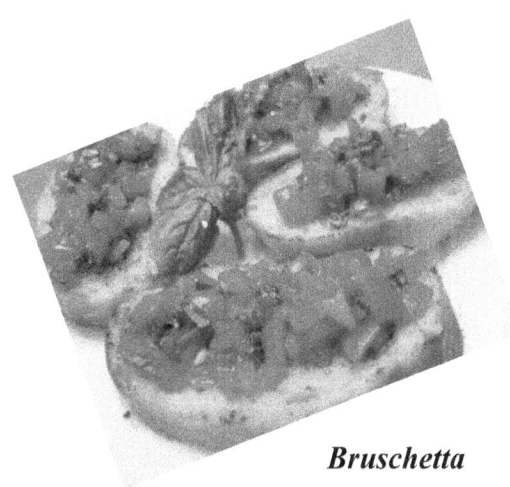
Bruschetta

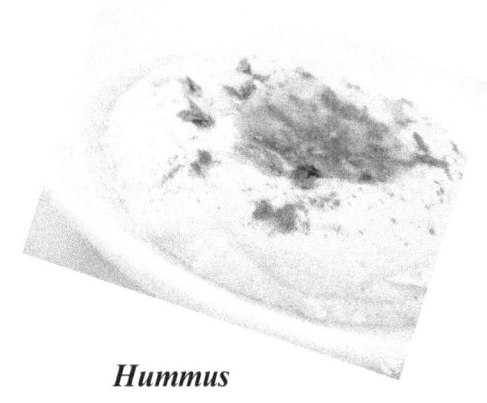
Hummus

ANTIPASTO

    4-6 oz. prosciutto   Radishes
    4-6 oz. capocollo   Black & green olives
    4-6 oz. boiled ham   Artichoke hearts
    4-6 oz. mortadella   Green onions
    4-6 oz. salami
    4-6 oz. soppressata

All meats should be sliced thin and arranged attractively on a large platter. Garnish with radishes, olives, artichoke hearts, and green onions. Makes 6-8 servings. Any combination of meat, marinated vegetables, fresh fruit, and cheese can be used.

ANTIPASTO ROLLS

    Large round slices of salami   ¼ C mayonnaise
    Large round slices of mozzarella   1 hardboiled egg, chopped
    1 can of tuna   1 tsp. lemon juice

Mix together tuna, mayo, egg, and lemon juice. Stack one slice of salami, one slice of mozzarella, and spread enough tuna salad to cover it. Roll it up, and use toothpicks to secure if needed. Wrap each in wax paper and chill. Slice in half or thirds to serve. Can be made ahead because it also freezes well.

FRITTO MISTO

This is a classic Italian dish that can consist of vegetables, meats, croquettes, or seafood. It can be served as an antipasto or a main dish, each food group piled separately on a platter with parsley and lemon wedges. I like to do each food separately. This recipe is *fritto misto* with vegetables.

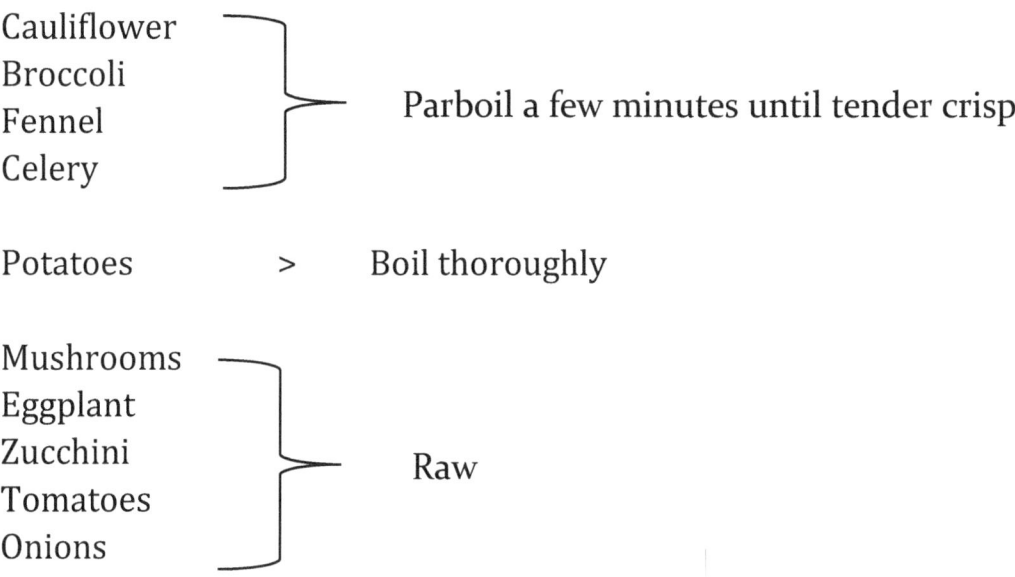

Cauliflower, Broccoli, Fennel, Celery — Parboil a few minutes until tender crisp

Potatoes > Boil thoroughly

Mushrooms, Eggplant, Zucchini, Tomatoes, Onions — Raw

Coat the vegetables with frying batter and fry crisp and golden in olive oil. Drain on paper towel and serve.

FRYING BATTER:
- ½ C flour
- ½ tsp. salt
- 2 T olive oil
- ½ C warm water (a little more if needed)
- 1 white of one egg

Sift flour and salt into a bowl. Stir in oil and water forming a smooth fairly stiff batter. Beat well and refrigerate for one hour. Just before using, beat egg white and fold gently into batter. Batter can be increased as needed.

SMOKED FISH DIP

Prep. Time: 5-10 minutes. Chilling time: 1 hour. Makes 3 ½ cups.

    ½ lb. any smoked fish   2 tsp. minced onion
    1 C sour cream   ½ tsp. salt & pepper, or to taste
    2 T lemon juice   ¼ tsp. dried rosemary
    2 tsp. chopped chives   parsley for garnish

Flake fish. Combine all ingredients except parsley. Mix well. Chill at least one hour before serving.

* This makes good deviled eggs when mixed with the yolks of hard boiled eggs.

** If you cut the eggs horizontally and remove a small slice of the white from each end so they stand, they look like little cups. A trick I learned when my daughter-in-law Sharon Lednak took me to a cooking school as a Christmas gift. It was wonderful.

TIKI SNACK MIX

8 thick slices of meaty bacon
3 C salted roasted peanuts
4 candied pineapple rings cut into 1/3 inch triangles
2 T sesame seeds
1 T low-sodium soy sauce
1 T honey
¼ tsp. cayenne pepper
Kosher salt

Preheat oven to 350°. Arrange bacon in a single layer on a rack set over a rimmed baking sheet. Bake about 30 minutes until bacon is crisp. Drain on paper towels and cut crosswise into 1/2 inch strips. In a bowl, toss the bacon strips with all remaining ingredients except salt. Bake for 20 minutes, stirring once, until bacon is browned. Season with salt and let cool, stirring occasionally.

* This is very different and very good.

Tiki Snack

BABA GANOOJ

(Pronounced "baba ganoosh")

1 large eggplant
Lemon juice to taste
2 large garlic cloves, crushed
½ tsp. salt
3 T tahini (sesame paste)
Parsley, chopped

Poke eggplant with fork and bake in 350° oven until soft. Scoop out pulp and drain in colander for several hours. Add lemon juice, garlic, salt, and tahini to eggplant pulp. Mix and mash together. After it cools, drizzle a little olive oil over it and sprinkle with chopped parsley. Serve with small pieces of Syrian break (pita) as a dip. Everyone just dips in with their bread.

PIZZA FINGERS

½ lb. salami or pepperoni
½ lb. brick cheese
1 large green pepper
1 small can tomato paste
Melted butter

2 large loaves sandwich bread (white, sliced)
1 T Italian seasoning
Grated Romano or Parmesan

Put meat, cheese, and green pepper in food processor. Process until smooth. Add seasoning and tomato paste and mix well in processor. Cut crust from sliced bread and roll each slice thin with rolling pin. Spread with meat mixture and sprinkle with grated cheese. Roll each slice like a jelly roll. Refrigerate or freeze until ready to use. Before serving, brush each roll with melted butter and place on well-greased cookie sheet. Bake at 375° for 15-20 minutes. Makes about 48.

BRIDE'S FINGERS

1 lb. phyllo dough *
1 lb. rendered butter **

STUFFING:
½ lb. beef or lamb, ground
1 small onion chopped
½ C pine nuts
Salt & pepper to taste

> To make stuffing, combine all ingredients in a frying pan and sauté until meat is cooked and onions are transparent.

To assemble fingers:
Lay 2 layers of dough flat and cut into 6-inch squares. Put a tablespoon of stuffing onto the bottom of squares and roll into a cigar shape, tucking in the sides as you roll to enclose the stuffing. Place on well-buttered baking sheet and brush generously with melted rendered butter. Bake at 350° until lightly golden, about 8-10 minutes. Serve with yogurt.

* Keep phyllo between damp cloth while working.

** Rendered butter is also known as ghee, drawn butter, or clarified butter.

To make rendered or clarified butter:
Heat butter in a sauce pan. The butter breaks down into 3 layers. Top layer will be foam. Use a large spoon to remove foam and discard. The milk solids will settle on the bottom. Remove from heat and pour off clear butter into a container with a lid. (Cook it a little longer if you want a nutty flavor to the butter.) Discard milk solids. Butter will keep several months in a container with a lid. Keep refrigerated. You will lose about 25% of the butter you start with.

HUMMUS / CHICKPEA DIP

2 C chickpeas
½ C tahini (sesame paste)
Juice of 2 lemons
2 cloves garlic, crushed

¼ C olive oil
¼ tsp. salt
Parsley
* 2 tsp. cumin and/or coriander

Drain chickpeas, reserving liquid. Blend in food processor. Blend tahini with a small amount of reserved liquid and salt. Add crushed garlic and half the olive oil. Add all the chickpeas and blend. If mixture is too thick, add more reserved liquid. Garnish with parsley and remaining olive oil.

* Can be added if you like.

** The new thing is to add anything you like. For example:
Roasted peppers, roasted carrots, basil and lemon, Kalamata olives, spinach, parsley, salsa. I have even seen fruit added.

*** Hummus comes out the best if you use my secret. It is all in the order you put the ingredients in the processor!
First put in the tahini & lemon juice. Process really well, then add the other ingredients with reserved liquid as needed.

BRUSCHETTA

This recipe is so easy, I almost forgot to include it. It is very basic, but there are hundreds of variations. To make bruschetta, you need Italian bread, olive oil, garlic, and a topping of your choice.

    Slice bread about ½ inch thick.
    Fry the bread lightly on both sides. *
    Rub one side with cut garlic.

In a bowl: seed and chop tomatoes. Add some chopped basil, cracked black pepper, salt to taste, and add a drizzle of olive oil. **

Spoon onto bread.

* The bread can be grilled or toasted in the oven on a tray with some olive oil.

** To this tomato base you can add chopped green peppers, chopped black olives, etc.

*** Or ... Spread the toasted bread with ricotta cheese and roasted garlic. Drizzle with honey or sliced Italian meats and sliced tomatoes.

**** Also ... See Blue Cheese Walnut Toast. It is one of my favorites.

KIBBE NAYYE (Raw kibbe)

Prounounced "ki-bee nay"

2 lb. ground lamb or beef *
1 ½ C fine wheat (bulgar)
1 large onion, chopped
Allspice to taste

Salt & pepper to taste
½ C cold water
Good olive oil & butter (melted)
Mint

Rinse wheat then cover with enough water to cover wheat. Soak 30 minutes to 1 hour to soften. While wheat is soaking, put meat and onion in food processor. Add salt, pepper, and allspice. Remove from processor. Knead with hands adding olive oil and cold water as needed if too dry. Refrigerate. Allow to rest. Knead again. Adjust seasoning.

To serve:
Shape kibbee on a serving dish. Make indentations with the back of a spoon. Drizzle on a little rendered butter. **

* I like using lamb and I shape the kibbee into small balls piled on one another on a platter. This way I add the melted butter to the meat as I knead.

** See Bride's Fingers for instructions to make rendered butter.

CROSTINI *
Italian Chicken Liver Paste

1 lb. chicken livers	¼ - ½ lb. butter
½ lb. chicken giblets	2 T tomato paste
3-4 cloves garlic	½ - 1 tsp. sage
1 small onion finely chopped	2-4 T capers, chopped
Salt & pepper to taste	Anchovies: 3-4 small ones, or to taste
2-3 T chopped parsley	Toasted Italian bread

Simmer giblets until tender. Drain and save some of the water. Chop giblets. Melt butter in skillet. When butter foams, add giblets and onion. Sauté over medium heat until golden. Add chicken livers. Sauté 3-5 minutes or until lightly browned. Add tomato paste and a little water from the giblets. Cook 2-3 minutes. Blend in food processor. Add sage, parsley, anchovy fillets, and capers. Turn processor on and off a few times. Spread on Italian bread which has been toasted golden brown on both sides.

* This is an old recipe given to me by my mother, Jennie Landi. She always made it for New Year's Eve.

POLPETTES
Neapolitan Meat Cakes

1 lb. ground beef
¼ lb. ground pork
¼ lb. ground veal
2 T parsley, minced
2-3 T toasted pine nuts, chopped

½ C bread crumbs
Salt & pepper
3-4 T raisins
2 eggs, beaten
2-3 cloves garlic, minced

Mix beef, pork, and veal together. Add parsley, bread crumbs, garlic, salt, pepper, and toasted pine nuts. Soak raisins in warm water until soft, drain and chop coarsely. Add to meat mixture. Stir in lightly beaten eggs. Form into small flattened cakes. Coat with fine bread crumbs and a good amount of salt & pepper. Sauté in oil and butter 2-3 minutes each side.

A good appetizer to carry – good served at room temperature.

BAGNA CÀUDA
"Hot Bath"

Bagna Cauda is a great party dish. It can be the start of a party, or a great party all by itself. Prounounced "ban-ya cow-da"

Clean fresh vegetables – the more different kinds of vegetables, the more fun you will have around the Bagna Càuda. Most all vegetables in this dish are raw, but the one I like best is cabbage, and I like it blanched. Some vegetables to use: cabbage, broccoli, celery, spinach, red and green peppers, zucchini, tomatoes, mushrooms, etc. Have fun!

Bagna Càuda

(Pronounced "ban-ya cou-da")

¾ C olive oil	Small can of anchovies
½ stick of butter	Very little salt/black pepper to taste
6 cloves garlic, chopped	

Heat butter & olive oil over <u>low heat</u>. Add garlic and anchovies. Mash anchovies. Do not let garlic brown.

Keep mixture warm any way you can. For example: candle, warming tray, electric skillet. Using a slice of Italian bread to catch the drippings, dip the vegetables in the sauce and enjoy. At last, you eat the bread.

You can double or triple this recipe.

I have seen tuna fish and/or cream added to the sauce.

CAPONATA
Italian Eggplant Appetizer

1 large or 2 small eggplant
4 T salt
½ C olive oil
1 large onion or pearl onions
4-5 stalks celery
8 cloves garlic

1 C pitted black olives
¼ C sugar
½ C wine vinegar
2 T tomato paste
1 green pepper
Some capers

Rinse and cube eggplant. Sprinkle with salt. Let stand 15 minutes, drain and pat dry. Heat oil in heavy sauce pan. Sauté onions, celery, garlic, and pepper. Do not burn garlic. Remove vegetables. Add more oil if needed. Sauté eggplant until slightly brown. Return vegetable mixture along with all other ingredients. Cook until most of the liquid evaporates. Pack in jars and refrigerate. Makes 4-6 cups. Makes a great "take along gift".

* As a kick I stir in ¼ - ½ C vodka at the end!

CAPONATA / Quick & Easy Method

Can of caponata
Can of oil packed tuna

Pearl onions
Capers

Mix – Jar – And who's to know!!

HAWAIIAN MEATBALLS

I like to think I taught my lovely daughter-in-law, Sharon, how to cook. This is one recipe she taught me. It is easy, fast, and very good. It can be served hot or room temperature.

    1 lb. bulk sausage (Bob Evans)*
    1 small can crushed pineapple (well drained)

Mix together. Form into small balls. Roll in corn flake crumbs. Bake in 375° oven for 25 minutes.

To double recipe: use 2 lb. sausage and 1 large can of pineapple

* I have tried different sausages: maple, hot, breakfast. They are all good.

STUFFED PEPPERONCINI

    3 slices of bacon
    2 shallots, minced (¼ cup)
    ½ med. red pepper
    1 3-oz. pkg. cream cheese, softened
    2 tsp. milk
    About 28 pepperoncinis

Brown the bacon, crumble and drain on paper towels. In two tablespoons bacon drippings, sauté red pepper and shallots about 4-5 minutes. In mixer on medium speed, cream the cheese and add the milk. When smooth, add bacon and shallots. Cut slit into each pepperoncini, drain and remove seeds. Using a small plastic bag, cut off ¼ inch of a corner and squeeze the cream cheese mixture into the pepperoncinis.* They can be refrigerated up to 2 days. Let stand one hour before serving.

* I find it easier to stuff pepperoncinis using my fingers. You can also cut them in half to stuff.

TIROPETES

These take time, but are worth it. They can be a little tricky to roll. Just take your time. The good news is that they freeze well. You can make a large batch, freeze some, and pull them out and reheat when you need them. They are phyllo cheese triangles, pronounced "tri-*pets*".

> 1 large cream cheese ... or
> > Mix 1 small cream cheese & 1/3 lb. feta cheese
>
> 3 oz. Gruyere or Swiss, finely shredded
> 1 egg, slightly beaten
> 2 T chopped parsley
> 5 sheets phyllo dough (about 14 x 20 inches)
> Melted butter

Cream the cream cheese. Add egg and parsley. If using the 3 cheeses, cream together and add egg and parsley. Mix well. Lay out 1 sheet of phyllo and brush with melted butter. Layer the remaining phyllo sheets buttering each one. Cut into 3-inch wide strips about 14 inches long. Place one heaping teaspoon of cheese in one corner. Fold the corner of the phyllo, making a small triangle over the filling. Fold as you would an American flag. Bake at 375° for 10 minutes on an ungreased sheet, or until puffed and golden. After cooling, they may be frozen. To reheat, place frozen on baking sheet at 375° for 10 minutes.

Sharon Lednak

ITALIAN RICE BALLS

There are many variations of this recipe. My favorite is made with chicken gizzards and lemon. Some use ground meat, and many use diced mozzarella cheese. Still some add a little tomato paste. I have even seen them made into a sweet version made with sugar, plumped raisins, butter, and rum. Be creative!

RICE BALLS -- CROQUETTES

2 C short grain rice	Salt / pepper
4 T butter	Cooked chopped gizzards
½ to 1 C Parmesan cheese	Olive oil
Rind & juice of 1 lemon	2 eggs, beaten
4 eggs, beaten	Bread crumbs

Cook rice in salted water – al dente – tender but firm, for about 12 minutes. Drain rice and spread out on tray to cool. When rice is cool, combine with butter, Parmesan cheese, lemon juice & rind, 4 beaten eggs, and cooked chopped gizzards, salt & pepper. Shape into croquettes.* Roll in flour, then 2 beaten eggs, then bread crumbs. Chill about an hour. Fry in hot olive oil until golden on all sides. Drain on paper towels.

* Can add a chunk of mozzarella in the center of each croquette. Croquettes are egg-shaped. Can be served hot or at room temperature.

PIZZA RUSTICA: Full Pie or Holiday Pie

I am not sure if this is an appetizer, a lunch with a salad, or an evening snack with a glass of wine, but it was always around at Christmas and Easter time.

PIE CRUST

2 C flour	3 T shortening
2/3 tsp. baking powder	1 egg, beaten
1/3 tsp. salt	½ C ice water

Sift dry ingredients together. Blend shortening into flour with fork or pie blender. Mix egg with cold water. Add to flour and mix until a ball is formed. Refrigerate.

FILLING

1 lb. ricotta cheese	4 oz. capicola
2 eggs, beaten	4 oz. genoa salami
4-6 T grated cheese	1 lb. sausage, cooked
Salt & pepper	8 oz. mozzarella
2 hardboiled eggs, sliced	¼ lb. prosciutto or ham
¼ lb. sliced pepperoni	

Combine ricotta, salt, pepper, and grated cheese. Add 2 beaten eggs. Roll out crust and line a 10-inch deep pie pan. (I use a black iron skillet.) Prick crust with a fork; sprinkle bottom crust with a little flour. Layer ricotta mix, meats, cheese and hardboiled eggs until all ingredients are used.* Repeat layers as needed. Cover with top crust. Cut slits and sprinkle top crust with a little water. Bake at 400° for 15 minutes, then at 325° for 45 minutes.

I start layering with a little flour, sliced meat, ricotta, hard egg, and sausage, repeating all ingredients. <u>Only</u> flour the bottom. There is no set way to layer everything in the pie. You can use any combination of meats and cheese you like. Some people chop the meat, cheese, and eggs and mix it all into the ricotta, then stuff the pie. I do it the way my grandmother and my mother did it: in beautiful layers.

    I won First Place in The Villages, Florida Cooking Contest with this recipe. First Place was $200.

SWISS CHEESE SPREAD

1 ½ lb. Swiss cheese, shredded
1 bunch green onions, chopped fine, including green parts
1 pint Miracle Whip, <u>not</u> mayo

Mix all ingredients together and serve with crackers or party bread. Better if made the day before. Can be put in the oven and served hot. I like it cold or at room temperature. Very easy – Very good.

PINEAPPLE CHEESE BALL

2 pkgs. (8 oz.) cream cheese, softened
1 can (8 ½ oz.) crushed pineapple, drained
2 C chopped pecans
¼ C finely chopped green pepper
2-3 T minced onion
1 T seasoned salt

Cream the cheese. Add all ingredients using half of the pecans. Shape into a ball or log. Roll in remaining pecans. Wrap in plastic wrap and refrigerate overnight. You can garnish with pineapple rings, cherries, and parsley.

APPETIZER HOLIDAY PIE

1 -8 oz. cream cheese, softened
2 T milk
1 -2 ½ oz. jar sliced dried beef, chopped or snapped w/ scissors
2-4 T minced onion
2-4 T chopped green pepper
½ C sour cream
1/8 tsp. pepper
¼ to ½ C walnuts, coarsely chopped

Blend cream cheese and milk. Stir in beef, onions, green peppers, and black pepper. Mix well. Stir in sour cream. Spoon into 8-inch pie plate or small shallow baking dish. Sprinkle walnuts over top. Bake in moderate oven 350° for 15 minutes. Serve hot with assorted crackers and/or party bread.

Old but good recipe.

HOT JALAPEÑO PEPPER CHEESE BALL

1 -8 oz. cheddar cheese, grated
1 -8 oz. hot pepper cheese, grated
2 -8 oz. pkg. cream cheese, softened
1 tsp. Worcestershire sauce
3-6 tsp. hot sauce (Tobasco)

Put all the cheeses into a bowl and let stand at room temperature for 4-6 hours. Blend Worcestershire sauce, onion, and hot sauce in blender until liquefied. With stand or hand mixer, mix cheese and liquid mixture. Shape into 3 balls. Roll in pecans or walnuts.

Freezes well. Very good.

PARMESAN ONION CANAPES

1 C Hellmann's Real Mayonnaise
1 C grated Parmesan cheese
½ C finely chopped onion
1 T milk
1 loaf sliced cocktail bread, toasted

Mix first 4 ingredients; spread on toast. Place on baking sheet. Broil 4 inches from source of heat for 2-3 minutes or until golden and bubbly. Makes about 36. Easy – Very good.

CORAL SEA SHELLS *

1 pkg. jumbo shells, 12-16 needed, some break
1 can 6-7 oz. seafood: tuna, crab and/or shrimp
1 T minced onion
4 T minced celery
½ tsp. ginger
½ tsp. basil
1 -8 oz. cream cheese
½ tsp. dill weed
1 T lemon juice
3 T olive oil

Cook shells, tender not mushy. Drain and rinse in cold water. Prepare stuffing combining everything but olive oil. Mix well and stuff shells using 3 teaspoons per shell. Rub outside of shells with olive oil. Chill and serve.

* Other varieties:
    Hen House Shells: stuff with chicken salad
    Bull Pen Shells: stuff with dried beef filling

SHRIMP STUFFED ENDIVE

    ½ lb. shrimp, cooked   1/3 C seeded diced cucumber
    1/3 C cream cheese   1 T thinly sliced green onion
1) 1 T chili sauce   1 -5 oz. can water chestnuts,
2) ½ tsp. sugar   drained & finely chopped
3) ½ tsp. lemon juice   32 Belgian endive leaves*
4) ¼ tsp. salt   (about 4 heads)
5) 2 drops hot sauce

Chop shrimp. Combine cream cheese and next 5 ingredients. Beat at medium speed. Add chopped shrimp, cucumber, green onion, and chopped water chestnuts. Cover and chill. To serve, spoon 1-2 T of mixture into each endive leaf.

* You can also use head lettuce or Romaine leaves.

SHRIMP TOAST – CHINESE

12 raw shrimp   ½ tsp. salt
1/3 C minced bamboo shoots   1 T cornstarch
    or water chestnuts   ½ T gin
1/3 C grated raw carrots   1 tsp. baking powder
1 egg   dash of pepper

Shell, clean and chop the shrimp. Mix with the bamboo shoots or water chestnuts (or a mixture of both), carrots, egg, salt, cornstarch, gin, baking powder, and pepper. Spread the mixture on thin sliced decrusted day old bread. Deep fry <u>upside down</u> – that is shrimp side down.
Hint: Use square sandwich bread cut in half or fourths before putting on shrimp. Have shrimp mixture at room temperature, and oil very hot.

This is a very tricky recipe. But it is delicious.

MILLIONAIRE CHICKEN

September 18, 1986, I won First Place in the Unilic Woman's Day Cooking Contest in DuBois, Pennsylvania, with "Millionaire chicken". September 18 is my husband's birthday, which turned out to be a lucky day for me!

1 chicken, cooked & cut up
Sauce:
4 T soy sauce   3 T peanut oil
2 T honey   2 scallions, sliced
1 clove garlic   4 slices ginger root

Place chicken in a stock pan with barely enough water to cover. Season. Simmer about 20 minutes or until chicken is cooked. Cool. Remove skin and bones. Tear or cut chicken into bite-sized strips. Set aside. Mix soy sauce, honey, and garlic. In a separate pan, heat oil, scallions, and ginger. Mix soy mixture with oil mixture and pour over chicken. Place on a bed of crisp lettuce. Makes 3-4 entrée servings. Makes 10-14 appetizers. To serve as appetizers, wrap chicken with sauce in lettuce leaves.

I served it as appetizers for the contest. This was way before anyone heard of wraps!

SHRIMP APPETIZERS

Prep time: 10-15 minutes. Makes 36.

36 large cooked & cleaned shrimp, tails on
2 tsp. crumbled blue cheese   ½ tsp. hot sauce
2 tsp. chopped celery   1 -3 oz. pkg. cream cheese,
2 tsp. chopped sweet pickle   softened
2 tsp. chopped green onions & tops

Split shrimp halfway through and spread open. Combine all ingredients. Mix well. Stuff each shrimp and chill.

CHOCOLATE COVERED BACON

Around 2010, chocolate covered bacon became a rage at state fairs. I tried it at one of my wine tasting parties and it was a hit! I used a head of cabbage to hold the skewers. It looked great. Go for it – It's fun!

    1 lb. thick sliced bacon
    Wooden skewers, about 12 inches, soak in water for 10 minutes
    1 C white chocolate chips
    1 C semi-sweet chocolate chips
    1 T shortening

Optional toppings: chopped dried fruit, crystallized ginger, finely chopped nuts, toasted coconuts, kosher salt, brown sugar, cayenne pepper, and coarsely ground black pepper.

Thread each bacon strip onto a wooden skewer. Place on a rack in a large baking pan. Bake at 400° for 20-25 minutes or until crisp. In a microwave, melt chocolate chips with half the shortening in each. Melt and stir until smooth. With pastry brush or spoon, coat bacon on both sides with chocolate. Top each strip as desired. Place on waxed paper-lined pan. Refrigerate until firm. Store in refrigerator.

SPINACH BALLS

    2 pkg. frozen spinach, cooked and drained
    1 large onion, chopped fine   1/3 tsp. salt
    4 eggs, beaten   ½ C Parmesan cheese
    ¾ C melted butter   2 C Pepperidge Farm Stuffing Mix

Mix everything together. Chill about ½ hour. Roll into balls. Place on greased baking sheet. Bake at 350° for 10-15 minutes. Freezes well.

SAUERKRAUT BALLS

One of my favorites!

½ lb. ground ham and ½ lb. bacon OR 1 lb. bacon
1 minced onion   ½ to ¾ C mashed potatoes (can use instant)
1 clove garlic   1-2 eggs
1 #2 can of kraut, drained & chopped (large can)

Sauté ham and fry bacon until crisp. Drain and crumble. In drippings, sauté onion and garlic until transparent. Blend in mashed potatoes. Add kraut, bacon, and ham. Cool. Form into balls. Roll in flour. Dip into beaten egg, roll in crumbs. Fry in drippings 3-5 minutes. Serve hot. Can be made 24 hours ahead. Cover and refrigerate. Reheat uncovered at 425° for 10 minutes. Freezes well.

OKEECHOBEE CAVIAR

I found this recipe when we moved from Pennsylvania to Okeechobee, Florida. With a few changes, I now have seen it named after just about every state in the USA!

2 cans of black-eyed peas, drained   ½ C chopped onion
1 -15 oz. can whole corn, drained   1 -8 oz. Italian dressing
1 -10 oz. can tomato & green chilies, Ro-Tel
½ C chopped fresh jalapeños   1 -4 oz. jar chopped pimento,
2 C chopped red bell peppers   drained

Mix all together. Serve with tortilla chips or scoops. Scoops work best.

Hint: I add a handful of chopped cilantro and the juice of 1 or 2 limes. Most times one can of black-eyed peas is enough. Any way you do it, it is great.

BLUE CHEESE WALNUT TOAST

This is very very good, and very easy. Use French or Italian bread, unsliced. Slice about ½ inch thick. Fry bread on both sides in olive oil. Rub one side with garlic. Top with blue cheese crumbles. Toast and chop walnuts. Put on top of cheese. Drizzle with honey.

I found that a small amount of cream cheese added to the blue cheese helps the blue cheese and toasted nuts stay on the toast.

Everyone loves this. When you are asked to bring something, this can't be beat.

HOT SAUSAGE HORS D'OEUVRES

1 lb. hot sausage
2 C grated sharp cheddar cheese
3 C biscuit mix

Mix all together. Roll into balls the size of large marbles. Bake at 350° for 15-20 minutes.

TOASTED SAUSAGE & HORSERADISH

8 slices white bread (2-day old)
¼ C soft butter
½ lb. sausage: skinned, chopped & fried
4 T sour cream

¼ C prepared horseradish
1 T flour
1 T sour cream

Spread each slice of 2-day old bread on both sides with soft butter. Cut in half. Mix sausage and sour cream and spread on bread (one side). Mix horseradish, flour, and sour cream, and spread over sausage. Bake at 450° for about 10 minutes. Makes 16. This is not pretty – But it's good.

TWO SAVORY CHEESECAKES:

Cheesecakes are not always sweet.

THREE-LAYER CHEESECAKE

Requires no baking.

- 3 -8 oz. pkgs. Cream cheese, softened and divided
- 3 T chopped pimento stuffed green olives
- 2 tsp. olive juice
- 1 T mayonnaise
- 1 C shredded sharp cheddar cheese
- 1 -2 oz. jar diced pimento, drained
- 1 tsp. grated onion
- ¼ C butter or margarine, softened
- 2 garlic cloves, pressed
- 1 tsp. dried Italian seasoning

Beat 1 pkg. cream cheese at medium speed with mixer until creamy. Stir in olives and olive juice. Spread mixture into bottom of a plastic wrap-lined 8 x 4 inch loaf pan.

Beat 1 pkg. cream cheese at medium speed until creamy. Add mayonnaise and cheddar cheese, beating until blended. Stir in pimento and onion. Spread over olive mixture.

Beat 1 pkg. cream cheese and butter at medium speed until creamy. Add garlic and Italian seasoning, beating until blended. Spread garlic mixture over pimento mixture. Cover and chill at least 3 hours or until firm. Serve with assorted crackers and fresh fruit.

ANOTHER SAVORY CHEESECAKE: SPINACH-HERB CHEESECAKE

Make this the star of your next wine and cheese party!

- 2 large tomatoes, sliced
- ¾ tsp. salt, divided
- ¾ tsp. pepper, divided
- ¼ C pine nuts or pecan pieced, toasted
- ¼ C Italian-seasoned bread crumbs
- 2 T butter, melted
- 3 -8 oz. pkgs. Cream cheese, softened
- 1 -15 oz. container ricotta cheese
- 1 -8 oz. pkg. feta cheese, crumbled
- 3 large eggs
- 4 C loosely packed shredded spinach
- 2 garlic cloves, pressed
- 2 T flour
- 1 T chopped fresh dill

Garnish: fresh dill sprigs

Sprinkle tomato slices with ¼ tsp. salt and ¼ tsp. pepper. Drain on paper towels for 10 minutes. Process nuts in a food processor until ground. Stir together pine nuts, bread crumbs and melted butter. Press into bottom of a 9-inch spring form pan. Bake at 350° for 10 minutes. Cool in pan on a wire rack.

Beat cream cheese at medium speed with an electric mixer until creamy. Add ricotta cheese, feta cheese, and eggs, beating until blended. Stir in spinach, garlic, flour and dill, remaining ½ tsp. salt, and remaining ½ tsp. pepper.

Pour into prepared crust. Bake at 325° for 15 minutes.

Top with tomato slices, and bake for 30 more minutes or until set. Turn oven off. Leave cheesecake in oven 20 minutes.

Cool on a wire rack 10 minutes. Gently run a knife around edge of cheesecake, and carefully remove sides of pan. Cool 10 more minutes. Serve warm or cold. Makes 12 appetizer or 8 main-dish servings.

STUFFED MUSHROOMS
CRAB STUFFING

24 large mushrooms
Crab Stuffing: *
1) ½ to ¾ lb. crab
2) 4 oz. Mascarpone
   (can use cream cheese)
3) 1 tsp. mayonnaise
4) 1 T minced onion

½ C Parmesan cheese

5) 1 T minced celery
6) Hot sauce to taste
7) Salt

Heat oven to 350°. Mix the 7 ingredients together. Remove stems from mushrooms and save.** Wipe caps clean. Arrange caps on baking sheet and fill caps with the mixture. Add ½ C water to baking sheet. Sprinkle with Parmesan cheese. Bake 20-25 minutes.

SAUSAGE STUFFING

I also stuff mushrooms with crumbled Italian sausage mixed with frozen spinach, thawed and drained. Cook sausage, mix with spinach and a little Parmesan cheese. Bake.

MUSHROOM STUFFING

Remove stems. Dice and fry in butter with finely chopped onion, diced pepperoni, garlic, salt & pepper. Crush Ritz crackers, add to fried mixture with a little water. Fill caps. Put a little water in the baking sheet. Bake 20-30 minutes.

CRISPY PARMESAN CHICKPEAS

Makes two.

2 cans 15 oz. each chickpeas
½ C grated Parmesan
1 T olive oil
½ tsp. garlic powder

½ tsp. kosher salt
¼ tsp. black pepper
Pinch of cayenne pepper
(optional)

1) Rinse chickpeas under water. Spread on paper towels and let dry 15 minutes. Pat dry with additional paper towels. Discard any loose skins.
2) Heat oven to 400°. In a large bowl, whisk Parmesan, oil, garlic powder, salt, pepper and cayenne if using. Add chickpeas and toss to coat.
3) Spread chickpeas on baking sheet and roast, tossing twice, until dried and very crisp, for 50-60 minutes. Let cool completely on baking sheet.

To give as a gift:

Soak chickpea can in warm water to remove label. Dry well and fill with roasted chickpeas. Cut a square of wax paper, place over opening and secure with ribbon. A pretty square of material or pretty paper napkin looks good.

* For Christmas: Stick on a label "Peas On Earth." You can also mix in some dry roasted nuts.

FRENCH FRIED CHEESE

My daughter Melissa goes wild over fried cheese. It can be fried in sticks or rounds. Serve with a side of marinara sauce for dipping.

    Beaten egg
    Bread crumbs
    Oil
    Assorted natural cheeses:
        Hard: cheddar, Edam, Gouda, etc.
        Semi: Mozzarella, brick, etc.

Dip cheese in egg then in crumbs. Repeat. Fry in deep hot fat.

Melissa Lednak

NEW POTATOES W/SMOKED SALMON

24 pieces

12 small new potatoes (same size)
4 oz. smoked salmon
6 oz. cream cheese, softened
1 T shallot, minced
White pepper
Dill sprigs

Steam potatoes until barely cooked. Cool. Purée salmon and cream cheese with shallots. Season with white pepper. Cut potatoes in half and hollow out with a Parisienne scoop. Pipe salmon into potatoes in a decorative swirl. This appetizer can be held up to 24 hours in the refrigerator. To serve, place on a doily-lined tray with dill sprigs.

CHERRY TOMATOES W/PESTO TUNA

2 pt. cherry tomatoes
7 oz. canned tuna (in water)
2 tsp. garlic, minced
¼ C fresh basil, minced
¼ C mayonnaise (approx.)
2 T Parmesan cheese, grated
3 T toasted pine nuts
Salt, white pepper
1 large bunch parsley, washed & dried

Cut tops off tomatoes and discard. Hollow out tomatoes, salt cavities and place upside down on a towel to drain. Drain tuna well and crumble into fine flakes. Blend with garlic, basil, mayonnaise, Parmesan and pine nuts. Use only enough mayonnaise to bind. The recipe can be held at this point up to 24 hours in the refrigerator. When ready to serve, stuff tuna mixture into tomatoes. Remove stems from parsley and completely line a tray with parsley tops. Makes 24 pieces

FRIED CALAMARI

8 oz. flour
8 oz. corn starch
2 oz. corn meal
¼ tsp. sea salt
¼ tsp. black pepper
2 T dry parsley
¼ tsp. crushed red pepper
1-2 lbs. calamari rings

Mix all together except the calamari. Soak the calamari rings in milk for about 1 hour. Shake in a bag or dip into flour mixture. Fry in hot oil until golden. Do not overcook, they will get rubbery.

CALAMARI W/ A DIFFERENT BREADING

¾ C flour
6 egg whites
2 ½ C panko
Salt & pepper

Mix flour and egg whites together until smooth. Dip calamari into egg white batter, then toss calamari into panko, (Japanese style bread crumbs) a few rings at a time. Fry in hot oil until golden. Do not overcook. You can use a heavy skillet with hot oil, or a deep fryer works well. I sometimes add strips of red and green peppers to either batter, and fry with calamari. Serve with marinara sauce or lemon wedges. Either of these batters is good with shrimp also.

Caramelized Onions & Apple Cream Cheese Spread

4 T butter, divided
2 medium sweet onions, chopped
2 T brown sugar
2 T balsamic vinegar
2 cooking apples, cored, peeled & finely chopped
¼ tsp. cinnamon
Small container of whipped cream cheese

In a large non-stick skillet, melt 2 T butter. Add chopped onions. Cook, covered, over medium-low heat for 13-15 minutes or until onions are tender, stirring occasionally. Uncover. Cook and stir over medium-high heat until onions turn light brown. Stir in brown sugar and vinegar. Cook, stirring for 1 to 3 minutes or until liquid evaporates. Remove from skillet. Set aside.

Wipe skillet out with paper towel and melt the remaining 2 T in same skillet. Stir in apples and cinnamon. Cook and stir over medium heat about 5 minutes or until slightly softened. Remove from heat. Cook at least 30 minutes.

In a medium bowl, stir together apple mixture and cream cheese. Stir in about ¾ of the onion mixture. Spread on crackers* and top with remaining onion mixture.

* Keebler Topper Crackers work best.

PIMENTO CHEESE DEVILED EGGS

12 large eggs
2 oz. sharp yellow cheddar cheese, grated
2 oz. Monterey Jack cheese, grated
¼ C mayonnaise
¼ C jarred, drained, sliced pimentos, plus more chopped for topping
Salt & pepper

Put eggs in large pot. Fill with enough water to cover by about 1 inch. Bring to a boil over high heat. Immediately remove from heat. Cover pot and let stand 10 minutes. Drain, then plunge eggs in ice water. Peel eggs. Working 1 egg at a time, slice bottom quarter from wider, round end. Using a small spoon, carefully scoop yolk into a bowl. Slice pointed end of egg flat (remove about ¼ inch) so that it stands up to make a cup. Repeat with remaining eggs, reserving 8 yolks in a bowl and discarding 4.

Combine cheeses, mayonnaise and pimentos in a food processor. Process until evenly mixed but still chunky. Stir in reserved egg yolks, mashing to combine. Season with salt and pepper.

Spoon cheese mixture into a re-sealable plastic bag. Press out air and seal. Snip a bottom corner of bag to make a 1/3 inch opening. Pipe cheese mixture into each egg cup, filling all the way up to the top. Top with chopped pimento.

Pimento Cheese Deviled Eggs

BACON-WRAPPED FIGS

2 T goat cheese
6 figs, cut in half lengthwise
6 slices bacon, cut in half crosswise

Heat broiler. Spread cheese onto cut-sides of figs. Wrap with bacon, overlapping ends of bacon under figs. Place figs, cut-sides up, in a shallow pan. Broil 6 inches from heat for 8-10 minutes or until bacon is crisp. Drain on paper towel.

CUCUMBER CUPS

Peel and score cucumbers with a fork. Cut into sections about 1 ½ inch thick. With melon baller, scoop out cucumber sections to form cups. Plunge into boiling water and then into ice water to hold color. Pat dry. Sprinkle with salt and pepper. Fill with filling of your choice: shrimp salad, crab salad, egg salad, etc.

BREADS & BREAKFAST

THE PERFECT FRIED EGG

1. Heat a large skillet over low heat for 5 minutes with 1 or 2 Tablespoons of oil.

2. Crack 2 eggs in each of two small bowls. Sprinkle with salt & pepper.

3. Turn up heat under skillet to medium. Add 1 or 2 Tablespoons butter.

4. Slip eggs into skillet – 2 eggs on each side of the skillet.

5. Cover with lid for 1 minute.

6. Remove from heat – Keep lid on for 15 seconds to 1 minute, depending on how much you want the yolk to set.

The edges will be crisp, the whites tender, and the yolks set.

                              Perfect!!

PERFECT HARD BOILED EGGS

Place eggs in a saucepan. Cover with cool water by 1 inch. Bring water to a boil over medium heat. Remove pan from heat. Cover with lid. Let stand for 12 minutes. Cool eggs under cool water to stop cooking.

Peel eggs. To peel, crack shells gently. Starting at broad end of egg, release membrane (air pocket) with side of thumb. Release shell. Fresh eggs do not peel well.

PERFECT SOFT BOILED EGGS

Bring a saucepan of water to a boil. Lower room temperature eggs into water carefully. Boil gently for 4 minutes. Lift out, crack, and eat.

Boiling for 3 minutes are what my family knows as "sick eggs". Crack eggs, scoop into a bowl, and break up a slice of dry toast. This always made the kids feel better. Big Rich still calls me when he wants a "sick egg".

PERFECT SCRAMBLED EGGS

The key to making perfect scrambled eggs is whisking the eggs vigorously before cooking. Overcooking is another problem. Use a nonstick pan and a rubber heat-resistant spatula.

    8 eggs
    2 T clarified butter or whole butter
    1 C whole milk
    Salt & pepper to taste

* Crack the eggs into a bowl and heat them until they turn pale yellow. Beat vigorously.

Heat a heavy-bottomed non-stick sauté pan over medium-low heat. Add butter & let it melt.

Add the milk to the eggs. Season with salt & pepper. Again, whisk the eggs for all you're worth.

When the butter is melted and hot, pour in the eggs. Do not stir. As the bottom starts to set, with a heat-resistant spatula, gently push one edge of the egg into the center of the pan while tilting the pan to allow the liquid eggs to flow underneath. Repeat around pan until there is no liquid left. Turn off the heat and continue gently stirring until any uncooked parts become firm.

There is no limit to the variations you can create by adding ingredients to this basic scrambled egg recipe.

* If you crack an egg on a flat surface rather than on the edge of a bowl or counter, you will never get shells in the eggs -- Remember -- Flat.

SCOTCH EGGS

6 eggs
1 lb. sausage, such as Jimmy Dean
3 T chopped mixed herbs
    (parsley, thyme, sage, etc.)
Pinch of ground mace
1 T mustard

Splash of milk
Flour
Breadcrumbs or panko or
    corn flake crumbs
Vegetable oil, to cook

Put 4 eggs into a pan, cover with cold water, and bring to a boil. Turn down the heat and simmer for 5 minutes, then put straight into iced water for at least 10 minutes.

Put the sausage, herbs, mace, and mustard into a bowl, salt & pepper if needed, and mix well with your hands. Divide into 4 balls. Carefully peel the eggs. Beat the 2 raw eggs together in a bowl with a splash of milk. Put some flour in a second bowl and season, then put breadcrumbs into a third bowl. Arrange in an assembly line. Put a square of wax paper on the work surface, and flour lightly. Put one of the meatballs in the center and flour lightly, put another square of wax paper on top. Roll or press out meat large enough to encase an egg. Remove top sheet of paper. Roll the egg in flour and place it in the center of the meat. Using the wax paper, bring up the sides of meat to cover the egg. Smooth the meat into an egg shape to cover the egg using your hands. Dip egg into flour, then egg, then breadcrumbs, then repeat egg & breadcrumbs.

In a pan, fill with vegetable oil several inches deep and heat oil. Cook the eggs several at a time, about 7 minutes, until crisp and golden. Drain on a paper towel before serving.

A nice picnic snack. As an appetizer, I cut them in half.

BISCUITS & GRAVY

1 lb. fresh sausage (Jimmy Dean, Tennessee Pride, etc.)
Drippings from sausage & 3 T butter **
¼ C flour
3 C milk
½ tsp. salt
¼ tsp. pepper

Brown sausage. Remove sausage and set aside. To the pan drippings, add butter, flour, salt, & pepper. Cook stirring constantly over medium low heat until flour begins to brown. Slowly whisk in milk. Bring to a boil. Reduce heat and cook about 1 minute. As gravy cooks, it will thicken – if needed, add milk. Return sausage to gravy and simmer 2-3 minutes over low heat.

Make or buy biscuits*. Split biscuits and cover with sausage gravy.

* Biscuits in a tube work well and are good.

** Can use shortening instead of butter and/or bacon drippings.

Richard making pancakes. Not sure what the beer is for!

ICE CREAM BREAD

Makes one 8" Loaf

1 pint (2 C.) ice cream, softened (any flavor)
1 ½ C self-rising flour

Stir together just until flour is moistened. Spoon batter into a greased and floured 8" x 4" loaf pan. Bake at 350° for 40-45 minutes, or until wooden pick comes out clean.

* Can divide batter between two 5" x 3" pans. Bake at 350° for 20-25 minutes.

This Ice Cream Bread is a lot of fun to make. Only 2 ingredients and everyone that tries it has a hard time believing it is made with ice cream. It works with any flavor. I love Buttered Pecan.

GORILLA BREAD

½ C sugar
3 tsp. cinnamon
½ C butter (1 stick)
1 C packed brown sugar
1 (8-oz.) packet of cream cheese
2 (12-oz.) tubes refrigerated biscuits (10-count)
1 ½ C coarsely chopped walnuts

Preheat oven to 350°.

Spray a Bundt pan with non-stick cooking spray. Mix sugar and cinnamon. In a saucepan, melt the butter and brown sugar over low heat, stirring well; set aside. Cut the cream cheese into 20 equal cubes. Press the biscuits out with your fingers and sprinkle each with ½ tsp. of cinnamon-sugar mixture. Place a cube of cream cheese in the center of each biscuit, wrapping & sealing the dough around the cream cheese. Sprinkle ½ C of the nuts into the bottom of the Bundt pan. Place half of the prepared biscuits in the pan. Sprinkle with cinnamon-sugar, pour half of the melted butter mixture over the biscuits, and sprinkle on ½ C of nuts. Bake 30 minutes. Remove from oven and cool 5 minutes. Place a plate on top and invert.

BUTTERSCOTCH PUDDING MONKEY BREAD

1 pkg (3 ½ oz.) cook & serve butterscotch pudding mix – NOT INSTANT
¾ C sugar
1 T cinnamon
½ C finely chopped pecans
½ C butter, melted
3 tubes regular-sized refrigerated biscuits

In a plastic bowl with a tight-fitting lid, combine pudding mix, sugar, cinnamon, and pecans. Pour melted butter into a shallow bowl. Cut biscuits into quarters. Dip several pieces into butter, then place in the bowl with dry ingredients. Replace lid and shake.

Line a 10" well greased Bundt pan with coated biscuit pieces. Continue doing in batches until they are all piled on top of each other in the Bundt pan. You may need to melt a little more butter to finish up biscuit pieces.

Bake at 350° for 30-35 minutes until golden brown. Cool 30 minutes in pan. Place large dish over Bundt pan and invert. Before lifting pan, tap bottom of pan all over. Lift gently off.

NEW ORLEANS BREAD PUDDING
With Bourbon Sauce

¼ C raisins
2 T bourbon
1 ½ C milk*
1 C heavy cream*
  * Or use Half & Half
½ C sugar

1 T vanilla
½ tsp. cinnamon
¼ tsp. nutmeg
Dash of salt
4 or 5 eggs, lightly beaten
4 ½ C cubed French or Italian bread

Combine raisins and 2 T bourbon. Let stand. Drain bourbon after 30 min. Save bourbon. Cut bread into ½" cubes. Toast in oven. Combine saved bourbon, milk, cream, sugar, vanilla, cinnamon, nutmeg, and salt. Add beaten eggs. Whisk over low to medium heat to make custard. When it starts to thicken, remove from heat. Pour over toasted bread. Butter or use non-stick spray in a 9" x 13" baking dish. Spoon half the mixture into prepared dish. (You may need to add more bread and custard. I use more of all ingredients to fill a 9x13 dish.) Sprinkle raisins on and add second half of bread mixture. Bake at 350° for 30 minutes, covered. Uncover and dot top with chunks of butter. Bake another 10 minutes uncovered.

Bourbon Sauce

½ C sugar
¼ C light-colored corn syrup
¼ C butter
¼ C bourbon

Combine sugar, corn syrup, and butter in a saucepan over medium heat. Bring to a simmer. Cook 1 minute, stirring constantly. Remove from heat. Stir in bourbon. Serve over bread pudding.

KRISPY CREAM BREAD PUDDING

2 dozen broken glazed Krispy Creams
2 eggs, beaten
1 pt. cream or Half & Half
½ to ¾ C sugar
Raisins (optional)
1 tsp. vanilla

Butter a 9" x 13" glass baking dish. Break up Krispy Creams into chunks. Combine all ingredients. Pour over broken Krispy Creams. Bake at 300° for 45 min. to 1 hour, or until set.

* I sometimes use more eggs and cream so that there is custard in the pudding.

** I use Krispy Creams, but any donuts you like will work. You can make this with bread or a combination of donuts and bread.

MEXICAN CORNBREAD

1 ½ C self-rising corn meal
½ tsp. salt
1 tsp. sugar
1 C buttermilk
3 eggs, beaten
1 C grated sharp cheese
1 bell pepper, chopped
1 tsp. baking powder
2/3 C cooking oil
½ tsp. hot liquid pepper
2-3 jalapeños, chopped
1 C creamed corn
1 large onion, chopped

Grease a 9" x 13" pan. Mix all ingredients well and pour into a well-greased pan that has been sprinkled with corn meal.

Bake at 400° for 35-40 minutes.

BROWNED BUTTER & SOUR CREAM CORNBREAD

4 T butter
1 tsp. veg. oil
1 ½ C stone-ground cornmeal
½ C flour
¼ C sugar

2 tsp. baking powder
1 tsp. salt
¼ tsp. baking soda
2 eggs, beaten
1 C sour cream

Melt butter in small saucepan over medium heat, swirling often until lightly browned, about 4 minutes. Pour into medium bowl and set aside to cool.

Preheat oven to 400°. Rub 8" cast iron skillet* with oil; place skillet in over to heat. In a large bowl, combine cornmeal, flour, sugar, baking powder, salt, and baking soda. Add eggs and sour cream to cooled butter, whisking well. Pour into dry ingredients, stirring just until combined. Pour batter into skillet. Bake until golden and toothpick inserted in the center comes out almost clean, about 20 minutes. Let cool in skillet 5 minutes, then turn out and slice.

* If you do not have a cast iron skillet, you can use a well-greased pan or casserole.

ARTISAN BREAD

On next page

ARTISAN BREAD

Makes one 1½-lb. loaf

You need an iron pot with a lid. Dutch Oven Pan and lid will be placed in hot oven at 450° to preheat pan and lid**. The water in this recipe must be exact: 1 ½ C + 2 Tablespoons. I don't know why.

    3 C flour, more for dusting
    ½ tsp. dry yeast, rapid rise
    1 ¾ - 2 tsp. salt
    1 ½ C + 2 T water

In a large bowl, combine flour, yeast and salt. (If you want to add herbs or cheese, add it to dry ingredients.) Add room-temperature water to dry ingredients. Mix with a wooden spoon until blended. Do not knead. The dough will be shaggy and sticky. Cover with plastic wrap. Set aside in a draft free place for 12-18 hours overnight. The dough will get spongy as it sets.

Preheat oven 450° - Preheat pan and lid in oven for 20-30 minutes. On a tea towel (not terry cloth), sprinkle flour (about ¼ C). Place bread on one end of well-floured cloth. Quickly shape dough into a ball. (Shape isn't real important, bread is rustic looking.) Fold other end of floured tea towel over dough. Let rest 15-20 minutes while pan and lid are heating.

<u>Carefully</u> remove hot pan and lid from oven. Turn oven down to 375°. <u>Plop</u> dough into pan. Do not touch pan, it is very hot. With pot holders, shake pan once or twice to center dough. Replace lid. Bake at 375-400° for 1 hour. It takes about 45 minutes to bake. It will look done before it is. After 45 minutes it should be done and it will be browned. If you think it should be browner, remove lid for the last 10 minutes. It does not seem to take the whole hour – check after 45 minutes.

* The bread looks nice if you cut an X or slash marks before baking.

** I have heard that this can be made in a cold iron pot – but I have never tried. You can!

TUSCAN BREAD

Yields Two Loaves

2 pkg. dry yeast
1 ½ T sugar
1 1/3 C warm water
¾ C flour
1 ½ - 2 tsp. olive oil
1 tsp. salt
1 lb. (4 C) flour
Cornmeal to dust

In a mixer:
Mix yeast, sugar, water and ¾ C flour for 2 minutes to form sponge and let it sit for 15 minutes. Next, fit the dough hook on and add the olive oil, salt, and half the flour and mix. Then add the rest of the flour and mix until dough clears the bowl. Knead for about 3-5 minutes until dough is shiny and springy. Place into a well-greased pan and let proof for 1 ½ hour.

With a fork, pull the dough out and portion into two equal parts. Form into rounds or long loaves. Place on a sheet pan that has been dusted with a mixture of cornmeal and flour. Score the dough, brush with water, and dust with cornmeal and flour mixture. Let proof for 1 ½ hrs. In a preheated oven, bake 350° for 18 minutes, or until bread sounds hollow.

SHARON'S PIZZA BREAD

Sharon is my wonderful daughter-in-law. This is her recipe. She makes it for her family and as a take-along dish.

    Frozen bread dough
    Green peppers
    Onions
    Pepperoni
    Mozzarella cheese

Thaw frozen bread dough overnight. Let rise. Push down. Roll out. Sauté green peppers and onions. Cut up pepperoni into small chunks. Mix peppers, onions, and pepperoni with shredded Mozzarella cheese. Place mixture on dough and roll to form a loaf.

Sharon puts everything in the middle of the dough and brings up both sides. She divides one frozen loaf of bread dough to make 2 Pizza Bread loaves. The peppers, onions, pepperoni, and cheese amounts are whatever is needed to fill the loaf.

Bake at 350° for about ½ hour.

Everyone loves this, and Sharon does a wonderful job.

OLD-FASHIONED CRACKLING BREAD

1 ½ C cracklings*
1 ½ C cornmeal
3 T flour
1 egg, beaten

1 tsp. salt
1 tsp. baking soda
2 C buttermilk

Mix cracklings with dry ingredients. Add buttermilk and egg. Pour mixture into a hot greased skillet. Bake at 450° for about 25 minutes, or until golden brown.

* Cracklings are pieces of pork fat and skin that have been deep fried so they turn crispy and golden.

This is a very old recipe. It goes back to my grandmother. When people slaughtered pigs in the old days, they made cracklings and used them in cooking. They were used in beans and bread that I can remember. If you look, you can find them in some supermarkets.

EASY HOLIDAY BREAKFAST BAKE

2 (12-oz.) pkgs. bulk sausage
1 C chopped bell peppers
½ C chopped onion
3 C frozen hash brown potatoes
2 C shredded cheddar cheese
1 C Bisquick mix
2 C milk
¼ tsp. pepper
4 eggs

Heat oven to 400°. Cook sausage, bell pepper and onion over medium heat, stirring occasionally. Drain. Combine sausage mixture, potatoes and 1 ½ C cheese in a greased 9" x 13" pan or baking dish. Stir Bisquick mix, milk, pepper and eggs. Pour into baking dish. Bake uncovered 40-45 minutes. Sprinkle with remaining cheese. Bake 1-2 minutes or until cheese is melted. This serves 10-12. Good for A.M. company.

LOAF BLINTZ

1 stick of butter
1 ½ lb. small curd cottage cheese
½ C Bisquick
3 T sugar
3 eggs

Melt 1 stick of butter in a glass loaf pan in a microwave. Pour melted butter in mixer with 1 ½ lb. small curd cottage cheese. (Use buttered loaf pan to bake blintz.) Mix until smooth. Add ½ C Bisquick slowly. Next add 3 T sugar. Add 3 eggs one at a time. Bake at 350° for 40-45 minutes.

Serve with sour cream and jelly.

ITALIAN BREAKFAST STRATA

This one you make the day ahead -- Refrigerate overnight.

½ C sun-dried tomatoes*
1 lb. sweet Italian sausage
1 C chopped red peppers
1 C chopped green peppers
1 loaf Italian bread

8 eggs
1 C milk
basil leaves
1 C Mozzarella, shredded

Soak ½ C sun-dried tomatoes in hot water for 10 min. Cook 1 lb. sweet Italian sausage. Remove casings. Cook 1 C each red and green peppers for about 4 minutes. Drain sun-dried tomatoes and chop. Stir into sausage mixture in skillet. Cut 1 large loaf of Italian bread into 1" cubes in a very large bowl.

In a medium bowl, whisk 8 eggs, 1 C milk, and 1/3 C torn basil leaves. Stir sausage mixture into bread along with 1 C shredded Mozzarella. Pour egg mixture over bread and sausage and stir to moisten. Coat a 2 ½ - 3 quart baking dish with non-stick spray. Pour bread mixture into prepared dish. Cover with plastic wrap and refrigerate overnight.

Heat oven to 350°. Sprinkle dish with 1 C shredded mozzarella. Cover dish with foil. Bake covered at 350° for 45 minutes. Uncover and bake for 15 minutes. Cool slightly before serving.

* I sometimes use fresh tomatoes, cut and squeeze out seeds. I also add mushrooms while frying the peppers.

PEACHES & CREAM FRENCH TOAST

½ C butter
1 C brown sugar
2 T corn syrup (Karo)
1 ½ C peaches (29 oz. can, drained, or 6 peaches peeled & sliced
1 loaf French bread, cubed
8 oz. cream cheese, cut into small chunks
12 eggs
1 ½ C Half & Half
1 tsp. vanilla

Heat butter, sugar, and syrup in saucepan until bubbly. Pour into a greased 9" x 13" baking dish. Cover syrup mixture with peaches. Spread cubed French bread over peaches. Scatter cream cheese through bread.

In blender, mixer, or whisk very well, all remaining ingredients. Pour over bread and cream cheese. Cover and refrigerate for at least 1 hour or overnight. Bake at 350° uncovered for 50-60 minutes.

ITALIAN EASTER BREAD

My Grandmother, my Mother, my Godmother, and my second cousin all made Easter Bread, and every recipe was a little different. This recipe is a combination of all of them. You can shape them in round loaves or braid them with egg.

8 C flour	2 envelopes active dry yeast
1 ½ C whole milk	1 C butter, melted
½ C sugar	8 eggs
1 orange, juice & zest	1 tsp. salt
1 lemon, juice & zest	½ - 1 tsp. Anise oil

1) Place flour in a large mixing bowl. Set aside

2) Heat the milk in a small saucepan. Scald milk. Allow to cool.

3) Place sugar in a small bowl and add the zest from the orange and lemon. With your fingertips, rub the zest into the sugar until completely incorporated and sugar is moistened.

4) When the milk is cooled to lukewarm, stir in the sugar & zest mixture, stirring to dissolve the sugar. Add the yeast, stir, and let sit for 10-15 min.

5) Add the milk & yeast mixture to the flour and begin to mix into a dough. (It will be shaggy at this point.)

6) Next, add melted butter & continue to mix. Add orange & lemon juice and mix to combine.

7) In a small bowl, beat with a fork: the eggs, salt & Anise oil. Add to dough and continue to mix.

ITALIAN EASTER BREAD, continued

8) At this point, you may need to add more flour to get the dough to come together. Once you have a sticky ball of dough, turn it out onto a floured surface and knead for about 5 minutes or until soft and elastic.* It will remain slightly tacky.

9) Place the dough in an oiled bowl, turning to coat, and cover with plastic wrap. Let rise double in volume, about 1 hour.

10) Oil pie pans. Divide dough into round loaves. Place round loaves in pie pans. Cover and let dough rise in pans for 45 min. – 1 hour.

11) While dough is rising, preheat oven to 350°.

12) Bake 40 min. to 1 hour.

13) Once the bread is out of the oven, beat an egg and brush the bread & sprinkle with sugar. You can also sprinkle with small colored sprinkles. If you prefer, you can glaze the bread.
    FOR GLAZE: 2 C powdered sugar
    ¼ C milk
    Sprinkles, if desired

* You may need to add more flour to get the dough soft & elastic. I use a 5 lb. bag of flour, about 12-15 C, and more to knead and shape dough.

** If you want to braid the dough:
    Roll 2 pieces of dough 24" long. Loosely twist the ropes together. You can insert raw eggs into the braid. Allow to rise on a baking sheet, with parchment paper, for 45 min. to 1 hour. You can color the raw eggs or not. They cook as the bread bakes.

NUT BREAD

2 eggs
2 C sour milk or buttermilk
4 C flour
½ tsp. salt

1 tsp. baking powder
2 tsp. baking soda
1 C broken walnuts

Beat eggs & sugar. Add sour milk and beat. Add flour, salt, baking powder, and baking soda. Bake in waxed paper* lined loaf pan** at 350° for 1 hour. Flavor improves after 12 hours.

LEMON BREAD

½ C butter
1 C sugar
2 eggs
1 2/3 C flour

1 tsp. baking powder
½ C milk
½ C chopped nuts
Grated rind of 1 lemon

Mix as for nut bread. Bake at 350° for 1 hour in 9" x 5" pan. Pour topping on bread while hot.

TOPPING: ¼ C sugar & juice of one lemon. Can use powdered or white sugar.

* You may like to grease pans rather than using waxed paper.

** Can be baked in soup cans for round slices. Nice for party sandwiches with cream cheese.

BREAKFAST ROLLS

    2 loaves frozen bread dough, thawed, not raised
    Chopped nuts
    ½ C packed brown sugar
    2 small boxes of vanilla pudding, not instant
    ½ C milk

Spread the nuts on a buttered 9" x 13" pan. Cut each loaf into 4. Place in pan on nuts. Mix brown sugar with boxes of vanilla pudding and milk. Pour over bread. Refrigerate overnight. Bake at 350° for 30 minutes.

SAUSAGE HASH BROWNS & EGGS

6 eggs	1 ½ C frozen hash browned potatoes, thawed
1/3 C milk	
¼ tsp. salt	¼ C chopped onion
6 oz. bulk sausage	1 C (4 oz.) shredded cheddar cheese
	Chopped fresh parsley or flakes

Whisk eggs, milk, parsley, and salt. Set aside.

In skillet, cook sausage over medium heat until no longer pink. Remove and drain. In same skillet, cook potatoes and onions for 5-7 minutes or until tender. Return sausage to pan. Add egg mixture. Cook and stir until almost set. Sprinkle with cheese. Cover and cook 1-2 minutes until cheese is melted.

STUFFED PICNIC LOAF

1 large round crusty loaf bread
Extra virgin olive oil
12 slices of salami
5 oz. cheddar cheese, sliced
12 slices of ham
1 ¾ oz. rocket leaves, trimmed (arugula)
3 vine-ripened tomatoes, sliced
20 basil leaves
black pepper

Start by preparing the bead the night before you plan to eat it. Slice off the top of the loaf and put to one side to use as a lid later. Remove all the soft bread filling from the inside of the loaf, leaving the crust to form a case. Brush the inside of the bread with a little olive oil.

* Layer the loaf with your chosen fillings, pressing well on each layer and seasoning with salt and freshly ground black pepper as you go along.

When the bread case is full, drizzle with a little olive oil and replace the lid. Press the lid firmly in place and wrap the loaf in a couple of layers of cling wrap. Place in the fridge with a weight or heavy breadboard on top to chill overnight.

Transport to the picnic wrapped in the cling wrap. To serve, unwrap and cut the loaf into wedges with a sharp knife.

Make the loaf at least 8 hours in advance of eating.

* Choose the filling ingredients to suit your taste. As a variation, try using thinly sliced, grilled aubergine, roasted red peppers, or marinated artichokes.

CHEESY JALAPEÑO PULL BREAD

1 rustic loaf of bread, unsliced, either Italian or French
12 oz. shredded Monterey Jack cheese
¼ C chopped pickled jalapeños (more or less to taste)
¼ C chopped green onions, including greens
¼ C (4 T) butter, melted

Preheat oven to 350°. Slice the bread almost all the way through (not all the way) in a cross hatch patter, spacing an inch between the slices.

Place the shredded cheese in a large bowl. Toss with the green onions and jalapeños. Pour the melted butter over it and use your clean hands to toss, to distribute the butter evenly through the cheese.

Place the bread on a large sheet of aluminum foil (large enough to wrap the bread) on a baking sheet. Stuff every crevasse with the cheese mixture. Wrap with the aluminum foil. At this point you can make ahead and refrigerate until ready to bake.

Place in the oven for 15 minutes. Then uncover the foil from the bread and cook for 10 minutes more, until all of the cheese has melted. Place on a serving board or plate to serve.

Decorative Bread Cut

BAKED ITALIAN SANDWICH LOAF

    1 crusty round loaf of bread
    6-8 oz. Italian sandwich meats
        (pepperoni, salami, Mortadella, Capicola, etc.)
    6 oz. Sliced Mozzarella or Provolone cheese
    1 C chopped Vlasic Farmer's Garden pickles, any variety
    1 T olive oil
    1 tsp. Italian seasoning

Preheat oven to 350°.

Slice the bread into half-inch slices, being careful not to slice all the way through, and leaving about 1/2" uncut at the bottom. Fill every other slice with meats, cheeses, and chopped pickle mixture. Drizzle loaf with olive oil and sprinkle with Italian seasoning. Wrap tightly in foil and bake in preheated oven for 25-30 minutes until cheese is melted and sandwiches are warmed through. Slice sandwiches apart at the unstuffed cuts and serve warm.

SOUPS, ZUPPA, AND MINESTRONE

It doesn't matter how you say it, soup is good. It's not the first thing you think of when you think of Italian food, but in many Italian families it was the whole meal. Soup can be made with almost anything or almost nothing. Plain chicken or beef broth when you don't feel good; or meat, sausage, chicken, vegetables, rice and pasta for a special soup. Minestrone when everything in the soup was from the garden. On a cold winter day, brown flour in olive oil until golden, add water, salt and pepper, and simmer for 20 minutes. Dip in with a slice of toasted garlic bread. It warmed you. You could add a beaten egg and it becomes stracciatella ("little rags"). That is what the beaten eggs look like in the broth. Stracciatella is often added to chicken soup.

A good broth makes a good soup. Most of the work in making soup is getting all the meat and vegetables ready – lots of chopping!

Never boil soup. You may let it come to a boil and then turn it down. Simmer, simmer, and simmer.

My mother made soup in a huge soup pot. We had it for days. We teased her that she put everything that was in the refrigerator in the pot. But how I wish I could make soup half as good as my mother.

One more thing – I have never seen a recipe for Italian Wedding Soup in an Italian cook book. I think it is an American thing, but I will share my recipe. I have never seen Italian Wedding Soup as we know it in Italy.

What better reason for hot soup!!!

Nice smiles.

I created this soup for my niece Nancy and her husband Steve Vankerkhove. They were kind enough to permit me to use this picture of them skiing in the buff! So, in their honor, and to warm them up, here is:

BARE BUTT SKIERS SOUP

1/3 C olive oil
- ¾ C sweet potatoes, peeled & cubed
- ½ C onions, chopped
- ¼ C red bell pepper, chopped
- 3 cloves garlic, chopped fine
- ½-1 jalapeño, seeded & chopped fine

2 C cooked chicken breast, cubed
- ½ C salsa
- ¼ tsp. ground cumin
- 1 (16 oz.) can or box chicken broth
- 1 (15 oz.) can Healthy Choice Chicken & Rice Soup, undiluted
- 1 (15 oz.) can black beans, drained

3-4 T creamy peanut butter

In a heavy soup pot, add enough olive oil just to cover the bottom of the pot. Add the next 5 ingredients and sauté 5 or 6 minutes. Add the chicken and the next 5 ingredients and bring to a boil. Reduce heat and simmer 10 minutes. Whisk in the peanut butter and simmer 2 minutes more.

This makes enough for Nancy and Steve and the rest of their cold friends.

My dad, Frank Landi, had a favorite meal, and that was soup – soup of any kind. He could eat soup every day. Minestrone was a staple in our home when I was a young girl. I don't believe my mother had a recipe. It was made with what she had in the house, the refrigerator, or the garden. My Dad called it "Minestra". It was great.

MINESTRONE "As I Remember"

Quantities of all ingredients are "about" that amount

- 3 medium carrots
- 3 celery ribs
- 2 medium onions
- 2 large potatoes
- ¼ lb. green beans
- 2 medium zucchini
- Small head of cabbage
- 1/3 C olive oil
- 3 T butter
- 4-6 garlic cloves

- 15-20 C beef broth
  (Broth made from a bone, some soup meat, celery, carrots & onions)
- 1 large can Italian plum tomatoes
- Salt & pepper to taste
- 1 can cannellini beans
- parsley to taste

Start your broth (vegetables in broth will be discarded). While broth is cooking, wash and coarsely chop carrots, celery, onions, potatoes, green beans, zucchini, and cabbage. (You may want to add a green pepper.) Chop garlic. Heat oil and butter in a large skillet over medium heat. Sauté all vegetables, starting with the ones that take the longest (carrots & potatoes). Sauté and season with salt & pepper. I add the chopped cabbage to the broth last, and do not sauté. Add the tomatoes with the juice. Add the parsley. Heat to boiling; reduce heat to low. Simmer covered stirring occasionally, about 1 ½ hour. Add cannellini beans to soup which have been drained.

ITALIAN WEDDING SOUP

Chicken Stock:

    1 chicken, about 4 lbs., or parts including necks, wings, backs

    2 celery ribs with leaves

    2 carrots

    1 large onion

    Salt & pepper

Put everything in a large soup pot and cover with 5 quarts of water. Simmer over low heat about 3 hours. Water should barely move. Strain and discard vegetables. Add 1 lb. of curly endive or escarole coarsely chopped, the meatballs, and thinly sliced or chopped carrot. When greens are tender add the pasta (ditalini, stars, orzo, or macaroni rings if you can find them). Any small pasta works.

Meatballs:

Roll into 1-inch balls the following:

1 small onion, grated	1 slice white bread made into crumbs
1/3 C chopped parsley	½ C grated Parmesan cheese
1 egg	8 oz. ground beef
1 tsp. minced garlic	8 oz. ground pork
1 tsp. salt	Black pepper

Mix all together and form into balls. You can use bought chicken broth. Sometimes I will whisk eggs and Parmesan cheese together, then drizzle into simmering broth, stirring gently with a fork to form strands of eggs.

Season soup with a little Parmesan.

SPASATINI / SPEZZATINO / VEAL STEW

This soup is like a thick Italian stew. The amount of ingredients depends on how much you want to make. It is different from any other recipe I have ever seen for Spasatini. My grandmother and my mother made it this way and I never changed a thing. It is a very old family recipe that is not made by the younger cooks in the family, but it is a recipe that should not be lost. Don't be afraid to try it!

- ½ to 1 lb. chicken gizzards
- 2 lbs. stewing or rump veal
- 2 lg. cloves of garlic
- 1/3 C olive oil, more if needed
- 2 T tomato paste, diluted in broth
- 1 C broth, beef or chicken, or water
- 1 lg. onion chopped
- 1-2 celery ribs, chopped
- Parsley
- 1 bay leaf
- Salt & pepper
- Mushrooms:
    - cut halves or quartered
- 1 C wine, dry red or white
- 1 box frozen peas

Simmer gizzards in water until tender, 30-45 min. Cool and chop. Sauté garlic in oil until golden. Discard garlic. Cut veal into small bite-size pieces. Add veal to oil and brown on all sides. Salt & pepper veal. Add chopped onions, celery, mushrooms and gizzards. Season. Sauté until tender. Add tomato paste with your choice of liquid plus the wine. Cover and simmer about an hour. Add peas & simmer 5 min. Add more liquid as needed. Should be on the thick side.

MEXICAN ALPHABET SOUP
SOPA DE LETRAS

    1 ½ lbs. fresh ripe tomatoes, quartered,
        or whole canned tomatoes, drained
    1 garlic clove, peeled
    ¼ C coarsely chopped white onion
    1 C water
    3 T vegetable oil
    2 C alphabet-shaped pasta (12 oz.), or any other small-shaped pasta
    1 tsp. kosher or coarse sea salt, or to taste
    8 C chicken or vegetable broth

Place the tomatoes, garlic, onion and water in a blender or food processor. Puree until smooth.

Heat the oil in a large soup pot over medium-high heat. When the oil is hot, but not smoking, add the pasta, stirring continuously. As you fry the pasta, it will change in color from a deep white to a deep brown. Take care not to burn it! You want to cook it until it smells toasty, but not bitter like burned toast, about 2-3 minutes.

Pour the tomato puree over the pasta, sprinkle in the salt, and stir. Be careful, as the puree will want to jump all over your burners. It's a good idea to cover it partially with a lid. Let the tomato base cook and thicken for about 6 minutes, stirring often, until it becomes a deeper red and has thickened to the consistency of a thick puree. Keep on stirring, so the pasta doesn't stick to the bottom of the pot. You will see the base of the pot as you stir, but the sauce will not be dried out. Cooking the tomato puree to this point will give the soup a really nice depth of flavor.

Pour in the broth, stir, and when it comes to a boil, reduce the heat to medium and simmer for another 10 minutes. Taste for seasoning and serve.

CHICKEN & DUMPLINGS SOUP

Oh so easy and a great crowd pleaser. My grandchildren, Richard and Stephanie, like it!

  6 C water

  1 (10 ¾ oz.) can of chicken broth

  1 (10 ¾ oz.) can cream of chicken soup

  1 (10 ¾ oz.) can cream of mushroom

  1 tsp. garlic powder

  Salt & pepper to taste

  1 medium onion, chopped

  2-3 lbs. boneless chicken, cut into bite-sized pieces*

  1 (16 oz.) pkg refrigerator biscuits**

Bring water, broth, soups, and seasonings to a light boil. Add chicken and return to a slow boil. Add biscuits and continue to boil covered until biscuits are done. About 20 minutes.
* You can use fresh chicken tenders, or cut up cooked chicken.
** Any biscuits will do: buttermilk, cheese, plain, etc. I cut biscuits in half or fourths. Sometimes I use 2 tubes of biscuits.

Stephanie and Richard III

CHEDDAR CHEESE & BEER SOUP

¼ lb. butter
1 C flour
1 ½ tsp. hot chicken broth
1 ¼ lb. sharp cheddar cheese
½ C mixed, finely chopped, parsley, chives, onions & carrots
1-3 drops Tabasco
1 T butter
1 C warm beer

Melt ¼ lb. butter. Add flour, whisk over heat until golden brown. Add hot broth, continuing to whisk until boiling. Add chopped vegetables and cook over medium heat for 20 minutes. Strain. Put cheese in double boiler with 1 Tablespoon butter and allow to melt, or you can do the same in a microwave. Add cheese to soup mixture blending well. Just before serving, add Tabasco and warm beer.

This is a fluffy soup. Serve with a sprinkle of popcorn or broken pretzels for garnish.

ITALIAN SAUSAGE SOUP

¾ lb. hot sausage
¾ lb. sweet sausage
1 large onion
2 green peppers
2 garlic cloves, chopped or sliced
1 C red wine

Break and fry sausage. When it starts to brown, add onions, peppers, and garlic. Cook until onions are transparent. Add beef stock, wine, basil, tomatoes, tomato paste, salt, pepper, and chopped parsley.

Simmer and add cooked pasta.

I like bow ties. The amounts in this recipe depend on your taste, and how much you want to make.

CINCINNATI CHILI

1 lb. ground beef

2 medium onions, chopped

2 cloves garlic, minced

1 C thick BBQ sauce

½ C water

1 T chili powder

1 tsp. black pepper

¼ tsp. cinnamon

¼ tsp. ground cloves

¼ tsp. ground coriander

½ tsp. salt

½ oz. unsweetened chocolate, grated

¼ tsp. ground cumin

¼ tsp. turmeric

¼ tsp. allspice

Tomato juice as needed

9 oz. spaghetti, cooked & lightly buttered

1 (16 oz.) can kidney beans, drained

1 lb. cheddar cheese, shredded

Crackers as garnish

Brown meat with half the onions and garlic, stirring to keep it loose. (Set the remaining onions aside to top the chili.) Drain any fat from the pan. Add BBQ sauce and water and bring to a boil. Add spices. Cover the pan and lower the heat. Simmer 30 minutes, stirring occasionally. The chili will thicken as it cooks. Add tomato juice as necessary to create a brew that ladles up easily. Allow the chili to "rest" at least 30 minutes in a covered pan at room temperature.

To place: Start with a layer of spaghetti and top with hot chili; then beans that have been drained and heated; then chopped onions to taste; and last the cheese.

Any of the spices can be changed to your taste. Elbow noodles can be substituted for spaghetti.

LENTIL SOUP

1 lb. dried lentils (wash them first)	1 ½ tsp. salt
2 medium onions, diced	½ tsp. pepper
3 cloves garlic, minced	1 tsp. oregano
2 tomatoes, peeled and quartered	½ C olive oil
2 carrots, peeled and diced	1 qt. water

In a large pot, bring water to a boil. Add all ingredients at one time. Allow to boil 15 minutes, then simmer on low heat for 30 minutes. You can add cooked rice or macaroni at the end if you want a thicker soup.

LENTIL, POTATO & BROCCOLI SOUP

1 lb. (about 2 heads) broccoli	3 bay leaves
1/3 C olive oil & more for serving	1 lb. lentils
2-3 potatoes, peeled & cut into ½" cubes	Salt
6 cloves garlic	Pepper
1 onion, chopped	Grated cheese
10 C hot water	

Cut the florets from the broccoli stalks. Cut the florets into pieces about ½ inch. Trim the bottom of the stalks. Trim and cut into small chopped pieces.

Heat oil in a heavy 4-5 quart pot over medium heat. Add the potatoes and cook, stirring until golden and they start to stick. No problem – the brown bits from the potatoes that stuck will add flavor. Crush garlic with the flat side of a knife and add to pot. Cook a few minutes, stirring occasionally. Add chopped onion. Pour in hot water and bring to a boil, stirring to get up all the brown bits. Reduce heat. Toss in bay leaves. Cook for 15 minutes. Stir in lentils, let simmer 15-20 minutes. Stir in broccoli. Season soup with salt & pepper. Simmer until broccoli and lentils are tender. Skim any foam from top of soup. Remove bay leaves. Let soup rest off the heat, covered, 10-15 minutes. Ladle soup into bowls and drizzle with olive oil and grated cheese.

MUSHROOM SOUP

Vegetable cooking spray
1 ½ tsp. butter or margarine
¾ C chopped green onion
1 clove garlic, crushed
2 (8 oz.) pkgs. presliced mushrooms
¼ C flour
About 3 ½ C chicken broth

1 tsp. dried basil
¼ tsp. salt
1/8 tsp. pepper
1 bay leaf
2 T cornstarch
2 T water
1 ¼ C of 2% milk

Coat a large Dutch oven with cooking spray. Add butter and place over medium heat until butter melts. Add green onions and garlic. Sauté 2 minutes. Sprinkle flour over vegetables. Stir and cook 1 minute. Gradually add broth and next 4 ingredients, stirring with a wire whisk until blended. Bring to a boil and reduce heat and simmer uncovered for 5 minutes.

Combine cornstarch and water. Stir well and add to mushroom mixture. Stir in milk. Bring to a boil over medium high heat and cook 1 minute or until thickened, stirring constantly. Discard bay leaf. Garnish with parsley if desired.

POTATO SOUP

5 C cubed & peeled potatoes*	½ tsp. dried parsley
¼ C chopped onions	2 C chicken bouillon
2 C water	2 ½ C milk
1 ½ tsp. salt	3 T flour
Dash pepper	6 slices bacon

Combine potatoes, onions, and water in a 3-quart sauce pan. Bring to a boil. Add salt, pepper, parsley, and bouillon. Cook covered 20 minutes or until potatoes are tender. Meanwhile, fry the bacon in a skillet until crispy. Drain and crumble bacon. Combine 1 cup milk and flour, blending thoroughly. Add milk and flour mixture to soup. Simmer until slightly thickened, stirring constantly. Add remaining milk. ** Heat until hot.

Serve topped with shredded cheese and crumbled bacon.

* I like my potatoes sliced, not cubed.

** Add drained clams for clam chowder.

POTATO SOUP – The Way I Like It!!

In a skillet, sauté chopped celery and sliced onion in a small amount of butter. Add to a soup pot along with thin sliced potatoes and cover with water. Simmer. Add salt & pepper to taste, and some chopped parsley.

This soup is easy, fast, and good. I never was one for creamed soups.

SEAFOOD GUMBO

Make a roux of ½ oil to ½ flour. Cook to a new penny color. Add celery and onions. Cook until tender. Add chicken stock and Andouille sausage, cut into slices. Simmer. Add fish, crab, clams, mussels, scallops, and shrimp. You may add all or any combo of the seafood. You can also add canned tomatoes and/or frozen okra. Makes it special.

STUFFED PEPPER SOUP

2 green bell peppers, chopped
1 onion, chopped
1 lb. ground meat
36 oz. spaghetti sauce

4 C beef broth
½ C water
2 C cooked rice

Cook together peppers, onion, and ground meat. Drain and add rest of the ingredients. Simmer until hot.

TANGY BEEF STEW

2 ½ lb. beef, cubed and browned
Beef broth and/or wine

Garlic
Thyme

Sauté the above ingredients and simmer 1 hour.

Add potatoes, carrots, and onions. Mix 1 cup water (or any liquid you like) with about ¼ cup flour. Add to soup and simmer until vegetables are tender. Serve over rice or noodles.

TEXAS CHILI: TEXAS RED AND A LONGNECK*

- 2 T vegetable oil
- 2 lbs. stewing beef, cubed
- 1 C chopped onions
- 1 green bell pepper, chopped
- 1-2 cloves garlic, minced
- 1 (12 oz.) can tomato paste
- 2 ½ C water
- 2 pickled jalapeños, rinsed, seeded, and chopped
- ½ tsp. crushed red pepper
- ½ tsp. salt
- ½ tsp. oregano
- ½ tsp. cumin
- 1 ½ T chili powder
- 1 (15 oz.) can pinto beans, drained

In a heavy pan, heat oil and brown beef cubes on all sides. Add onions, green peppers, and garlic. Fry for 5 minutes. Add all remaining ingredients except beans. Simmer the chili for 1 ½ hour, or until the meat is tender. Add beans until heated through.

* A Long Neck is a Texas beer, but any bear goes good with chili!

PASTA E FAGIOLI (Beans & Macaroni)

1 ¼ C dried navy beans, washed[1]
6 C water
Smoked pork bones or ham hocks[2]
½ tsp. salt
Pepper to taste
Olive oil
1 lg. onion
2-3 celery ribs, chopped
1 carrot, chopped
3 strips bacon, chopped[3]
1 can Italian crushed tomatoes[4]
Ditalini pasta
Parmesan cheese

Add 6 cups water to the navy beans. Heat over high heat to boiling; boil for 2 minutes. Remove from heat, cover, and soak 1 hour with smoked pork bones or ham hocks. Do not drain.

Add the salt, and pepper to taste. Sauté in some olive oil the onion, celery, carrot, and bacon, all of which have been chopped.[5] Add sautéed vegetables to beans along with Italian crushed tomatoes. Bring to a boil. Lower heat and simmer about 1 hour. Remove a large spoonful of means and mash. Return to pot. Add cooked (al dente) pasta. Ditalini pasta works best. Add chopped parsley.

Serve with Parmesan cheese. Remove any bones and salt pork if used.

[1] The soup can be made with canned beans – it is a quick way to make beans & macaroni.
[2] Meat from ham hocks can be chopped and added
[3] You can use a piece of salt pork (¼ lb.). Do not chop so salt pork can be removed.
[4] I like mine white not red, so I use 1 or 2 tablespoons tomato paste, not tomatoes, and more onion and celery.
[5] Add some red pepper flakes when sautéing vegetables.

HEARTY PASTA E FAGIOLI SOUP

I like my *Pasta e fagioli* on the "white" side, but for those of you that like it on the "red" side, here it is.

2 T olive oil	¼ C chopped basil
1 lb. ground beef	2 bay leaves
Salt & pepper to taste	1 (28 oz.) can crushed tomatoes
3 garlic cloves, chopped	1 (14.5 oz.) can of beef broth
1 onion, chopped	1 C ditalini pasta, cooked & drained
2 celery ribs, chopped	1 (15 oz.) can Cannellini beans
¼ C red wine	½ C grated Parmesan cheese

In a large skillet over medium heat, sauté beef until browned. Season with salt & pepper. Add garlic, onion and celery, sauté until soft. Add wine and scrape bottom of skillet to deglaze. Add basil, bay leaves, crushed tomatoes, and broth. Simmer for 30 minutes. Add pasta, beans with juice, and cheese; stir to combine. Season with additional salt & pepper if needed.

WEIGHT LOSS MAGIC SOUP

Olive oil

2 cans chicken broth*

3 C V-8 juice, or tomato juice

3 cans Italian diced tomatoes

1 small onion

3 cloves chopped garlic

1 pkg. sliced mushrooms

3 carrots, peeled & sliced

1 zucchini, diced or sliced

1 yellow squash, diced or sliced

2 C fresh or frozen green beans

1 can kidney beans, drained & rinsed

3-4 C shredded cabbage

1 tsp. Italian seasoning

Salt & pepper to taste

In 2 T. of olive oil, sauté garlic, onions, carrots, and mushrooms for 5 minutes. In a large soup pot, place garlic and sautéed vegetables and all other ingredients. Bring to a boil. Reduce heat and cook until vegetables are tender. Add any and all seasonings you like.

* You can just use water for the liquid in this soup, and add a lot of herbs and seasonings.

ARTICHOKE SOUP

Cleaning artichokes can be a job, and you discard so much of the artichoke, so I now use the frozen artichoke hearts. They are good and work well in the soup.

    2 boxes frozen artichoke hearts
    2/3 C olive oil
    1 ½ lbs. russet potatoes, peeled & cut into ½" cubes
    2 leeks, white & pale-green parts, sliced, washed well
    3 shallots, chopped
    6 garlic cloves, chopped
    1 T fresh thyme leaves, or 1 tsp. dry
    1 T kosher salt
    1/8 tsp. red pepper flakes
    4 quarts cold water*
    2 T chopped Italian parsley
    Grated Parmesan cheese for serving

Heat olive oil in a soup pot over medium heat. Add the potatoes and cook until they begin to stick to the bottom of the pot, about 5 minutes. Add leeks and shallots, and cook until softened, about 10 minutes. Add the garlic, thyme, bay leaf, salt & pepper. Cook until the garlic is fragrant, about 1-2 minutes. Pour in water & bring to a boil. Add artichokes and bring soup to a rapid simmer. Cook uncovered until potatoes and artichokes are tender, and the potatoes have broken down to thickened soup, about 1 ½ hour.

* Chicken stock can be used in place of water.

** Add 2 Tablespoons creamed cheese to make soup creamy.

DRIED BEAN SOUP

Dried beans are the base for many soups. Any dried beans you like will work. You start by rinsing the beans and then cover and let beans stand overnight. Drain beans. Add water: about 2-3 quarts with 1 or 2 bay leaves. Bring to a boil, adjust heat, and simmer until beans are tender, about 1 ½ hours. *

1. At this point, you can add washed and chopped escarole, along with 6-8 cloves of garlic that have been sautéed in about ¼ cup olive oil. Check seasoning. Add salt & pepper to taste. Add some red pepper flakes and a little more olive oil if needed.
I have also browned chicken in olive oil & garlic and added to the beans before adding the escarole. Escarole cooks in about 15 minutes.

2. Another version: You can add chopped carrots, onions, and potatoes to the beans, along with canned crushed tomatoes, some parsley, rosemary, red pepper flakes, olive oil, garlic, salt and pepper.

You can make bean soup by adding anything you like: celery, cabbage, green beans … It's your choice.

Some beans to think about using:
    Cannellini (white kidney beans)
    Great Northern
    Lima
    Chickpeas

* Do not add salt while cooking the beans, it will toughen them. Do add herbs and spices that you like. A little olive oil never hurts. When the beans are tender, you can add salt and proceed from there.

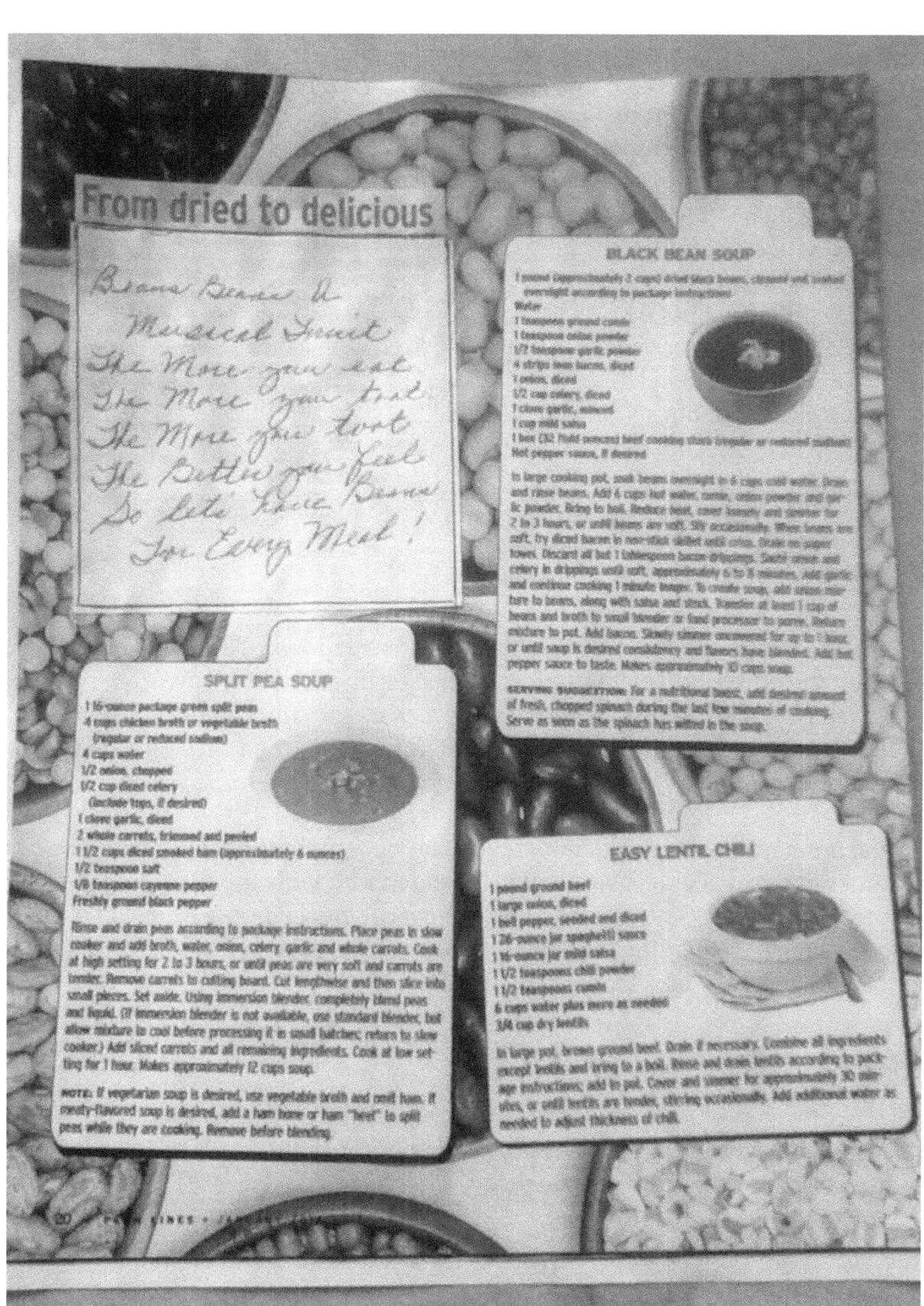

The above bean soup recipes are typed below.

SPLIT PEA SOUP

1 (16-oz.) pkg. green split peas
4 C chicken broth or vegetable broth
　　(regular or reduced sodium)
4 C water
½ onion, chopped
½ C diced celery (include tops, if desired)
1 clove garlic, diced
2 whole carrots, trimmed and peeled
1 ½ C diced smoked ham (approx. 6 oz.)
½ tsp. salt
1/8 tsp. cayenne pepper
Freshly ground black pepper

Rinse and drain peas according to package instructions. Place peas in slow cooker and add broth, water, onion, celery, garlic and whole carrots. Cook at high setting for 2-3 hours, or until peas are very soft and carrots are tender. Remove carrots to cutting board. Cut lengthwise and then slice into small pieces. Set aside.

Using immersion blender, completely blend peas and liquid. (If immersion blender is not available, use standard blender, but allow mixture to cool before processing it in small batches; return to slow cooker.) Add sliced carrots and all remaining ingredients. Cook at low setting for 1 hour. Makes approximately 12 cups soup.

NOTE: If vegetarian soup is desired, use vegetable broth and omit ham. If meaty-flavored soup is desired, add a ham bone or ham "heel" to split peas while they are cooking. Remove before blending.

BLACK BEAN SOUP

1 lb. (approx. 2 cups) dried black beans,
    cleaned and soaked overnight according to package instructions

Water	1 onion, diced
1 tsp. ground cumin	½ C celery, diced
1 tsp. onion powder	1 glove garlic, minced
½ tsp. garlic powder	1 C mild salsa
4 strips lean bacon, diced	Hot pepper sauce, if desired
1 box (32 fl. oz.) beef cooking stock,	
(regular or reduced sodium)	

In large cooking pot, soak beans overnight in 6 cups cold water. Drain and rinse beans. Add 6 cups hot water, cumin, onion powder and garlic powder. Bring to boil. Reduce heat, cover loosely and simmer for 2-3 hours, or until beans are soft. Stir occasionally. When beans are soft, fry diced bacon in non-stick skillet until crisp. Drain on paper towel. Discard all but 1 tablespoon bacon drippings. Sauté onion and celery in drippings until soft, approximately 6-8 min. Add garlic and continue cooking 1 min. longer.

To create soup, add onion mixture to beans, along with salsa and stock. Transfer at least 1 cup of beans and broth to small blender or food processor to puree. Return mixture to pot. Add bacon. Slowly simmer uncovered for up to 1 hour, or until soup is desired consistency and flavors have blended. Add hot pepper sauce to taste. Makes approximately 10 cups soup.

Serving Suggestion:
For a nutritional boost, add desired amount of fresh, chopped spinach during the last few minutes of cooking. Serve as soon as the spinach has wilted in the soup.

EASY LENTIL CHILI

1 lb. ground beef

1 lg. onion, diced

1 bell pepper, seeded and diced

1 (26-oz.) jar spaghetti sauce

1 (16-oz.) jar mild salsa

1 ½ tsp. chili powder

1 ½ tsp. cumin

6 C water plus more as needed

¾ C dry lentils

In large pot, brown ground beef. Drain if necessary. Combine all ingredients except lentils and bring to a boil. Rinse and drain lentils according to package instructions; add to pot. Cover and simmer for approximately 30 minutes, or until lentils are tender, stirring occasionally. Add additional water as needed to adjust thickness of chili.

BARLEY, SPLIT PEA & HAM HOCK SOUP

- 2-3 smoked ham hocks
- 1 C chopped onions
- 1 C chopped celery
- 1 C carrots, chopped
- 1 C leeks, white part only, diced
- 2 potatoes, diced
- 8 C water, more if needed
- 1 C corn
- 1 C baby spinach
- 2 C split peas
- ½ - 1 C barley
- Salt & pepper
- Red pepper flakes
- Grated cheese

Soak smoked ham hocks while chopping vegetables. Drain ham hocks. In a soup pot with a little olive oil, add diced potatoes & leeks. Add salt, pepper, and a little red pepper flakes. Next, add chopped onions, celery and carrots. Sauté a few minutes. Add 8 C boiling water, ham hocks, barley, and split peas. Simmer 40 minutes. Add corn and baby spinach. Simmer another 10 minutes. Check for salt and pepper. Hocks can be removed and the meat chopped and returned to soup, or left whole. Serve with grated cheese.

It's time for Soup!!!

Su standing on the Continental Divide

Su & Jeannine: July in Colorado

SAUCES, PASTA, POLENTA, RICE, and BEANS

PASTA

Pasta is all about the sauce. Red sauce or tomato sauce is the most popular. There are many variations of tomato based sauces. Too many to start to name, but something should be said about the making of a good tomato sauce.

1. Fresh garden tomatoes are the best. Having said that, there are excellent canned tomatoes on the market today. For example, Roman or egg-shaped, whole, crushed, diced, it's up to you.

2. Don't overcook the sauce. With today's high-speed gas or electric stoves, it does not have to cook all day.

3. Americans tend to use much more sauce on their pasta than Italians. The sauce should season, moisten, and coat each strand. The pasta should not be swimming in the sauce.

There are a few simple rules to keep in mind when cooking pasta.

1. Use plenty of water and add salt to the water.

2. I discourage adding oil to pasta-cooking water. Your sauce will adhere to the pasta better without it.

3. My mother always spooned the sauce over the pasta in a serving bowl if she made a very large pot of sauce. If on the other hand you make just enough sauce for the amount of pasta you are making, scoop out the pasta and finish cooking it in a big skillet of sauce.

4. Always bring water to a full boil before adding pasta. Cover the pot with a lid, propped open at an angle to bring it back to the boil quickly and prevent the water from boiling over. Water must be boiling before the pasta is put in. All the pasta should go in at the same time. Long pasta (spaghetti) will have to be pushed down with a spaghetti fork or a wooden spoon.

5. Stir frequently during cooking.

6. Do not overcook. Cooking time varies with the shape and thickness of the pasta, so taste it. Remember, all pasta should be al dente, that is "firm to the tooth".

7. Drain pasta immediately. Do not rinse in cold water.

8. When you see "grated cheese", always understand that it means grated Parmesan cheese.

9. Serve immediately.

My mother never put onions in her sauce, nor do I. Olive oil and garlic* and pork neck bones is the way I start. Meatballs, then anything goes: sausage, clams, shrimp, mushrooms, vegetables, nuts, breadcrumbs, the list goes on.

* You will see over and over again, "Do Not Burn the Garlic".

THE AUNT'S BOOK OF SAUCES

I made the following book of sauces with the help of family members to be used as favors for my daughter-in-law Sharon's wedding shower. After all these years, I thought it would be nice to pass it on.

TABLE OF CONTENTS

Aunt Ella...Page 2

Aunt Helen..Page 2

Uncle Herman..Page 2

Aunt Maddie...Page 3

Aunt Marje..Page 3

Aunt Mill...Page 4

Aunt Rosemarie..Page 4

Aunt Rosemary...Page 5

Aunt Vera...Page 5

Aunt Sammy..Page 6

Aunt Sandy..Page 6

Nana Landi..Page 7

Amy Lednak..Page 8

Amy Lednak..Page 9

Macaroni Casserole

1 pound Medium sea shells
1 pound ground meat
1 medium onion chopped
1 medium green pepper chopped
1 can Campbells tomato soup

Boil shell aldenti. Drain and put shells in baking dish. Saute onion, green pepper and meat in that order. Add a little nutmeg ($\frac{1}{4}$ to $\frac{1}{2}$ t.). Mix ground meat mixture into shells. Heat soup with half a can of water. Add to shells. Add your own sauce folding a little in and spoon over top.

A good canned or prepared sauce can be used or any leftover sauce you may have. Good recipe to serve to a party or group.

Aunt Ella

No Work Bar-B-Que Sauce

Equal parts of Coke and ketchup. Good on anything - chicken, hamburgers, chops, ribs, etc.

Aunt Helen

Tuna Sauce

Saute large onion and garlic in oil. 1 large can of tomato paste - refill can with water 3 times. Pour over onions and garlic. Add 2 cans of Imported Italian Tuna in oil. Cook 2 hours. Much better if made the day before.

Uncle Herman

Alfredo Sauce

1 stick of butter or oleo - melted.
Stir in 1 cup of cream and 1 cup of parmesan.

Do not let it boil but keep it hot. Cook and drain fettucini. Toss with sauce. Sprinkle with ¼ cup more of Parmesan cheese.

Aunt Maddie

White Clam Sauce

2 cans whole clams
2 cans white clam sauce (Progresso)

In oil, saute 4 cloves of garlic and a handful of chopped parsley. Drain whole clams and save the liquid. Saute clams in oil, garlic, and parsley for a few minutes. Add clam liquid and white clam sauce. Salt and pepper to taste. Enough sauce for 1 pound of fettuccini.

Aunt Marie

Pesto Sauce

2 cups fresh basil
10 cloves garlic
1 cup olive oil
3/4 cup pine nuts or walnuts
1/2 cup parmesan cheese

Blend in blender. Toss about 4 T. over pound of hot pasta. Sauce keeps in refrigerator about a month. Likes using springs or shells because the sauce sticks in crevices.

Aunt Mill

Marinara Sauce

1/2 cup good olive oil
8 cloves garlic

Saute garlic till soft. 2 large cans whole tomatoes. (Break tomatoes with hands) (Aunt Rose likes Hunts). Add 2 T. basil. Salt and pepper to taste.

Let cook 35 to 40 minutes.

Aunt Rosemarie

Basic Sauce

Saute garlic and onions. Add to fresh tomatoes. Black pepper to taste. 1/3 to 1/2 cup medium dry wine (red or white). 1/2 cup chopped parsley. 1 to 2 t. basil. Simmer 1/2 hour to 45 minutes. Add small can of paste with equal amount of water. Simmer another 10 minutes. Optional additions - Chicken sauteed, ground meat sauteed, tuna fish, or shrimp.

Aunt Rosemary

Ground Meat Spaghetti Sauce

Saute onions and garlic in oil. Remove from pan and drain. Brown ground meat. Add a small handful of Italian Seasoning to meat. Add one large can of puree along with one large can of tomato paste and one small can of paste. Rinse puree and paste cans with small amount of water and add to sauce, plus one puree can of water. Add salt and pepper to taste. Cook slow about 1½ hours. Added touch - Brown sausage, drain and add to sauce.

Aunt Vera

Always On the Stove Spaghetti Sauce

Meatballs: Ground meat - beef and pork. 2 eggs to a pound of meat. Bread crumbs, salt, pepper, grated cheese (1 t. to a pound). Mix and allow to stand awhile.

Brown meatballs in oil. Set meatballs aside. In oil in pan saute garlic, onion and parsley. Add tomatoes, then paste. Cook just a little while, then put sauce in a deep sauce pan and add meatballs. Cook slow from 20 to 30 minutes.

Aunt Sammy says, "Sauce is better if cooked the day before."

Aunt Sammy

No Fuss Sauce

2 lb. ground meat
1 onion diced
1 stalk celery diced
1 can tomato paste (Contadina)
2 cans tomato sauce
1 cup Ragu Homestyle
1 clove garlic
¼ cup grated cheese
Salt & pepper.

Brown ground meat, onions and celery. Drain grease. Put remaining ingredients in pan and let simmer.

Aunt Sandy

Every Sunday Spaghetti Sauce

½ cup olive oil, 4 cloves garlic — saute until garlic is soft, not brown.

1 quart tomatoes (home cooked)

Add tomatoes to garlic. Cook for about ½ hour. Add ½ t. salt, ½ t. pepper and 1 scant t. sugar, 2 T. chopped parsley, simmer ½ hour.

Brown sausage and or meatballs. Add to sauce. Cook 1/2 to 3/4 hours. Last 10 minutes of cooking add one can of tomato paste and one can of water.

* Pork neckbones make a good sauce starter. In small amount of oil in iron skillet, brown neck bones long and slowly. Flavor well with salt and pepper. Add to tomato sauce.

Nana Landi

Primavera Sauce

Use any combination of vegetables you like. Blanch each raw vegetable separately in boiling water and drain. Green beans, asparagus tips, broccoli, cauliflower and unpeeled zucchini takes only about 2 to 3 minutes each. Snow peas and green peas, fresh or frozen, no more than 15 seconds if at all.

Heat olive oil in a skillet until haze forms above it, then stir in blanched vegetables. Turn vegetables in the oil until they are hot but still crisp, no more than 3 or 4 minutes. Add vegetables to any hot boiled and drained pasta. Top with parmesan cheese.

If you like, you can saute onions and or garlic in oil, then add blanches vegetables.

Other suggestions:

Frozen artichoke hearts
Small peeled and quartered ripe tomatoes
Fresh mushrooms
Carrots, cut into thin strips
Eggplant
Chick Peas (garabanzos)

Amy

Seafood Sauce

Using any combination of fresh seafood you like, steam seafood separatly and set aside. (I like cod, catfish, shrimp and scallops).

Make a light red sauce using 2 cans of good crushed tomatoes.

Saute garlic and onion in olive oil. Add a handful of chopped parsley and crushed tomatoes. Cook about 15 minutes.

Using any combination of canned seafood, add to suace. (I like tuna (drained), clams whole and chopped and crab). Last add fresh steamed seafood.

Salt and pepper to taste.

Hint: Do not over stir sauce and break up seafood. You can steam fresh seafood with Old Boy Seasoning in water.

Amy

And that is

"The Aunt's Book of Sauces"

HAND-MADE PASTA

Or as my Dad called it:

Fatto Mano

"Made by Hand"

3 C flour
4 eggs
2 tsp. olive oil
½ tsp. salt
warm water if needed

You can make a well in the flour, add the eggs, salt, olive oil, and a little warm water as needed. Then you knead.

I find it much easier and just as good if you use a food processor.

In a food processor with a metal blade, spoon in 2 2/3 C of the flour. In a small bowl, beat the eggs, olive oil, and salt together until blended. With the motor running, pour egg mixture into processor. Process until a rough and sticky ball of dough is formed. If mixture is too dry, drizzle a very small amount of warm water into the processor. Remove dough to a work surface and knead with remaining flour for about 5 minutes. Flour work surface and hands if dough sticks.

Roll the dough into a smooth ball. Cover with plastic and let rest for 30 minutes to 1 hour.

Use a Pasta Machine to roll and cut pasta.

Use this dough for fettuccini or ravioli.

MY SPAGHETTI SAUCE

This is the way I make my spaghetti sauce. You will need:

2 or 3 cans of crushed tomatoes	fresh basil
olive oil	pork neck bones
garlic	salt& pepper for seasoning
parsley	

In a sauce pan, put the crushed tomatoes on medium heat to simmer while you brown the neck bones in a skillet with olive oil and garlic. Do not let garlic burn. Salt & pepper the neck bones very well. When the neck bones are well browned, add to tomatoes. At this point I will add about 2 T clean olive oil and new garlic to the skillet, and when the garlic starts to turn light golden, it is also added to the tomatoes. Add a few basil leaves and check for seasoning. Stir sauce – do not let it stick on bottom of sauce pan. While sauce is simmering, make the meatballs. You will need:

1-1 ½ lb. of ground meat	Salt & pepper
Bread crumbs (I prefer day-old Italian bread)	Grated Parmesan cheese
Minced garlic	
Chopped parsley	A beaten egg

If you use day-old Italian bread, wet with cold water, then squeeze out excess water. Mix all of these ingredients together. Roll into balls. Brown in olive oil and garlic. (Do not let garlic burn. Change oil and garlic as needed as not to burn.) You can also brown Italian sausage to be added to the sauce. Once you add the meatballs and sausage to the sauce, you only cook the sauce long enough to finish cooking the meat. Remember to stir the sauce.

About 10 minutes before the sauce is done, add a small can of tomato paste and about 2-3 cans of water. Stir in the paste. Depending on the tomatoes (if they are tart), you may want to add a little sugar.
* Check seasoning. You may want to use a little dry Italian seasoning if you like. But remember that my grandmother, my mother, and I never put onions in our sauce or meatballs!

ROTOLO di PASTA

This is a real show stopper! A little tricky, but so worth it. *Rotolo* means "to roll up". That is just what you do. First you make a pasta dough. Let it rest, then roll it in a pasta machine. Do not roll the pasta as thin as you would for just making pasta. The Rotolo needs some body to hold its shape.

Once you have rolled the pasta sheets, lay them on a work surface that has been lightly floured. Overlap the sheets slightly to create one large sheet. Use a rolling pin to smooth out overlap. Scatter the filling of your choice.
Examples of fillings:
- Spinach & ricotta
- Pumpkin & ricotta
- Potato & salami
- Mushroom
- Pancetta & Parmesan

The choices are endless. I like ground meat, Italian sausage, and Parmesan. Sometimes I add a little spinach.

Roll the pasta up like a log, sealing the ends. Wrap it firmly in cheese cloth and tie it in intervals with kitchen string to keep the pasta in shape. Leave enough string at the ends to tie the roll up off the bottom of the ban. A large oval roaster with handles works well.

Once the salted water has come to a boil, turn it down and tie your Rotolo in the pan and let it simmer until it is cooked. This can take 45 minutes to an hour. Remove from water. Unroll and slice.* Top with a little sauce** so they can see the rolls and pass more sauce and cheese.

* I never cut mine into slices. I love bringing it to the table on a large platter with a small amount of sauce and slicing it in front of my guests. Pass the sauce & cheese.

** Depending on your filling, you might want a butter or alfredo sauce.

It's a little work, but try it. You can make it the day before and reheat it in simmering water, or in the oven with sauce.

Rotolo di pasta

AMALFI CALAMARI PASTA

1 ¼ C flour
¼ C cornstarch
1 tsp. coarse salt
½ tsp. baking powder
¼ tsp. cayenne pepper
1 lb. squid rings
2 C olive oil

2 C canola oil
1 lb. spaghetti
¼ C butter, diced
3-4 T fresh lemon juice*
½ C chopped parsley, divided
Lemon wedges
Salt & pepper

Line a rimmed baking sheet with several layers of paper towels. Wisk flour, cornstarch, salt, baking powder, and cayenne pepper in a medium bowl.** Working in batches, toss squid rings in flour mixture to coat, then place rings in single layer on a sheet of foil. Pour both oils into a large deep skillet. When oil is hot, working in batches, add squid rings to hot oil and cook until light golden and crisp, 2-3 minutes per batch. Using a slotted spoon, transfer squid to towel-lined baking sheet to drain.

Meanwhile, cook pasta in boiling salted water. Drain, reserving 1-1 ½ C pasta water. Return pasta to pot. Add butter and lemon juice. Toss to coat pasta. Add ¾ C pasta cooking water and toss. Mix in 1/3 C parsley. Season to taste with salt & freshly ground pepper. Add more lemon juice and pasta water if desired. Transfer pasta to a serving bowl; top with calamari. Sprinkle with remaining parsley. Serve with lemon wedges.

* Along with the lemon juice, I sometimes add the lemon zest.

** This flour mixture is very good on any seafood.

PASTA with CRAB

In a large skillet, melt butter, do not let it brown.* Add 2 garlic cloves mashed, 3 T chopped onion, and some chopped celery with leaves. Salt & pepper for seasoning. Add 1 C chopped tomatoes, 1 C tomato sauce, 2 tsp. Worcestershire (that's different), and 1 lb. lump crab*. Heat through – Do not over cook. Toss with cooked pasta.

I use about 3-4 T butter and add 1 T of olive oil. It helps the butter not to brown.

* If you like, you can use imitation crab that is now on the market.

PASTA with SHRIMP SCAMPI

3-4 T butter	1/3 C chopped parsley
3-4 T olive oil	½ lemon zest
4 cloves garlic, minced	¼ C lemon juice
1 lb. cleaned shrimp	1/8 tsp. red pepper flakes
Salt & pepper to taste	2-3 thin lemon slices

In a heavy bottom pan, melt butter & olive oil. Add garlic. Sauté 1 minute. Careful not to burn. Add shrimp, salt & pepper. Sauté until shrimp turn pink, about 4 minutes, stirring often. Remove from heat, add parsley, lemon juice and zest. Check seasoning. Toss with hot pasta of your choice.

BROCCOLI & SCALLOPS with LINGUINE

Heads of broccoli, chopped to bite size *
1 lb. bay scallops (reserve liquid) *
1 small onion chopped
½ tsp. each, dried basil & oregano
½ C chopped parsley
½ C olive oil
¾ stick of butter
3-6 cloves garlic, crushed
1/8 tsp. red pepper flakes, if you like

milk
flour

Steam or microwave broccoli until tender but firm. Set aside. In a jar, mix scallop liquid, a little milk and some flour. Shake until smooth. Heat oil over low heat in a large skillet. Add garlic & onions. Do Not Brown. Add butter and let melt. Add broccoli, crushed pepper, parsley, basil and oregano. Cook 2 minutes. Add scallops, cook & stir for 5 minutes. Remove from heat. Add enough of the flour mixture slowly while stirring to thicken slightly. Serve over cooked linguine.

* I have used cauliflower in place of broccoli, omitted the scallops, and used chickpeas in their place.

BUCATINI with TOASTED BREAD CRUMBS

Italian day-old bread
1 ½ T coarse salt
1 lb. bucatini or perciatelli*
½ C olive oil

3 T sliced garlic
1 tsp. dried oregano
3 T fresh parsley, chopped
½ C grated Parmesan cheese

Remove crust from bread. With your fingers, tear the interior of the bread into irregular shreds about ½-inch. For a pound of pasta, shred 2 full cups of rough crumbs. In boiling water, cook the pasta until al dente. As soon as you put the pasta in boiling water, pour ½ C olive oil in a large skillet over medium-high heat and scatter in the garlic slices. Cook for a couple of minutes until garlic is sizzling and fragrant, but still pale. Drop in the torn bread crumbs & stir to coat with oil. Keep tossing as they start to toast and color. Sprinkle over the oregano & keep stirring & tossing to avoid burning. As soon as the crumbs are deep gold & crisp, turn off heat.

When the bucatini is al dente, lift out the pasta with tongs or a spider. Let the water drain off for just a second, then drop pasta into skillet. Turn the heat up a bit & toss the pasta with the bread crumbs. Sprinkle on ½ tsp. salt & keep tossing. If the crumbs absorbed all the oil, and the pasta seems dry, drizzle over 2 or more T olive oil & toss. Check seasoning. Sprinkle on parsley & grated cheese.

* Bucatini is a long hollow pasta, as is perciateli.

** Spaghetti can be used.

FETTUCCINE ALFREDO

Alfredo is the specialty of my son Richard Lednak, and a favorite of his children, Richard and Stephanie.*

    3 T butter   2 C heavy cream
    2 T olive oil   Salt & pepper
    2 cloves garlic, crushed   ½ C grated Parmesan cheese

Melt butter & olive oil in a large skillet. Add garlic. Do not brown. Add cream and grated cheese.** Cook slow over low heat. Salt & pepper to taste. Sauce will thicken as it cooks. Add cooked fettuccine.

* Try as I might, Richard & Stephanie like their Dad's the best!

** Move it up a notch by adding ¾ C Mozzarella or Fontina cheese along with the grated cheese. Amounts can be increased depending on the amount of sauce you need.

Pasta & pizzelles keep them running!

BAKED LINGUINE

Spray a spring form pan. Mix together:

2 C ricotta	Salt & pepper
2 eggs, well beaten	½ C Parmesan cheese
Chopped parsley	½ C shredded Mozzarella

Sauce:

Heat oil. Add onions & garlic. Cook until translucent, not brown. Add juice & rind of a lemon. Cook linguine al dente. Drain & add to pan of sauce. Toss well.

Layer into spring form pan using ½
    Pasta
    Ricotta mixture
    Sliced fresh tomatoes
    Salt, pepper & basil
    Top with shredded Mozzarella cheese

Repeat layers ending with tomatoes and cheese. Bake until set at 350° for 30-45 minutes.

SPAGHETTI with HARICOTS VERTS, SHRIMP & SCALLOPS

¼ C olive oil
6 garlic cloves, crushed
3 C peeled & chopped tomatoes
　or 1 -14 oz can crushed or diced
1 tsp. crushed red pepper flakes
1 lb. spaghettini (thin spaghetti)
6 oz. haricots verts or thin young string beans, cut to 1-inch

8 oz. sea scallops, quartered
8 oz. peeled large shrimp
1 T chopped parsley

In a large skillet, heat 2 T oil. Add garlic, cook until lightly browned, about 2 minutes. Stir in tomatoes & red pepper flakes. Bring to a boil, reduce heat & simmer 15 minutes. Remove & discard garlic. Set sauce aside. Cook spaghettini (thin spaghetti) & haricots verts (or green beans) together in boiling salted water for about 7 minutes, or until pasta & beans are tender.

Meanwhile, in a large skillet, heat remaining oil on medium to high heat. Add scallops, cook 2 minutes, turning once. Stir in shrimp, cook 1 minute. Stir in tomatoes, bring to a boil. Reduce heat. Stir in parsley. Drain pasta and stir with ½ the sauce. Add a little pasta water & oil if dry. Top with remaining sauce & serve.

PESTO

The word "Pesto" means pounded or ground. That is precisely how pesto is made. Classic pesto is bright green and made with the freshest, most tender basil leaves, extra virgin olive oil, the best-quality garlic, pine nuts (I like to toast them), cheese, Pecorino Romano and/or Parmigiano-Reggiano, and sea salt.

Set up your blender or food processor. Assemble the ingredients you are using for your pesto. Put the basil, olive oil, nuts, and garlic in blender or food processor and whisk to a thick paste. Add cheese and taste to see how much salt you need. You can add a little soft butter to smooth out the pesto. One or two tablespoons of milk will mellow the pesto. This is optional. Pesto can be made with any number of variations:

Walnuts, almonds, parsley, capers, anchovies, mint leaves, green beans, asparagus, etc.

A red pesto can be made by using fresh or canned tomatoes, tomato paste, or roasted red peppers.

MOSTACCIOLI with TOMATO PESTO

1 6-oz can of tomato paste
¾ C olive oil
½ C pine nuts
¼ tsp. sea salt
¼ to ½ tsp. crushed red pepper

2 T tomato juice or water
2-3 garlic cloves
1 lb. Mostaccioli, penne or rigatoni
Grated Parmesan cheese

Combine ingredients in a blender and blend to a smooth purée. Boil pasta in boiling salt water. Save a cup of pasta water if needed for sauce. Pour room temperature tomato pesto over pasta.

PESTO with POTATOES, PASTA, & GREEN BEANS

    3-5 new potatoes or red potatoes
    ½ lb. green beans
    1 lb. pasta*

Boil potatoes with skins. Peel & quarter. I do not peel the red potatoes. Cook green beans until just tender crisp.

PESTO: In a blender or food processor, combine: **
    2 C fresh basil   2-4 cloves of garlic
    ½ C olive oil   melted butter
    3-5 T pine nuts, toasted

Stir in Parmesan cheese, salt & pepper to taste.

* Best if made with rigatoni, penne, or bow ties.

** The amounts of everything is just a guide. More potatoes, less potatoes, more green beans, less green beans, more or less pesto, it is up to you.

*** My wonderful daughter-in-law, Sharon Lednak, loves this dish. She says it is easy to make and take when you need to bring a dish to share. Good hot, room temperature, or even cold.

SPAGHETTI with TUNA & LEMON

    2 T fresh lemon juice
    ½ C olive oil + more to toss with pasta
    1 ½ C best-quality canned Italian tuna in oil
    1 tsp. dried oregano – crush between fingers
    2 tsp. finely chopped oregano
    1-2 fresh hot peppers, seeded & chopped
        OR 1/8 to ¼ tsp. cayenne
    1 tsp. capers
    16 black oil-cured olives, pitted & chopped
    2 T chopped parsley
    4 small cooked & peeled potatoes, cut into ¼ " dice
    1 lb. spaghetti
    Lemon wedges (optional)

Cook spaghetti in boiling salted water. Reserve a cup of pasta water for sauce if needed. Whisk lemon juice & olive oil together. Add remaining ingredients. Toss to combine. In a large bowl, toss spaghetti with 1 or 2 tablespoons of olive oil. Add enough pasta water to moisten & coat spaghetti. Add the tuna & potato mixture and toss well. Serve right away. Pass lemon wedges to spritz over pasta.

PASTA with PASTA WATER SAUCE

Cook pasta in salt water. While pasta is cooking, heat oil & butter in deep skillet. Add onions and garlic. Do not brown. Remove pasta from water with tongs or spider. Add pasta to skillet to finish cooking. Add pasta water to loosen pasta. Add cheese, black pepper, parsley, and a little more butter. Be sure and add enough pasta water to loosen dish. Very good -- Fast -- Easy!!

LINGUINE with MOZZARELLA, EGG & CAPOCOLLO

3 large eggs, room temperature
½ C grated Parmesan cheese
Pinch of salt
4 T olive oil
3 oz. (1/2 to 2/3 C) chopped capocollo*
2 tsp. coarsely chopped <u>fresh</u> sage, not dried
1 lb. linguine
6 oz. fresh Mozzarella

Mix eggs, cheese & salt together and set aside. Heat oil, capocollo, and sage in a fry pan over moderate heat. Cook stirring from time to time until capocollo begins to crisp. Ladle ½ C pasta water into fry pan and cook until most of the liquid is gone. Set aside over lowest heat. If it becomes too dry, add a little more pasta water. Cook pasta in boiling salt water until al dente. Just before draining pasta, scatter mozzarella in fry pan to soften. Drain pasta, and reserve some water. Add pasta to fry pan and toss to combine with mozzarella. If too dry, add a little pasta water. It will be string like. Off the heat, fold in eggs and cheese. If eggs do not thicken, stir over very low heat until eggs cling to pasta. Serve immediately.

* You can substitute equal amounts of prosciutto or Italian salami for capocollo.

Serve with extra cheese.

Capocollo can be spelled capicola.

PASTA FOR A CROWD

5 lbs. pasta (macaroni, not spaghetti)

3 peppers, diced   4 cloves garlic, crushed
2 onions, diced   4 lb. ground meat

Brown the meat in a skillet. As the meat browns, add the peppers, onions, and garlic. Sauté until soft and the meat is browned. Salt & pepper to taste.

Make a sauce using:
4 cans tomato soup. Refill 2 cans with water. Add 2 to 3 quarts of tomato sauce and 2 small cans of tomato paste. Refill each paste can with water. Season sauce and heat. Cook pasta al dente. Drain. Add peppers and meat mixture to pasta and stir to mix lightly. Add ½ to ¾ sauce. Lightly mix. Top with remaining sauce and cheese.

I make this in a large 18-20 quart electric roaster.

This recipe came from my Aunt Ella, my father's sister. She was a cook at the Italian Club and made this for large groups. She always used a pasta, a macaroni that the name on the bag or box was "Gnocchi".

SPAGHETTI ALLA CARBONARA

This dish is very good, but it can be a little tricky. So here are a few tricks that I have learned to make it easier.

1. Cook the spaghetti while making the sauce. Cook it in half the salted water you would normally use to cook spaghetti. The water will be starchy, and the starch will let the sauce adhere to the spaghetti and not clump. Be sure and save 1 cup of the pasta water, you will need it to loosen the sauce.
2. Start the chopped bacon in a skillet with a little water or white wine. When the liquid has evaporated, add 3 T olive oil and cook until the bacon browns and is a soft crisp. Add chopped garlic and cook another minute. Set aside, but when adding to pasta be sure it is very hot.
3. Beat eggs, cheese and black pepper together. Temper the egg mixture by whisking in 1 T hot bacon drippings.
4. To the drained pasta, you will toss in the very hot bacon, garlic and drippings. Then immediately pour on the egg mixture and toss well. Add pasta water as needed. Start with 1/3 cup. Do Not Scramble the eggs. It should be silky and creamy.

   1 lb. spaghetti (can use fettuccine or linguine)
   ½ lb. bacon, cut into ½" pieces (can use pancetta)
   4 eggs, beaten
   ½ C grated Parmesan cheese
   Chopped parsley for garnish
   Salt & pepper

Put the drained pasta back into the hot pot it was cooked in and add the bacon and egg mixture to pot. It must be hot so that the eggs cook. Work fast and serve immediately.

Some people add a little cream to the eggs. Top with more grated cheese and parsley. I have also seen it with some frozen peas tossed in after they were heated.

Many Italian babies grew up eating tiny pasta, cooked & drained, and a beaten egg tossed in. The heat of the pasta cooked the egg just enough.

SPAGHETTI with ANCHOVIES
Spaghettini alle Acciughe (ah-Lee-chee)

This is one of my very favorites. It is always on the Christmas Eve table.

    1 lb. spaghettini (thin spaghetti)
    1 C olive oil
    4-6 cloves of garlic, chopped sliced
    1 or 2 cans of flat anchovies, chopped
    Salt & pepper to taste
    ¼ C chopped parsley

Heat the olive oil and garlic in a large skillet over moderate heat. Keep a close eye on the skillet as you want the garlic to cook slowly, just to golden – Not a Hint of Browning. Add anchovies and the oil they are packed in. Simmer 2-3 minutes. Add parsley.

Cook spaghettini (see box) 6-7 minutes. Drain and mix with the sauce.*

* Save a little pasta water to loosen dish if needed.

SPAGHETTINI AGLIO-OLIO
Spaghetti with Olive Oil & Garlic

This dish is made like Acciughe, just leave out the anchovies and add a little butter.

LASAGNA (MEAT)

There are many different lasagnas. The most well known is a meat lasagna.

    Tomato sauce with meat   Parsley
    3 lb. Ricotta   Onions
    1 lb. Mozzarella   Garlic
    Parmesan cheese   Spices

    1 lb. lasagna noodles (will not use them all)

SAUCE: You start with a tomato meat sauce. In a Dutch oven, or heavy bottom sauce pan, sauté garlic and onions about 5 minutes. Add ground chuck and pork; sauté until well browned. Add tomatoes, tomato paste, parsley, small amount of sugar if needed, basil, oregano, salt & pepper to taste.

Bring to a boil; reduce heat and simmer covered, stirring occasionally not to let it stick on bottom. Simmer about an hour or so.

ASSEMBLE: Boil noodles in salted water al dente. Remove to a pan of cold water until you are ready for them. In a 9 x 13 inch pan or baking dish, layer noodles, starting with a little sauce on the bottom. Using a large container of Ricotta, beat 3 eggs, ½ cup Parmesan cheese, and some parsley into the Ricotta. Layer noodles, Ricotta mixture, sprinkle on shredded Mozzarella cheese & sauce. Repeat layers until all ingredients are used, ending with sauce.

Bake at 350° covered for 30 minutes. Uncover and bake another 30-40 minutes. Let set 20 minutes before you cut.

SEAFOOD LASAGNA *

1 green onion, finely chopped	¼ tsp. white pepper, divided
2 T oil	½ C flour
2 T plus ½ C butter, divided	1 ½ C milk
½ C chicken broth	1 C heavy whipping cream
1 bottle (8 oz.) clam juice	½ C shredded Parmesan cheese, divided
1 lb. bay scallops	
1 lb. small uncooked shrimp, peeled & deveined	
1 pkg. (8 oz.) imitation crab meat, chopped	
9 lasagna noodles, cooked & drained (al dente)	

In a large skillet, sauté onion in oil and 2 Tablespoons butter until tender. Stir in broth and clam juice; bring to a boil. Add all seafood and 1/8 tsp. white pepper; return to a boil. Reduce heat; simmer uncovered 3-4 minutes or until shrimp turn pink and scallops are firm and opaque, stirring gently. Drain, reserving cooking liquid; set seafood mixture aside.

In a large saucepan, melt the remaining butter; stir in flour until smooth. Combine milk and reserved cooking liquid; gradually add to the saucepan. Add salt & remaining white pepper. Bring to a boil; cook and stir for 2 minutes or until thickened. Remove from heat; stir in cream and ¼ C Parmesan cheese. Stir ¾ cup white sauce into the seafood mixture.

Spread ½ cup white sauce in a greased 9 x 13 inch baking dish. Top with three noodles; spread with half of the seafood mixture and 1 ¼ C sauce. Repeat layers. Top with remaining noodles, sauce and Parmesan cheese. Bake uncovered at 350° for 25-40 minutes, or until golden brown. Let stand 15 minutes before cutting.

* This is a very rich dish. Wonderful dish for company. Serves about 12.

CREAMY SEAFOOD LASAGNA

Quick & Easy Seafood Lasagna

¾ C chopped onion
2 T butter
8 oz. cream cheese, cubed
1 ½ C cottage cheese
1 egg, lightly beaten
2 tsp. dried basil
1 tsp. salt
¼ tsp. pepper
1 can cream of shrimp soup, undiluted
1 can cream of mushroom soup, undiluted
½ C white wine or chicken broth
½ C milk
2 pkgs. (8 oz. each) imitation crab meat, flaked
1 can (5 oz.) small shrimp, rinsed & drained
9 lasagna noodles, cooked & drained
½ C grated Parmesan cheese
¾ C shredded Monterey Jack cheese

In a large skillet, sauté onion in butter until tender. Reduce heat. Add cream cheese; cook and stir until melted and smooth. Stir in cottage cheese, egg, basil, salt & pepper. Remove from heat and set aside.

In a large bowl, combine the soups, wine or broth, milk, crab and shrimp.

Arrange three noodles in a greased 9 x 13 inch pan or baking dish. Spread with a third of the cottage cheese mixture and a third of the seafood mixture. Repeat layers twice. Sprinkle with Parmesan cheese.

Cover and bake at 350° for 40 minutes. Uncover; sprinkle with Monterey Jack cheese. Bake for 10 minutes longer or until cheese melts. Let stand for 15 minutes before serving.

SEAFOOD FRA DIAVOLO*

This recipe was created in 2006 for the Winter Olympics that were played in Torino, Italy. The sauce can be hot and spicy. You can adjust the heat to your taste. This recipe is more flavorful than hot.

>   3 T olive oil
>   5 cloves garlic, coarsely chopped
>   1 (28 oz.) can crushed tomatoes
>   1 (28 oz.) can diced tomatoes
>   2 T dried oregano
>   1 tsp. dried basil
>   1 tsp. sugar
>   1 tsp. crushed red pepper
>   1 T salt
>   ½ tsp. black pepper
>   1 doz. little neck clams, cleaned**
>   2 lb. mussels, cleaned**
>   1 lb. shrimp, peeled & deveined
>   1 lb. spaghetti

In a large pot, heat the oil over medium heat & sauté the garlic until golden. Stir in crushed and diced tomatoes, oregano, basil, sugar, red pepper, salt & pepper. Reduce heat, cover and simmer for 25-30 minutes. Add the clams and mussels. Cover and cook for 5 minutes. Add the shrimp and cook 5-7 minutes, or until clams and mussels open and shrimp are pink.

Cook the spaghetti according to the package. Drain pasta. Discard any unopened clams or mussels. Serve sauce over pasta.

* **Fra Diavolo** translates to "Devil Brother", because it can be so spicy!

** Most clams and mussels are sold clean now, but if needed, wash them under cold running water and remove any black beard from each mussel.

CLAM SAUCE

WHITE CLAM SAUCE

1 onion, chopped
6 cloves garlic, chopped
¼ C olive oil
1 lb. linguine
4 (6.5 oz.) cans minced or chopped clams*

½ C butter
Salt & pepper to taste
2 T dry white wine

In a large skillet, sauté onions and garlic in olive oil until onions are translucent. Drain the clams, reserving the juice. Stir in the clams, ½ the reserved juice, butter, salt & pepper, and wine. Simmer about 20 minutes until sauce has reduced 1/3 and thickened. (You have more clam juice if needed.) Spoon clam sauce over cooked linguine. Top with chopped parsley.

RED CLAM SAUCE

Sauté onions and garlic until soft. Drain clams and set aside the juice. Add red pepper flakes and cook 30 seconds. Add one 28-oz. can whole or crushed tomatoes (crush whole tomatoes with your hands) and ½ the reserved clam juice. Increase the heat and bring to a boil. Reduce heat. Cover and simmer 15-20 minutes. During the last 5 minutes, stir in the clams, basil, parsley, salt & pepper, all to taste. Drain cooked pasta, add to sauce, and toss to combine.

* The clams can be minced, chopped, or whole, or a mixture to your taste.

MANICOTTI

In 1957 I won first place in the Nationality Division of the cooking contest held by the New Kensington Daily Dispatch. I was pregnant with my first child, Jeannine, and first prize was $10.00!!

  2 C flour
  1 C milk
  1 C water
  6 eggs

  ¼ tsp. salt
  Grated zest of one lemon
  4-6 T melted butter
  Vegetable oil or Pam spray for frying

Whisk eggs in a medium bowl until blended. Pour in milk, water and salt. Stir together until blended. Add lemon zest. At this point, if you like, you can add 1 tsp. or so of sugar. Gradually sift the flour into liquid, stirring constantly until the mixture is smooth. Stir in the melted butter. The batter will have the consistency of melted ice cream.

CREPES: Heat 1 Tablespoon of vegetable oil or Pam in a 5" – 8" crepe pan or skillet (non-stick is best). Pour off excess oil. Holding the pan at a 45-degree angle, pour about 3 Tablespoons of batter into the pan, allowing it to run down from the highest point. The secret of making crepes is to flex your wrist, distributing the batter over the entire bottom of the pan as quickly as possible before the batter sets. Cook only on one side. Put wax paper between finished crepes. Repeat making crepes, adding oil as needed.

FILLING:

  2 lb. or 15 oz. container of Ricotta cheese*
  ½ C Parmesan cheese
  1 (8 oz.) pkg. shredded Mozzarella cheese

  2 eggs, beaten
  4 T parsley, chopped
  Salt & pepper

In a bowl, combine all ingredients. Place about 3-4 T of filling down the center of each crepe; roll up. Spoon some sauce in the bottom of a 9 x 13 inch pan or baking dish. Place crepes, seam side down, over sauce. Spoon some sauce on top. Cover and bake at 350° for 20 minutes. Uncover and bake another 20 minutes. Sprinkle with some grated cheese & sauce.

* If the Ricotta is wet, you may want to drain it in a sieve before making filling.

MAKING MANICOTTI are Mrs. Richard Lednak, right, who won a prize in the nationality division of the Daily Dispatch Recipe Contest and her mother, Mrs. Frank Landi, left, both of 2005 Moore St., Arnold, who taught her how to make the Italian dish.

'Manicotti' Wins Award

College Student's Wife Wins Nationality Prize

Winning a $10 first prize in the Nationality Division of the Dispatch Recipe Contest was the first time Mrs. R. P. Lednak has ever won a contest.

A recipe for Manicotti, a main dish, earned her the prize. Mrs. Lednak, who is expecting their first child about June 1 is staying with her parents, Mr. and Mrs. Frank Landi of 2005 Moore St., Arnold, while her husband attends Pennsylvania State University. Mrs. Lednak, who hasn't been married quite two years, and her husband, who was stationed with the Army at Ft. Lewis, Wash., returned to Arnold from Ft. Lewis, Wash., at Christmas.

Manicotti has been a favorite dish of the Landis for years; Mrs. Lednak learned how to make it from her mother.

"We've made it for years," Mrs. Lednak said. "We liked lasagna but often couldn't find lasagna noodles so we started to make this — it's much easier."

See next page to read this article!

TEXT FROM 1957 NEWSPAPER ARTICLE:

New Kensington Daily Dispatch
Thursday, May 23, 1957

College Student's Wife Wins Nationality Prize

Winning a $10 first prize in the Nationality Division of the Dispatch Recipe Contest was the first time Mrs. R. P. Lednak has ever won a contest.

A recipe for Manicotti, a main dish, earned her the prize. Mrs. Lednak, who is expecting their first child about June 1 is staying with her parents, Mr. and Mrs. Frank Landi of 2005 Moore St., Arnold, while her husband attends Pennsylvania State University. Mrs. Lednak, who hasn't been married quite two years, and her husband, who was stationed with the Army at Ft. Lewis, Wash., returned to Arnold from Ft. Lewis, Wash., at Christmas.

Manicotti has been a favorite dish of the Landis for years: Mrs. Lednak learned how to make it from her mother.

"We've made it for years," Mrs. Lednak said. "We liked lasagna but often couldn't find lasagna noodles so we started to make this – it's much easier."

LINGUINE with TOASTED ALMONDS & JALAPEÑOS

In a dry skillet, toast 1 C almonds (more or less to your taste). Be careful not to burn almonds. In a food processor, whirl together:

  Toasted almonds
  1/3 C olive oil
  3 cloves garlic, chopped or sliced
  Parsley

In a large skillet, sauté 3-4 more cloves of garlic in about ½ C olive oil. Do not burn garlic. Add 1-2 seeded and sliced jalapeños. Lower heat. When jalapeños are soft, add mixture from the food processor. Add a pat of butter for richness, and the juice and rind of a lemon. Salt & pepper to taste. Put cooked linguine in skillet with sauce and toss to coat pasta.

Reserve about 1 C pasta water to loosen pasta if needed.

Serve with grated cheese and parsley.

Gnocchi

Gnocchi are not hard to make, but they can be tricky. The trick is to know that the less flour you add, the less you handle the dough. The less moisture in the potatoes, the lighter the gnocchi will be.

Potato Gnocchi

    4 large Russet potatoes, unpeeled & washed
    Salt
    2 eggs
    3 C flour, or as needed

Cook potatoes in a pot of enough cold water to cover, and cook until tender, about 35-40 minutes. Remove from water, and when just cool enough to handle, remove skins & mash. Spread them on a cookie sheet to allow steam (water) to dry out. When potatoes are cool, beat eggs and salt together. Working on a floured surface with floured hands, add the egg mixture to the potatoes. Work the mixture with both hands, adding as much flour as necessary to form a firm but moist dough. Do not over work dough.

Cut dough into about 6 parts. Using fingers and palms, roll each piece of dough into a rope about ½ -inch thick. Cut the rope crosswise into ½ -inch pieces. Using the floured tines of a fork, press down one side of each gnocchi, or if you get the hang of it, you can press and roll quickly with your thumb. It will either have 4 lines on the gnocchi, or a small dimple.

Lay the gnocchi on a floured kitchen towel as you make them. At this point the gnocchi must be cooked in boiling salted water, or frozen.

TO FREEZE: Place them on a cookie sheet. When frozen, put in plastic bags.

Serve cooked gnocchi with red sauce, or butter & garlic.

RICOTTA GNOCCHI

      1 ½ lb. Ricotta, drained*
      1 ¾ tsp. salt, + more for pasta water
      2 eggs
      ½ C Parmesan cheese
      ¼ tsp. nutmeg
      2 C flour

Make the same as potato gnocchi.

* To drain the Ricotta, drain in a fine mesh sieve for several hours or overnight in the refrigerator.

Ricotta gnocchi can be served with red sauce, or a sauce with butter & toasted pine nuts, cream and Parmesan cheese. Some crisp fried bacon and chopped parsley and/or basil.

RAVIOLI DOUGH & FILLINGS
Dough on next page

MEAT FILLING:
- 2 lb. ground beef
- ½ lb. ground pork or Italian sausage, casing removed
- ½ lb. ground veal or chicken
- Bread crumbs
- Parmesan cheese
- 6 eggs*
- Medium onion, chopped
- 3-6 cloves of garlic, chopped or sliced
- Parsley
- Salt & pepper
- 1 box frozen spinach

Sauté onion and garlic in a large skillet with all the ground meats in a little olive oil. Add salt & pepper to taste. In a small amount of water, cook and drain well, 1 box of frozen spinach. Add to meat. White meat is warm, add about ¾ C Parmesan cheese, and bread crumbs as needed. Mix in beaten eggs and parsley. Check seasonings.

* Rule of thumb: Use 2 eggs for every pound of meat

RICOTTA FILLING:
- 8 oz. Ricotta, drained**
- 1 to 1 ½ C Parmesan cheese
- ½ tsp. salt
- Hint of nutmeg
- 1 egg, slightly beaten

Mix all together.

** Drain in a fine mesh sieve for 2-3 hours

RAVIOLI DOUGH

3 C flour
4 eggs
1 tsp. olive oil

½ tsp. salt
Warm water as needed

Spoon 2 2/3 cups flour into a food processor with a metal blade. Beat eggs, olive oil and salt together. With motor running, pour egg mixture into processor. Process until a rough and slightly sticky dough is formed. If too dry, add a little warm water. Remove dough to a floured work surface and knead by hand for about 5 minutes. Roll dough into a smooth ball. Cover in a small bowl and let rest for 1 hour at room temperature, or up to 1 day in the refrigerator.

Roll dough into thin sheets with a pasta machine. Working on a lightly floured surface, lay out one sheet of dough. Place a scant Tablespoon of filling in spots about 2 inches apart. Cover with second sheet of dough. With fingers, press the top sheet of dough to the bottom, pressing out any air. With pastry cutter, cut into squares or rectangles about 2 ½" – 3". Be sure and seal edges.

POLENTA

In the "old days", polenta was cooked for hours. As a young girl at home, my memories of polenta was the way it bubbled up in the pan and splattered out like hot lava. Therefore, you needed a very long stick to stir the polenta, and I do mean long. My father, Frank "Dutch" (as he was known) Landi, sanded a broom handle and he called it a "Stoccola". I can remember eating polenta at my grandmother's house when she put down a white cloth on the table, poured the polenta onto the middle of the cloth, spooned on the sauce, and we all sat around and ate our way to the center.

Things change.

Now there is instant polenta, and though many Italians are turning over in their graves at the thought, It's Very Good! 10-15 minutes – you're done. Be careful, it still spits! The sauce is the thing – and there are many – anything you can think of to go on top. I did a dinner in Lakeland, Florida, for 300 people and had a choice of 2 sauces: chicken or sausage.

I had a party in my home with a group of well-to-do, sophisticated people, and used my grandmother's serving method: a white tablecloth with polenta in the center – It was great! They loved it! Now, very high class restaurants are serving polenta almost like a dish. They make it, let it get cold, cut it in squares or triangles, fry it, and top it with whatever.

When I was a young girl, leftover polenta was put into a loaf pan, sliced down, fried with butter, and served with maple syrup.

So buy the instant and just go for it. The instant is good. I have also seen it in the market, made into a roll. You just have to slice, heat, and eat with whatever you want to top it with. There is no end to how to serve polenta.

Some examples of toppings: sausage, chicken, red sauce, alfredo sauce, rabbit, venison, etc. Cool it, then slice it, dip it in egg and crumbs, and fry. Top it with meat or stew, or use it just as a side.

RISOTTO

Risotto, like polenta, has many different styles. What you must know: only short-grain rice is grown in Italy. Arborio is what you need.

BASIC RISOTTO

4-5 C chicken stock (hot)
3-4 T olive oil
1 medium onion, minced
1-2 cloves garlic, minced

2 C Arborio rice
Salt
2-3 T butter
Parmesan cheese

Heat the olive oil in a heavy bottom pan or skillet. Add onions and garlic, stirring until softened, 2-3 minutes. Add some of the rice and stir until toasted, 1-2 minutes. Season rice lightly with salt & ladle enough hot chicken stock into the pan to barely cover the rice. Bring to a boil, then lower the heat to a simmer. Cook, stirring constantly, until all the stock has been absorbed. Continue cooking & adding hot stock in small batches, just enough to moisten the rice, and cook until each batch of stock is absorbed. Stir constantly. The last liquid can be, if you like, a little white wine.

If you like a creamier Risotto, stir in a little more stock once the rice is al dente, but do not cook the rice any further. For a denser Risotto, keep the rice over the heat until the last addition of stock is absorbed. The general rule is, Risotto with seafood is looser, and risotto with meat, game or mushrooms is more dense. But the golden rule is, "How Do <u>You</u> Like It?"

Examples of different Risotto: Butter & cheese, chicken, asparagus, basil & parsley, mushrooms, Parmesan, sausage, different cheeses mixed, lemon, etc.

POLENTA with GAME

1 C cornmeal – Polenta   1 ½ C boiling water
1 C cold water   Salt

Add cold water to polenta & stir the mixture into the boiling water. Add salt to taste. Stir 45 minutes to 1 hour.* Careful – it spits!

Pheasant, rabbit, squirrel, deer, etc. Whatever they shot. In a roaster with the meat, add garlic, onion, rosemary, sage, salt & Pepper, and a mixture of ½ olive oil and ½ melted butter. Mix. Roast about 1-1 ½ hours at 325°. Add mushrooms, wine (red or white). Depending on how mush meat, 1-3 C of wine. Roast another 1-1 ½ hours until meat is tender.

Spoon over plates of Polenta.

* You can use instant polenta and save a lot of time and work. No game – use roasted chicken, sausage, anything you like. It's All Good.

NOT YOUR EVERY DAY SUNDAY PASTA SAUCE

4 T olive oil
½ C diced onion
4 oz. cooked ham
1 C Italian tomatoes w/ liquid
1 T basil
1 ½ C whipping cream*
¼ to ½ tsp. nutmeg
Salt & pepper

1 lb. spaghetti, cooked & drained
Parmesan cheese
2 large jars marinated artichoke hearts, chopped & drained
Toasted almonds, slivered or sliced

In a skillet with olive oil, add onions & ham and cook until onions are soft. Stir in tomatoes, breaking up with a wooden spoon or crushing in your hands before adding to pan. Add artichokes, basil and cream. Let it come to a boil, then simmer until sauce reduces, stirring to prevent sticking. Add salt, pepper & nutmeg to taste. Serve over spaghetti; top with Parmesan cheese. Garnish with almonds.

* Can use heavy cream or Half & Half.

BAR-B-Q BAKED BEANS

BEANS:
- 1 (10 oz.) pkg. frozen lima beans, cook & drain
- 3 (16 oz.) cans baked beans
- 2 (16 oz.) cans kidney beans
- ¼ C brown sugar
- 2 tsp. salt
- ¼ tsp. pepper
- 1 tsp. mustard

Mix all together in a large roasting pan. Set aside and make marble-sized meatballs.

MEATBALLS:
- 2 lb. ground meat
- 1 T salt
- ½ tsp. pepper
- 1 small onion, minced

Make into small balls and fry until brown in 1 Tablespoon shortening. Set aside. Make sauce.

SAUCE:
- 1 C ketchup
- 1 T vinegar
- 1 T brown sugar
- 1 T butter

Mix all sauce ingredients & simmer for 20 minutes.

Add sauce and meatballs to beans. Mix well. Add a jar of small white onions on top of beans and bake for 45 minutes at 375°.

WHITE BEANS with ROSEMARY & VINEGAR

    1 can of cannellini beans   2 sprigs fresh rosemary
    ¼ C olive oil   ¼ C red wine vinegar
    1 yellow onion, sliced   Salt & pepper to taste
    3 sliced prosciutto or bacon, chopped

Heat oil in a sauce pan or skillet. Stir in onions & prosciutto or bacon. Brown. Add drained beans, fresh rosemary & vinegar. Simmer until flavors have a chance to blend, about 15 minutes. Salt & pepper to taste. Remove rosemary and serve. A good side dish with grilled or roasted meats.*

* In the appetizer section, you will find a recipe for Italian Rice Balls. They make a wonderful side dish or a nice lunch with a green salad.

RICE with PORK from PUERTO RICO

1 onion, chopped fine
5-6 cloves garlic, chopped fine
½ green pepper, chopped fine
Cilantro & Oregano
Salt
Olive oil
Sazon Goya, sold in all markets in a box of foil packets

8 oz. can tomato sauce
Pork shoulder
Rice
1-2 T capers
Green olives with pimento

Two or three days before you make this dish:

Make a sofrito by first chopping fine the onion, garlic, green pepper, cilantro, oregano & salt. With a mortar & pestle, grind to a paste, adding oil up to a cup. If you do not have a mortar & pestle, use a food processor. To this, add Sazon Goya seasoning. Cut pork shoulder into chunks, bite-sized, and marinate 2-3 days in a zip lock bag, turning a few times.

Brown pork in seasoned oil and chopped sofrito. Sauté until onions are transparent. Add 8 oz. can of tomato sauce and rice. Add water to cover rice. Two to one, water to rice. When almost done, add capers & green olives with pimento.

PASTA with SAUSAGE & BUTTERNUT SQUASH

3 T olive oil, divided
1 lb. Italian hot sausage
1 C chopped onion
5 cloves garlic, thickly sliced
1 T chopped basil
1 T chopped fresh sage
¼ tsp. red pepper flakes (opt.)
1 C white wine
1 ½ C butternut squash, peeled, seeded & cut into ½-inch dice
2 ½ C chicken stock
2 T salt (optional)
1 lb. pasta: sea shells, penne rigate, or rigatoni
6 T Parmesan cheese
2 T softened butter

Pour 1 tablespoon of olive oil into a large skillet, and cook over high heat for 2 minutes. Take the sausage out of the casing and add it to the hot oil. Cook for about 3 minutes until it browns. Using the back of a wooden spoon, break the sausage up into small, bite-sized pieces while it is browning. Turn off the heat. Using a slotted spoon, place the sausage in a bowl; cover and set aside. Keep about 1 tablespoon of the oil and fat left in the pan, and discard the rest.

Add the remaining 2 tablespoons of olive oil to the pan, and cook over medium heat for 3 minutes. Add the onion, garlic, basil and sage, and cook for 4 minutes, stirring well, until the onion and garlic start to brown. (If you like it really spicy, add the optional ¼ tsp. of red pepper flakes.) Add the reserved sausage and cook for 2 more minutes, stirring well. Add the chicken stock, bring to a boil over high heat, and then reduce the heat and allow to simmer for 30 minutes.

While the sauce is cooking, bring a large pot of water to a boil. (If you wish, add the optional tablespoons of salt.) When the water reaches a rolling boil, add the pasta and cook according to the instructions on the package. When the pasta is cooked, drain it well in a colander over the sink. Pour the pasta back into the pot, add the sauce, and cook over medium heat for 3-5 minutes, stirring constantly. Remove the pan from the heat, add the Parmesan cheese and softened butter, and serve.

PASTA with TOMATO CREAM SAUCE

12 oz. linguine or other pasta
2 T olive oil
2 T butter
1 medium onion, finely diced
4 garlic cloves, minced
2 (15 oz.) cans tomato sauce
Salt & pepper to taste
Pinch of sugar
1 C heavy cream
½ C grated Parmesan or Romano cheese
Chopped fresh basil

Cook pasta according to package directions, and reserve a few ladlefuls of hot pasta water.

Heat olive oil and butter in a large skillet over medium heat. Add onion and cook until translucent, about 4 minutes. Add garlic and cook, stirring, for 1 minute more. Pour in tomato sauce and add salt, pepper, and sugar. Stir to combine and add more seasoning to taste, if desired. Cook sauce until warm, then stir in heavy cream. Add Parmesan and drained pasta. Toss to coat pasta in sauce and add hot pasta water to thin if necessary.

Top with fresh basil. Serve immediately.

SPAGHETTI with FRESH CLAMS, PARSLEY, AND LEMON

½ C extra-virgin olive oil
8 garlic cloves, thinly sliced
3 lb. fresh Manila clams or small little neck clams, scrubbed
¼ C plus 2 T chopped fresh Italian parsley
½ C dry white wine
¼ C fresh lemon juice
1 lb. spaghetti

Heat oil in heavy large pot over medium-high heat. Add sliced garlic and sauté until light brown, about 1 minute. Add clams and ¼ C chopped Italian parsley; stir 2 minutes. Add wine; simmer 2 minutes. Add fresh lemon juice. Cover and simmer until clams open, about 6 minutes (discard any clams that do not open).

Meanwhile, cook pasta in pot of boiling salted water until just tender but still firm to bite (al dente). Drain. Add to clams; toss to coat. Season with salt & pepper. Sprinkle with 2 tablespoons parsley.

EASY PAELLA

Green pepper	Shrimp
Onion	Mussels and/or clams
Garlic	Chicken broth
Chicken	Saffron – you can use Sazon Goya
Olive oil	(less expensive & easier to find
Paprika	in most supermarkets)
Salt & pepper	Rice
Dried oregano	Lemon
Chorizo sausage	Bay leaf
	Peas

It is essential to have all your ingredients ready ahead of time. Every paella starts with a "sofrito", which is a sauté of green peppers, onion & garlic, fried in a tomato base or sauce.

To start, cut up one chicken and season pieces with 1 T olive oil, 1 T paprika (sweet or smoked), 2 tsp. dried oregano, salt & pepper to taste, and 2 cloves garlic, minced. Set chicken aside.

Sauté 1 lb. of chorizo sausage (links cut into quarters) in a heavy skillet in olive oil 2-3 minutes. Set aside.

In the same skillet, sauté seasoned chicken pieces, browning on sides to a golden color. Set aside.

In some clean oil, sauté cleaned shrimp for 1-2 minutes. Set aside.

In a paella pan or stainless steel pan, heat 2 T olive oil, 1 large onion diced, and sauté about 2 minutes. Add 1 green pepper chopped, and 2 large cloves of garlic, and sauté over low heat another 2 minutes. Do not burn garlic. Add 1 or 2 peeled, seeded, and finely chopped tomatoes, and simmer until juices have reduced. Add 2 C short grain white rice and sauté an additional 4-5 minutes.

EASY PAELLA continued ...

To 4 C of chicken broth, add 10-15 saffron threads, 1 bay leaf, the juice and zest of 1 large lemon. Simmer broth 5-10 minutes. Remove bay leaf. Add broth 1 C at a time to rice, stirring to mix & distribute ingredients evenly in pan. THIS IS IT. DO NOT STIR AGAIN.

Place chicken & chorizo into rice, tucking it in along with the shrimp. If using mussels or clams, place them on rice, hinged side into rice. Scatter the peas over the top.

Preheat oven 375-400°. Place pan in lowest part of oven (some say the floor), and bake 25-30 minutes, or until all the liquid has been absorbed and the rice & the grains are tender but not soft. Remove from oven and drape a kitchen towel over the top. Let rest 8-10 minutes. Garnish with lemon slices and serve directly from pan.

This is not hard. Most of it is done ahead of time and you just put it in the oven when your company comes. It is lot of fun.

You can make it with just chicken, or add pieces of browned pork and/or fish and shellfish. It is up to you.

RICE & LENTILS
(Mujadara)

1 C lentils
1 C rice
1 large onion, chopped
½ C olive oil
Salt & pepper

Wash lentils and boil until tender, about 15 minutes. Drain. In another pan, cook washed rice in salted water, about 15 minutes.

In the meantime, slice or chop onion. In a skillet with ½ C olive oil, sauté onion until browned. (If you like, add 1 tsp. cumin seeds to oil before adding onions. Brown seeds about 1 minute.) Put drained lentils and rice into a pan. Pour oil & onion into rice mixture. Salt & pepper to taste. Simmer a few minutes to improve flavor.

I have seen this with the lentils & rice cooked together – I don't like the color.

I also add some butter to the olive oil and onions for flavor.

Serve with yogurt or sour cream.

LAMB RAGU SAUCE

2 T olive oil
2 large cloves garlic
½ lb. ground lamb*
6 or 7 green olives with pits,
  pitted & chopped
¼ C capers
2 ½ C cherry tomatoes, cut in half
¼ C minced parsley
Salt & pepper to taste
½ C grate Parmesan cheese

Heat the oil in a large sauté pan over medium heat & cook the lamb & garlic until the meat is no longer pink. Add the olives & capers and cook a few minutes. Add the tomatoes, lower the heat & cook the sauce for 15 minutes.**

Stir in parsley, salt & pepper to taste. Keep the sauce warm and covered until pasta is ready. This sauce goes well with bow-ties or wide egg noodles.

* If you are lucky enough to live by Jeannine and Su, you can make this with fresh ground goat meat.
** I double this sauce.

Jeannine

MEATS:

BEEF, CHICKEN, GOAT, PORK, and VEAL

ITALIAN ROAST BEEF

This roast beef is made for sandwiches, and the sandwiches are so good, they can be used for any occasion. They are served with a giardiniera, a mixture of vegetables in olive oil and vinegar: See the next page. But I like them best with fried or roasted sweet peppers. Do this the day before you want it.

> 5 lb. boneless bottom round, or rump roast*
> 3 cloves garlic, finely diced or minced
> 3 T olive oil ½ tsp. red pepper flakes
> 1 tsp. dried oregano 1 envelope onion soup mix
> ½ tsp. black pepper

In a small bowl, mix the garlic, oil, oregano, black pepper, red pepper and envelop of soup mix. With your fingers, rub the herb mixture all over the roast to cover it fully. In a preheated oven at 350°, roast the meat uncovered in a shallow roasting pan, about 30 minutes per pound, for about 2 ½ hours. Roast will be very rare. Don't overcook it. Good idea to check it after 2 hours.

Remove roast from pan. Let it cool. The roast must be cut very thin. It is easier if you refrigerate it after it cools. While the roast is chilling, make the gravy:

> 2 C boiling water Black pepper to taste
> 2 beef bouillon cubes, crushed Check for salt
> 2 tsp. dried oregano Tabasco sauce
> 1 tsp. dried thyme Worcestershire sauce

Add to the roast pan drippings, the boiling water, bouillon cubes, oregano, thyme, pepper and a dash of Tabasco sauce & Worcestershire sauce. Taste for salt & garlic, add some if you wish.

Slice beef very thin & marinate in the gravy overnight. Next day, reheat and serve on crusty Italian rolls.

* Chuck roast is a poor choice, too stringy.

GIARDINIERA for ITALIAN ROAST BEEF

¼ C each, Chopped into 1/8" to ¼" chunks:

Hot peppers	Celery
Sweet peppers	Cauliflower
Zucchini	Onion
Carrots	Fennel

3 cloves garlic, sliced	¼ tsp. pepper
½ tsp. basil	1 C oil
½ tsp. oregano	½ C vinegar
¼ tsp. salt	

Spoon vegetables into a clean jar. Pour in the mixed oil & vinegar. Use a knife to dislodge bubbles. Screw on lid. Olive oil will get cloudy in the fridge. Canola will stay clear. This will keep for weeks in the refrigerator. Or you can just buy a jar of giardiniera (mixed pickled vegetables)! But like I said, I like roasted peppers better.

EASY BEEF

The next three recipes are just easy things you can do with beef, and they are good for a crowd.

1. ROAST BEEF BAR-B-QUES

½ bunch of celery
1 green pepper
3 onions
1 T salt
1 tsp. pepper

1 C ketchup
3 T Bar-B-Q sauce
1 T Worcestershire
1 ½ C water
½ tsp. chili powder

Dice up celery, onions and green pepper. Combine all ingredients and pour over a 4-6 pound chuck roast. Cover and bake at 300° for 6 hours. Remove from oven and use two forks to flake the meat. Return to sauce. Serve hot on buns.

2. BEEF IN BEER

3-5 lb. roast*
1 can of beer

1 pkg. Lipton Soup mix
1 brown gravy mix

Cook in crock pot until meat is tender.

* You can use rump, bottom round, or chuck.

** If you cube the meat first, it is good over rice or noodles. If you leave the meat whole, take it out and chill (slight freeze), then slice and return to sauce. If you use chuck, it is easy to shred with forks.

*** If your meat is larger, just increase other ingredients.

3. BARBECUPS

Brown a pound of ground beef along with a small chopped onion. Drain.

Then add ½ C barbecue sauce and 1 T brown sugar. Now take 1 tube of Pillsbury Refrigerated Tenderflake Biscuits and press each into an ungreased muffin cup. Spoon meat mixture into cups and sprinkle with shredded sharp cheddar cheese. Bake at 400° for 10-12 minutes. Makes 12 -- A good snack or nice for a party.

SHARON'S MEATLOAF

1 ½ lbs. ground meat
½ C milk
2 T flour
½ tsp. baking powder
Salt & pepper to taste

Small onion, chopped
1 egg, beaten
2 slices bread, cubed
Cream of potato soup

Mix all ingredients together. Oil bottom of pan. Bake meatloaf for 1 hour at 375°. Take out of oven. Pour cream of potato soup mixed with a little water over meatloaf. Return to oven and bake another 30 minutes.

Sharon and Stephanie

MEATLOAF with MUSHROOMS

16 saltine crackers
½ lb. white mushrooms
½ lb. portabella mushrooms
1-2 T oil
1 onion chopped
4 cloves garlic, minced
1 lb. ground pork or Italian sausage

2 eggs
2 T Worcestershire
1 lb. ground beef
½ tsp. thyme
¼ C flour
2 ½ C chicken broth

Process the saltines in food processor or crush in plastic bag until they are finely ground. Remove & set aside 3 or 4 of each of the mushrooms. Process remaining mushrooms or chop until they are very fine. In the oil, sauté the onion until it is browned, about 5 or 6 minutes. Add processed mushrooms and ¼ tsp. salt. Cook until mushrooms begin to brown, about 4-5 minutes. Add the minced garlic and cook about 1 minute. Mix mushrooms and saltines in a large bowl and cool completely, about 15 minutes.

Once the mixture has cooled, add the pork or sausage, eggs, 1 tablespoon Worcestershire sauce, 1 tsp. salt and 1 tsp. pepper. Knead gently until it is mostly combined. Add the beef and knead until mixture is well combined. Shape into a loaf and bake at 350° for about 45-55 minutes. Tent it loosely with foil while making the sauce.

Using the meat drippings, sauté the remaining mushrooms that have been thinly sliced. If you do not have enough drippings, add a little butter. Sauté mushrooms until they are deep golden brown, about 6-8 minutes. Stir in thyme & salt. Add the flour & cook, stirring, until golden, about 2 minutes. Slowly whisk in the chicken broth & remaining 1 T Worcestershire sauce. Bring to a boil. Reduce heat & simmer, whisking occasionally, until thickened, about 10-15 minutes. Season with salt & pepper to taste. Slice meatloaf & serve with gravy.

* You might find it easier to make a slurry of the flour & chicken broth by mixing them in a jar with a tight lid & shaking until smooth, then adding to the sautéed mushrooms. Gravy won't be as dark, but no lumps.

COCA-COLA MEATLOAF

About 1 ½ lbs. ground beef	2 T ketchup
1 ½ C fresh bread crumbs	1 ½ T mustard
¼ C minced onion	1 tsp. salt
2 T finely chopped parsley	½ tsp. basil leaves
1 egg	1/8 tsp. pepper
½ C Coca-Cola	

In a bowl, break up meat with a fork; add crumbs, onion & parsley, mixing well. Beat egg, mix with remaining ingredients. Pour over meat. With fork, toss lightly to blend thoroughly. Mixture will be soft. Turn into a 9x5x3 inch loaf pan. Bake in moderate over at 350° for 1 hour. Let set about 10 minutes before slicing. This loaf will be moist and tender if you mix it lightly with a fork.

COCA-COLA GLAZE

Reduce Coca-Cola, 10-15 minutes. Add 1 T spicy mustard, ½ C ketchup and 1 clove garlic, minced. Simmer 15 more minutes. Will be almost syrup like. Serve on the side or on top of loaf.

Rachel, the lady who cooked at Mt. St. Peters Church, made a meatloaf with just meat, breadcrumbs, eggs, salt & pepper. But she would chop onions, celery and sometimes carrots and a little green pepper, and then she would sauté the vegetables in butter until they were soft. Let them cool and add them to the meat mixture. She said that way no one could pick out any one thing not to like. It all blended together and was very tasty.

BEEF BURGUNDY

4 lb. chuck roast, trim fat & scraps. Save.

Cut meat into chunks; salt & set aside.

In a roasting pan, add 6 oz. salt pork, diced, and all the fat from the chuck roast. Add a large tablespoon of butter.

On a baking sheet, spread 1 pound chopped crimini mushrooms and a box of frozen pearl onions. Toss with a little melted butter and sprinkle with 1 tablespoon or so of sugar. Place in a hot oven at 450° to caramelize, about 20 minutes. In roaster with salt pork, stir in about ½ C flour, 4 C beef broth, 2 C red wine, 4 T gelatin and 2 or 3 anchovies, or a tsp. or so of anchovy paste.

Place chunks of chuck roast in roasting pan on top of mixture in the roaster. Nestle the meat in the roaster, but <u>Do Not</u> cover or push the meat the whole way into the liquid. Roast for 3 ½ hours at 325°. Meat will be browned.

Remove chunks of beef and add meat to caramelized mushrooms and pearl onions. Set aside.

Add another 2 C red wine to roaster. Simmer to reduce sauce. Remove as much fat from top of sauce as you can.* Strain sauce into Dutch over and simmer on top of stove for about 20 minutes. Add beef, mushrooms and pearl onions. Add chopped parsley and serve.

* If you make it a day in advance, it is easy to remove fat from cold sauce.

GREEN CHILI BURGERS

3 jalapeño peppers
3 Anaheim peppers
1 large onion
2 T green chili

1 ½ lb. ground meat
Salt & pepper
Cheese slices

Cut peppers in half and remove seeds. Slice onion into thick slices. Place peppers and onions on a hot grill to char, 2-4 minutes. Place grilled vegetables in a bowl and cover with plastic wrap so they will steam. After a few minutes you can remove skins from peppers. Place peppers & onions along with 1 or 2 cloves of garlic in food processor and coarse chop. Careful not to over process.

Put about 2 T green chili in 1 ½ lb. ground meat with salt & pepper to taste. Shape ground meat into burgers, pressing an indentation into the center of each so they will not puff up and be rounded. Grill burgers on one side for 3-5 minutes. Remove from grill. Spoon green chili on grilled side of burgers and top with a slice of cheese.

Return burgers to grill and grill second side another 3-5 minutes. Serve on buns. Makes four 6-oz. burgers.

BEEF alla CERTOSINA

3 lb. eye of round
2 slices bacon, diced
2 T butter
2 T olive oil
½ tsp. nutmeg
The juice of ½ lemon

6 anchovy fillets, chopped
1/3 C parsley, chopped
1 C stock or water
1 T capers
Salt & pepper

Place bacon, butter and oil in a heavy pan, together with the beef. Brown meat on all sides, and then add all ingredients except the lemon juice and capers. Cover & simmer about 1 ½ - 1 ¾ hours. Add lemon juice and capers the last 5 minutes of cooking. Serve sliced with pan gravy.

THE BEST BAR-B-Q-RIBS

    1 or 2 slabs of ribs

Rub with a mixture of salt, pepper & brown sugar on both sides. Let it set in the refrigerator an hour or two. Grill ribs about 8 minutes on each side. When cool enough to handle, wrap ribs in saran wrap and then in foil. Place on baking sheet and into a 300° oven for about 2 ½ - 3 hours. Careful when you unwrap. Cover with your favorite Bar-B-Q sauce.

The secret is the saran wrap!

Rich at the Grill—In February!

ROUND STEAK PARMESAN

1 ½ lb. round steak
2 eggs, beaten
1/3 C Parmesan cheese
1/3 C bread crumbs

Oil
Flour
Salt & Pepper

Cut steaks into serving pieces and pound with meat mallet between parchment or waxed paper. Dredge in flour seasoned with salt & pepper. Dip into beaten eggs, and then into a mixture of bread crumbs and Parmesan cheese. Brown in oil. Use any good jarred sauce, or make a sauce.

SAUCE:

Sauté 1 small onion & 1 clove of garlic until tender in a little olive oil. Mix 1 12-oz. or 2 6-oz. cans of tomato paste with 3 cups of water. Add onions and garlic with oil, season and simmer for 10 minutes.

Lay meat in a baking pan. Pour ¾ sauce over meat. Top with slices or shredded Mozzarella cheese (about ½ lb.). Top with remaining sauce. Bake for 1 hour at 350°: 45 minutes covered with foil; Last 10-15 minutes uncovered. Sprinkle with Parmesan cheese.

CHICKEN KIEV

Boneless chicken breasts, skin removed
Snipped parsley
Chopped green onion (include green tops)
1 Stick butter, well chilled (frozen)
1 C fine dry bread crumbs
Shortening or cooking oil for deep frying

4 beaten eggs
4 T water
1 C flour
Salt & pepper

Place each piece of chicken between two sheets of plastic wrap or waxed paper. Pond out chicken to 1/8 inch thick (work from center out). Remove top piece of plastic or waxed paper. Sprinkle with parsley and chopped green onion. Season with salt & pepper. Cut butter into 8 pieces.* Place 1 piece of butter on each breast. Roll, folding in sides. Using 3 pie plates, combine beaten eggs & water in one, and flour with salt & pepper in the second, and fine bread crumbs in the third. Roll chicken in flour, then in eggs, and last in bread crumbs (use fingers to press on fine crumbs). Cover & chill at least one hour.**

Heat oil (enough to deep fry) to 375°. Cook for 5 minutes in the oil until golden. Drain on paper towel.

* Mix butter with herbs and roll into a log shape. Place each log on chicken & roll. You can mix shredded cheese of your choice in the butter along with some minced garlic. Shape into logs. Freeze butter logs. Place frozen logs on chicken and roll. You can deep fry to brown and finish in a hot over, 400-425° for about 20 minutes.

** I have found that it works better if after the chicken is dipped and rolled, you put it in the freezer an hour before frying.

ROASTED ITALIAN CHICKEN

This was a chicken recipe that I grew up with. My Mother would have this on Sundays after a nice dish of spaghetti. From time to time, my husband Dick will say, "Make the chicken on Sunday the way your mother did, and we will have spaghetti and your mother's chicken." You will need:

Chicken	Garlic cloves, peeled & halved
Fresh squeezed lemon juice	Salt & pepper
Fresh rosemary	Olive oil

Chop the rosemary and put it in a shallow roasting pan lined with foil, along with the olive oil, lemon juice & garlic. Put the chicken in the pan, and turn the pieces to coat with the mixture. Cover with plastic and place in the refrigerator for several hours or overnight.

Preheat oven to 450° and roast for 20 minutes. Turn the chicken pieces, coating them well. Reduce heat to 350° and roast for another 20-30 minutes.*

* When you lower the heat, you can add baby potatoes with the skins on. Serve chicken with a little chopped parsley on top.

CHICKEN with POTATOES, SAUSAGE & VINEGAR

1 or 2 frying chickens, cut into small pieces	10-12 small red potatoes
Salt & pepper	6 cloves garlic
¼ C olive oil	3 sprigs of rosemary
½ lb. sweet Italian sausage	¼ C red wine vinegar
	2 T chopped parsley

Preheat oven to 450°. Wash & pat dry the chicken. Season well with salt & pepper. Heat 2 tablespoons of oil in a wide heavy skillet over medium heat. Cut sausage into ½-inch to 1-inch lengths. Cook sausage, stirring often until lightly browned on all sides, about 3 minutes. Remove sausage with a slotted spoon to a roasting pan.

Season the chicken again with a little salt & pepper. Increase the heat to medium high and brown chicken on all sides, about 8 minutes. Remove to roasting pan along with sausage.

Add potatoes, cut-side down. You may need to add a little more oil to cook & brown potatoes. Sprinkle a little salt & pepper over potatoes, then transfer to roaster. Crush the garlic & scatter them and the rosemary over the contents of the roasting pan. Drizzle with remaining 2 tablespoons of olive oil and roast for 15 minutes, stirring once or twice. Sprinkle in the vinegar and continue roasting, stirring occasionally, until chicken is cooked and potatoes are tender, about 15 minutes.

Remove contents to a serving platter and sprinkle with parsley.

CHICKEN CACCIATORE

2 chickens, about 2 ½ lb. each
Salt & pepper
Flour
¼ C vegetable oil
¼ C olive oil
1 yellow onion, chopped (about 1 Cup)
½ C dry white wine
1 (28 oz.) can Italian plum tomatoes w/juice, crushed
1 tsp. dried oregano
2 C white mushrooms
2 C total of green, yellow, or red pepper, sliced

Cut up chicken. Season pieces generously with salt & pepper. Dredge in flour, coating them lightly and tapping off excess flour. Heat vegetable oil & olive oil in a large skillet that has a lid, or a large braising pan like a Dutch oven. Add as many pieces of chicken to the pan that will fit without touching. Do not crowd chicken. You may need to brown in batches. Remove all the chicken from the pan, add onion to the fat in the pan and cook 5 minutes.

Pour the wine in the pan and cook until it is reduced by half, about 3 minutes. Add the tomatoes and oregano, season lightly with salt & pepper and bring to a boil. Tuck the chicken into the sauce, lower heat to a simmer, cover pan. Cook, stirring a few times, for 20 minutes.

In another skillet, heat remaining 2 tablespoons olive oil over medium-high heat. Add mushrooms & peppers. Cook 7-8 minutes. They should be quite crunchy. Season with salt & pepper. Stir into chicken. Cook covered until everything is tender, 10-15 minutes. Check the liquid, there should be barely enough to cover the chicken. If needed, add a small amount of water or wine to maintain the level of liquid as the chicken cooks.

This dish is a real treat served with soft polenta, but you can serve it with mashed potatoes or crusty bread.

SHREDDED BAR-B-Q CHICKEN

Make this ahead of time. 22 minutes prep time, 7 hours in a slow-cooker.

    1-2 lb. skinned & boned chicken thighs
    1 T olive oil
    1 C ketchup
    ¼ C dark brown sugar
    1 T Worcestershire sauce
    1 T cider vinegar
    1 T yellow mustard
    1 tsp. ground red pepper
    1 tsp. garlic salt

Brown chicken 4 minutes on each side in the olive oil in a large skillet over medium heat. Place chicken in a 4 quart slow-cooker. Combine ketchup and the next 6 ingredients. Pour over chicken. Cover and cook on high for 1 hour. Reduce heat to low and cook for 5 to 6 hours. Remove chicken from sauce. Shred and return to sauce. Serve on buns with dill pickle slices.

CHINESE CHICKEN CASSEROLE

    2 (10 oz.) cans cream of mushroom soup
    ¼ C water
    1 (8 oz.) can water chestnuts,
        Drained & sliced
    1 C celery, chopped
    ¼ C onion, chopped
    2-3 C diced cooked chicken
    ¼ C cashew nuts
    Fresh or canned mushrooms,
        optional
    3 oz. can Chinese noodles

Combine all ingredients <u>Except</u> nuts & noodles. Grease a casserole. Put in ½ the mixture. Add noodles. Cover noodles with remaining mixture. Top with cashews. Bake at 325° for 30 minutes, covered. Uncover and bake 5 minutes more.

This is a good dish for a potluck.

COLONEL SANDERS CHICKEN

    3 lb. fryer parts, cut small

Make a paste using:
    2 pkg. Italian salad dressing mix (Good Seasons)
    3 T flour   ¼ C lemon juice
    2 tsp. salt   2 T butter

Wipe chicken dry. Brush with paste to coat chicken evenly. Stack pieces in bowl. Cover & refrigerate several hours.

1 ½ hours before serving, heat about 2 inches of oil in a pot or skillet to 425°. Dip pieces in milk, then in 1 ½ cups pancake mix combined with 1 tsp. paprika, ½ tsp. sage, and ¼ tsp. pepper. Coat well. Dust off excess. Lightly brown chicken on all sides, about 3-4 minutes each side. Place in a single layer in a shallow pan. Bake for 35 minutes at 350°. Serves 8.

BRUSCHETTA CHICKEN

    4 boneless skinless chicken breasts   3 T torn fresh basil
    ½ C flour   1 T olive oil
    2 eggs, beaten   2 garlic cloves, minced
    ¼ C Parmesan cheese   ½ tsp. salt
    1 T butter, melted   ¼ tsp. pepper
    Bread crumbs
    2 large tomatoes, seeded & chopped

Preheat oven to 375°. Dip chicken in flour, then in egg. Place in greased 9x13 baking dish. In a small bowl, mix cheese, bread crumbs & butter; sprinkle over chicken. Loosely cover baking dish with foil. Bake for 20 minutes. Uncover and bake 5-10 minutes longer. Meanwhile, in a small bowl, toss tomatoes with remaining ingredients. Spoon over chicken. Bake 3-5 minutes or until tomato mixture is heated through.

CLARK'S BARBECUED CHICKEN

Clark's is a famous barbecue restaurant in Tioga, Texas. They sell their sauce and their rub. I have worked this recipe out until it is just about the same – but this one is mine.

For the sauce, buy any good tomato base barbecue sauce, or make your own:
    Ketchup, brown sugar, a little hot sauce & some spices.

Next you will need a dry rub. I make a mixture of:
- 3 T coarse ground black pepper
- 3 T dark brown sugar
- 2 T salt
- 1 tsp. cayenne
- Some Season All

Now get ready for the chicken.
- 10 C cold water, or more if needed
- 2 C light brown sugar
- 1 T coarse salt
- 2 chickens halved, 3 ½ to 4 lb. each (I quarter my chicken)*

Mix water, sugar & salt in a large roasting pan. Add chicken, skin-side down in water mixture. Cover and refrigerate 12 hours or overnight. Preheat oven to 300°. Drain chicken, pat dry. Place chicken skin-side down on baking sheet with rim. Brush chicken on 1 side with 2 tablespoons barbecue sauce. Sprinkle with 1 ½ tsp. dry rub. Turn chicken over, brush second side with 2 tablespoons sauce, then sprinkle 1 ½ tsp. rub.

Bake chicken skin-side up until meat thermometer registers 185° and chicken is a deep mahogany color. Baste every 20 minutes. Bake about 2 hours 15 minutes.

* Chicken cut into quarters will not take as long to bake.

OVEN-FRIED CHICKEN

1 cut up chicken
½ C oil or French dressing
1 C corn flake crumbs
½ C grated Parmesan cheese
¼ C chopped parsley
1 clove garlic, minced
1 ½ tsp. salt
¼ tsp. pepper

Preheat oven to 350°. Marinate chicken in oil or French dressing for 1 ½ hours, turning occasionally. Combine crumbs, cheese, parsley, garlic, salt & pepper. Mix well. Roll chicken in crumb mixture, patting the crumbs on. Arrange chicken in a shallow pan without crowding. Bake about 1 hour.

FRIED & ROASTED CHICKEN

Skin and wash chicken. Marinate in buttermilk about 1 hour. Roll in seasoned flour. Ex., salt, pepper, garlic powder, paprika, poultry seasoning, Italian seasoning, etc. Whatever you like. Just be sure to use a lot of seasoning. Some will fall off while frying.

Brown in hot oil. Place chicken pieces on a shallow pan and bake in a hot oven (375-400°) for 20 minutes to 45 minutes, depending on the size of chicken pieces.

CHICKEN with RICE

"Funeral Chicken"

1 can cream of mushroom soup	1 ¼ - 1 ½ C raw rice
1 can cream of celery soup	¼ - ½ lb. butter
1 can cream of chicken soup	Cut up chicken

Melt the butter. Pour into a 9x13 pan or baking dish with all of the soups. Add the rice and stir. Do not add water or salt. Place chicken skin-side up on top. Sprinkle with paprika. Bake at 275° for 2 ½ hours.

I call this "Funeral Chicken" because in the '50s every funeral I attended, this chicken was served at the wake. I think it was because it could cook during the service.

CRISPY BREADED & BAKED CHICKEN WINGS

2/3 C bread crumbs	½ tsp. paprika
1 tsp. onion powder	1 egg
1 tsp. dried basil	1 T water
½ tsp. garlic salt	10 chicken wings*

1. In a large resealable plastic bag, combine the bread crumbs, onion powder, basil, garlic salt and paprika.
2. In a small bowl, whisk egg & water.
3. Dip the wings in egg, then place in bag & shake to coat.
4. Place on greased baking pan.
5. Bake at 425° for 30-35 minutes or until juices run clear.

* You can cut the wings into sections, or do them whole. Remember, the amounts are just a suggestion. I always use more.

CHICKEN WINGS

Restaurant-Style Buffalo Chicken Wings

½ C flour or Bisquick
¼ tsp. paprika
¼ tsp. cayenne pepper
¼ tsp. salt
10 chicken wings*

Oil for frying
¼ C butter
¼ C hot sauce
Dash of black pepper
Dash of garlic powder

1. In a small bowl, mix together the flour, paprika, cayenne pepper & salt. Place half the chicken wings at a time in a plastic bag with the flour mixture, & shake until evenly coated. Shake off excess flour. Refrigerate 60-90 minutes on a covered sheet pan in a single layer.

2. Heat oil in deep fryer to 375°. The oil should be enough to entirely cover wings. Combine the butter, hot sauce, pepper & garlic powder in a small saucepan over low heat. Stir until butter is melted & mixture is well blended. Remove from heat.

3. Fry coated wings in hot oil 10-15 minutes, or until wings start to turn brown. Remove from heat. Place wings in large container & toss with sauce. Serve on a plate with celery, carrots, and a blue cheese or ranch dressing.

* Wings can be cut into sections or left whole – I like them whole. Whole wings are hard to find in restaurants now.

CHICKEN with 40 CLOVES OF GARLIC

1 chicken, cut up
2 tsp. sea salt
40 cloves garlic (3-4 bulbs), peeled
4 stalks celery
2-3 carrots
1 large onion, sliced very thin
2-4 T olive oil
Crusty bread or garlic toast for serving

Fresh ground pepper
Nutmeg
Handful of parsley, chopped
½ - 1 C dry vermouth
Dollop of cognac
1/3 C chicken stock

Cut the celery and carrots into match sticks or slice very thin.

Heat the oven to 375°. Season chicken all over with salt. Arrange pieces, skin-side up, in a single layer in a baking dish or roasting pan. Scatter garlic & cut vegetables into the gaps between the chicken and over the top. Drizzle everything with olive oil. Grind some black pepper & a bit of nutmeg over the chicken & vegetables. Top with parsley. Pour in the vermouth, cognac, & chicken stock. Cover the pan tightly with double foil. Bake 1 ½ hour.

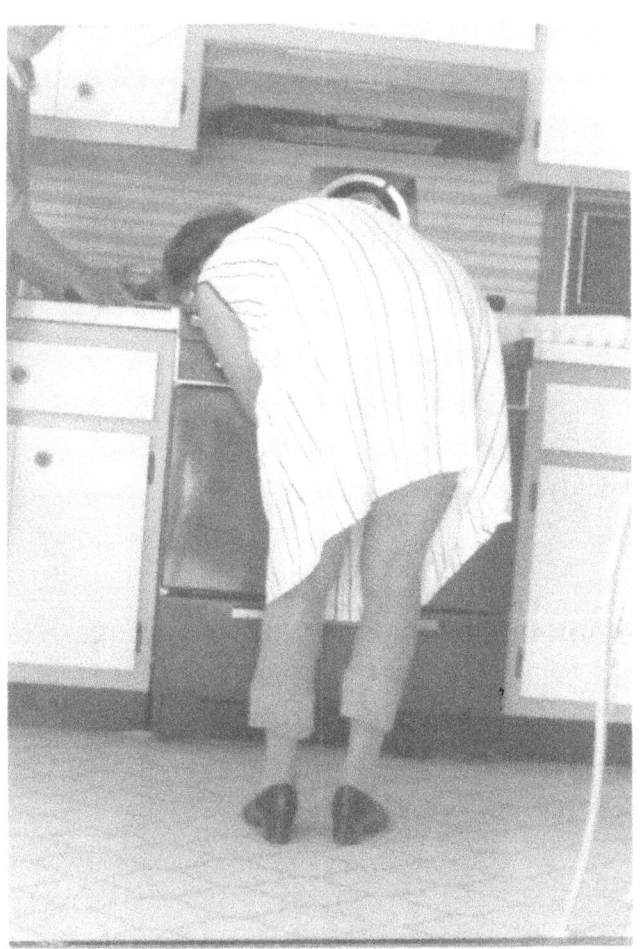

Do not remove foil (Do not peek). The chicken will be very tender & the garlic & vegetables soft enough to spread. Serve the chicken in shallow bowls with plenty of juice; spread the garlic & vegetables on bread and dunk into the juice as you eat the chicken.

My Mother made this many Saturday nights when Mary and Al Guerchoni came to play a spirited game of Pinochle.

My mother was not only a great cook. She really knew how to accessorize!

MOJO-MARINATED CHICKEN

½ C olive oil
1 C sliced garlic (2-3 whole heads)
1 jalapeño pepper, chopped
3 T ground cumin
1 tsp. oregano
½ C onions

½ C fresh orange juice
¼ C fresh lemon juice
¼ C fresh lime juice
1 tsp. chili powder
¼ C chopped cilantro
Salt & pepper

Heat oil in a skillet over medium-low heat until almost smoking. Add garlic. Shake pan until garlic begins to turn golden. Add onions & remove from heat. Add jalapeño, chile powder, cumin, cilantro, orange, lemon & lime juices. Season with salt & pepper. This is your mojo.

Stir the mojo well, then take out ½ cup, cover & refrigerate. Put remaining mojo in a large bowl and let cool to room temperature. Place a whole chicken, or cut chicken into parts, and place in a large zip-lock plastic bag. Add mojo. Seal bag, pushing out excess air. Refrigerate overnight or up to 2 days. Turn bag once a day or so.

Remove chicken. Pat dry with paper towels. Place whole chicken on a rack in a roasting pan.* If you cut up the chicken, place in a foil lined roasting pan. Roast at 350° for about 1 hour to 1 ½ hour. Remove from oven and let rest for 10 minutes.

To serve, heat reserved ½ cup mojo and spoon over chicken on a serving plate.

* You can put ½ of an orange and/or lemon inside chicken while roasting.

SALSA COUSCOUS CHICKEN

3 C hot couscous or rice
  (cooked as directed on pkg.)
1 T olive or vegetable oil
¼ C coarsely chopped almonds
2 garlic cloves, minced
8 chicken thighs, skinless,
  Deboned if you like

1 C salsa
¼ C water
2 T dried currants or raisins
1 tsp. honey
1 ¾ tsp. cumin
½ tsp. cinnamon

While couscous or rice is cooking, heat oil in large skillet over medium-high heat until hot. Add almonds; cook 1-2 minutes or until golden brown. Remove almonds from skillet with slotted spoon; set aside.

Add garlic to skillet; cook and stir 30 seconds. Add chicken; cook 4-5 minutes or until brown, turning once.

In medium bowl, combine salsa and all remaining ingredients; mix well. Add to chicken. Reduce heat to medium; cover and cook, stirring occasionally for 20 minutes or until chicken is fork-tender and juices run clear. Stir in almonds. Serve chicken mixture over couscous or rice.

Serves 4.

CHICKEN CASA AMELIA

2 fryers, cut up
Salt & pepper
Paprika
1 lb. chicken livers
1 C chicken broth
1 C white wine
1 lb. fresh mushrooms
2 T flour
Butter
Chives or parsley

Dust chicken parts with salt, pepper & paprika. Brown in ¼ lb. butter. Place in casserole with chicken broth and white wine. Cook 40 minutes at 300° until tender. Cover while cooking.

Sauté mushrooms in butter. In another pan, sauté chicken livers. Combine liquid from both pans and add flour. Arrange mushrooms & chicken livers on top of chicken in casserole, cover with liquid* and sprinkle with chives or parsley. Serve with rice & French bread.

* The liquid can be white wine and water, or chicken broth.

PRETZEL-CRUSTED CHICKEN

4 boneless, skinless chicken breast halves
¼ C honey mustard
8 thin slices deli ham
1 T butter, melted
½ C crushed pretzels

Spread honey mustard on chicken. Lay on 2 slices of deli ham. Fold chicken breast in half. Drizzle with melted butter. Coat with crushed pretzels. Bake on greased 9x13 baking sheet at 350°.

CHICKEN LIVER PATE

ASPIC:
- 2 T unflavored gelatin
- 1 C cold tomato, beef or chicken broth

Dissolve gelatin in broth; bring to a boil and remove from heat. Pour half the liquid into a loaf pan or mold you will use for pate, and chill. Decorate chilled aspic if you wish to do so.

PATE (Pâté):
- 6 T butter
- 1 lb. chicken livers
- 4 T chopped onion

Melt the butter in a sauce pan over medium heat. Add the chicken livers and onions. Reduce heat to low and sauté about 10 minutes, until chicken livers are tender and no longer pink. Pour into a food processor along with:*

- ½ tsp. salt
- 1 T Dijon mustard
- ½ tsp. Allspice
- ½ tsp. garlic powder
- ½ tsp. pepper
- 3 T sherry or cognac
- ½ C whipping cream
  or 3 oz. cream cheese
- Remaining broth

Process until very smooth. Spoon into loaf pan or mold, and refrigerate covered with plastic wrap 6-8 hours or overnight. Unmold by quickly dipping pan into hot water and running a knife around sides.

You do not have to unmold, just put the glaze on top, or it can be served without a glaze.

* A dash of hot sauce in the mix is a nice addition.

QUICK & EASY PATE

- 8 oz. Braunschweiger
- 3 oz. cream cheese, softened
- 2 T onion, finely chopped
- 1 T Worcestershire
- 2 T dry sherry
- ½ tsp. nutmeg
- Dash of hot sauce

Blend all ingredients in food processor & serve with crackers or cocktail bread.

GOAT

For my daughter Jeannine and her partner Su, I have to include two recipes for "Goat". They live in Colorado and had a goat farm. Don't be afraid to try these recipes, they are good and easy to make. The hard part will be finding goat meat, but look around, it's out there. If you just can't find it, use lamb.

Goat: Before and After

Billy Goat in Colorado

Jeannine cooking in the Woods

Jeannine & Su had to give up the goat farm when Jeannine was diagnosed with cancer. She is very strong and is amazing everyone with her recovery. Much of her recovery is due to Su, who is by her side at all times. Also, this book would never have seen print if it were not for Su, who flew from Colorado to Florida to do this book on a computer.

I thank God for Jeannine's recovery, and I thank God for Su, for being there for both of us.

****

AFRICAN GOAT STEW – BY WAY OF COLORADO

1 ½ lb. goat meat, finely diced
2 large onions, chopped
2 carrots, chopped
2 cloves garlic, minced
3 T butter
1 large can tomato puree
1 bay leaf
1/8 tsp. ground cloves

1/8 tsp. ginger
1 dash cayenne
Salt & pepper
½ freshly squeezed lemon juice, or 1 T vinegar
2 C beef stock
1 or 2 T peanut butter
2 T flour

Sauté meat & vegetables in a little olive oil & 3 T butter until onions are translucent. Then add tomato puree, spices, lemon juice & stock. Bring to a boil, reduce heat, cover and let simmer until meat is tender to your liking. About 1 ½ hours.

Warm up peanut butter and mix with flour and stir into stew. Let the stew simmer for about 10 more minutes & check for seasoning.

CURRIED GOAT

3 T oil
2 lb. goat meat
1 large onion
2 C vegetable or beef broth
1 tsp. Allspice
½ tsp. dried thyme
2 cloves garlic, minced
3 T curry powder

1 tsp. salt
1 tsp. pepper
1 T wine vinegar
3 dashes hot sauce
2 T brown sugar
1 T lime juice
1 C coconut milk
2 sliced scallions for garnish

Heat the oil in a heavy pan such as a Dutch oven. Brown the goat meat quickly and set aside. Turn the heat down & sauté the onions until soft. Add garlic and sauté 2-3 minutes. Add the broth, Allspice, thyme, curry powder, salt, pepper, vinegar, hot sauce, brown sugar, coconut milk, and the lime juice. Stir together. Put the meat back in the pot & simmer on low for 2 hours, or in a crock pot for 6 hours. Serve over rice.

Jeannine and her first two goats in Colorado.

PORCHETTA

Porchetta – one of my favorite meats, and the star of most of my buffet tables. It is made with a pork shoulder or a pork butt or, as some people call it, Boston butt. I have even made it with a fresh ham.

- 4-6 lb. pork shoulder, skin on
- Olive oil
- 6-8 cloves garlic, chopped fine
- Thyme leaves, chopped fine
- Rosemary, chopped fine
- Fennel seeds, crushed
- Parsley, chopped fine
- 1 ½ tsp. salt
- 1 ½ tsp. pepper

Chop fine and mix together: garlic, thyme leaves, rosemary, fennel seeds, parsley, salt & pepper. With a sharp knife, score pork skin in a diamond pattern, about 1/8 inch deep and about 1 inch apart. With a sharp paring knife, make incisions about ½ inch deep all over pork & stuff with herb mixture. Brush olive oil over the skin and rub all over with any remaining herb mixture.* Cover tightly & place in refrigerator overnight or up to 3 days.

Remove from refrigerator & bring to room temperature for 45 minutes to 1 hour. Preheat oven to 325° and roast for 30 minutes per pound. You can add a little red wine to pan while meat is roasting. Remove from oven, tent with foil, and let meat rest 15-20 minutes. Slice & serve.

Good hot or cold. Sliced thin and piled on an Italian roll makes a delicious sandwich.

* The roast can be butterflied and the herbs spread on meat, and then tied and rubbed with oil, salt & pepper, and allowed to marinate in refrigerator, and then roasted.

CITY CHICKEN

City Chicken should have a question mark after the name. It is anything but chicken. It is pork & veal on a stick. Sometimes it is pork & beef on a stick – but it is never chicken on a stick. This is a very old recipe. In the early 1900s & during the Depression, chicken was more expensive than pork & veal, so the less expensive meat was put on a stick to look like a chicken leg. Many young cooks today do not know what City Chicken is, but it is too good to be forgotten. You can do it on top of the stove, or in the oven. Whichever way you like it.

1 lb. pork shoulder, cut into 1- 1 ½ inch cubes
1 lb. veal, cut into 1- 1 ½ inch cubes
1 C flour
½ tsp. salt
½ tsp. pepper
½ tsp. thyme

2 eggs, beaten
8-10 wooden skewers, 6 inches
Oil for frying

Mix flour, salt & pepper in a bowl. In a second bowl, beat 2 eggs with a little water, salt, pepper & thyme. Slide pork & veal on skewers. Roll in flour mixture, then in egg, and back into flour.

In a large heavy skillet, heat oil then add skewers. Brown on all sides. At this point, there are 2 ways you can finish cooking the City Chicken.

1. Add some canned chicken broth, put a lid on the skillet, and simmer until meat is tender, about an hour. You can add some sliced onion and/or rosemary to the pan to flavor the gravy.

OR

2. You can remove the skewers after they are browned to a shallow roasting pan. Deglaze the skillet with some canned chicken broth or some white wine; add it to the roasting pan. Cover with foil and place in a 325° oven for about 1 – 1 ½ hours. Remove foil the last 15-20 minutes.

PORK CHOP CASSEROLE

In a glass casserole, empty a can of apple pie filling. Slice 1 or 2 fresh apples on top of pie filling. Put pork chops on top of apples. Mix stove top stuffing as directed on box and place stuffing on chops. Bake at 350° for 35-45 minutes.

This is very good and very easy. I find it has a better flavor if you brown and season the chops first, and bone-in chops have more flavor. If you cover the casserole with foil, you get a soft, moist top. If you bake it uncovered, the top is crispy.

ITALIAN SAUSAGE & PEPPERS

6-8 hot or sweet Italian sausages
2 T olive oil
1 large onion, halved & sliced
2 large red peppers, seeded & sliced
1 green pepper, seeded & sliced
3 cloves garlic, sliced
Salt & pepper to taste
Dried oregano to taste

Heat the oil in a large pan. Add the sausages and cook, turning frequently until browned all over. This takes a good 10 minutes. Add the onions & stir up any browned bits on the bottom of the pan. Add the peppers, garlic, salt, pepper & dried oregano. Lower the heat & cook another 10-15 minutes until peppers & onions are tender.*

* You can, if you like, add a small can of tomato sauce during the last 10-15 minutes.

HAM: EASTER, CHRISTMAS, OR ANY TIME

MAPLE-BOURBON GLAZED HAM

1 fully cooked ham, 7-10 lbs.*
½ C pure maple syrup
½ C packed brown sugar
1/3 C bourbon

2 T Dijon mustard
1 T soy sauce
Ginger ale

Preheat oven to 350°. Peel skin from ham. Trim fat to about ½ inch thick, then score in a cross-hatch patter, cutting through fat but not into meat. In a roasting pan, place ham flat side down. Pour enough ginger ale to cover bottom of pan by at least ½ inch. Cover tightly with foil and bake 1 hour.

GLAZE:
Meanwhile, make glaze: Mix remaining ingredients in a bowl. Remove ham from oven, uncover, brush generously with glaze.

At this point, if you wish, you can stud with whole cloves and decorate with pineapple rings & cherries. If needed, add more ginger ale to prevent drippings from burning. Drizzle more glaze & pan drippings over ham, basting about every 30 minutes until glaze is glossy & browned. Bake ham uncovered another hour to 1 ½ hour. Remove from oven & let rest 10 minutes before serving.

* Hams are generally sold in halves: the shank end and the butt end. The shank end is much easier to carve than the butt end, which included the hop joint.

SCALOPPINE SALTIMBOCCA ROMAN STYLE

* Scaloppine is thinly sliced meat.

Sautéed spinach
Veal, chicken, turkey or pork scaloppine for 4
4 slices prosciutto, cut in half crosswise
12 large fresh sage leaves, extra leaves for in the pan
3 T olive oil, more if needed
¼ C dry white wine
1 C chicken broth (can use bought)

Salt & pepper
Flour
6 T butter

Braise spinach in a skillet with olive oil & garlic. Add a little salt.

Veal rump, sliced thin. (If you partially freeze the meat, it is easier to slice thin.) Salt & pepper.

Pound meat with a meat mallet, working from the middle out. Have meat between parchment or waxed paper. With the back of a knife, press prosciutto, which has been cut in half crosswise, into the pounded veal so that it adheres to the meat. Center a sage leaf over the prosciutto & fasten it in place with a toothpick, weaving the toothpick in & out, like making a stitch. Dredge the scaloppine in flour to lightly coat both sides. Tap off excess flour.

Heat 3 tablespoons olive oil & 2 T butter in a large heavy skillet over medium heat until butter is foaming. Slip as many of the scaloppine, prosciutto-side down, into the pan as fit without touching. Cook just until prosciutto is light golden (about 2 minutes). Overcooking will toughen the prosciutto. Turn and cook second side until browned, about 2 minutes. Remove & drain on paper towels. Repeat until all scaloppine are cooked, adding more oil if necessary. Remove all scaloppini from skillet & pour off oil.

Return the pan to the heat and add ¼ C dry white wine. Add the remaining 4 tablespoons butter & cook until wine is reduced about half, about 3 minutes. Pour in the chicken stock & bring to a rigorous boil. Tuck the scaloppini into the sauce. Simmer about 3-4 minutes. Taste & season with salt & pepper. To serve, spoon the spinach in a mound in the center of each plate. Arrange the saltimbocca over the spinach & spoon on some pan juice.

STUPID-SIMPLE ROAST BEEF With HORSERADISH CREAM

1 C plus 1 tablespoon kosher salt
1   7-8 lb. top round beef roast, tied with the full fat cap on the roast
1 T freshly ground pepper, plus more for seasoning
1 C sour cream
½ C prepared horseradish

1. Set a rack over a baking sheet. Rub ½ cup of the salt all over the roast and let stand for 10 minutes. Repeat with another ½ cup of the salt. Transfer the roast to the rack and refrigerate uncovered for 2 days. Bring to room temperature 3 hours before roasting.

2. Preheat the oven to 450°. Season the meat with pepper and roast for 20 minutes. Reduce the oven temperature to 225° and roast for about 1 ½ hours longer, until an instant-read thermometer inserted in the center of the roast registers 120°. Let the meat rest for 30 minutes.

3. In a bowl, mix the sour cream with the horseradish and the remaining 1 tablespoon of salt and pepper. Slice the roast and serve with the horseradish cream.

Make ahead: The roast beef can be refrigerated for up to 2 days. Serve warm or chilled. The sauce can be refrigerated for up to 2 days as well.

SOUTHERN FRIED CHICKEN

2 ½ - 3 ½ chicken, cut up,
   Or your favorite parts
3 eggs, beaten
Salt & pepper

2 C self-rising flour
Crisco shortening or
   vegetable oil

Rinse the chicken & pat dry. Salt & pepper chicken pieces & return to refrigerator. Beat the eggs in a 9x13 pan. Lay the chicken pieces in the dish, turning each piece until well coated with egg. Place enough Crisco or vegetable oil in a cast-iron skillet, electric skillet, or a Dutch oven, to come up about halfway up chicken parts. Crisco or shortening should be moderately hot, 350-375°, just until smoking.

Place flour in a paper bag along with any seasonings you like (garlic powder, salt & pepper, paprika, poultry seasoning, etc.). Add the chicken pieces a few at a time & shake bag to coat. Remove with tongs, shaking off excess flour, & place in hot fat. Do not over-crowd.

Cover the pan, leaving a crack for steam to escape. Cook about 10 minutes, turn pieces & cook another 10 minutes on second side. Drain chicken on paper towels. Larger pieces may take a little longer. You may need to lower heat as you go. Also, you may need to add more oil or Crisco. Repeat until all chicken is cooked.

STANDING RIB ROAST

1. Allow roast to stand at room temperature 1 hour.

2. Preheat oven to 375°.

3. Rub roast with seasoning: salt, pepper, garlic powder.

4. Place roast on rack in roasting pan, fat-side up.

5. Roast for 1 hour at 375°.

6. Turn off oven. Leave roast in oven. Do Not Open Oven Door.*

7. ** 40 minutes before serving, turn oven on to 375°. At the end of 40 minutes, remove roast from oven.

8. Cover with foil – let heat 15-20 minutes.

* Remember, you cannot open the oven, so think what you will serve with the roast.

** Good idea that roast stays in oven about 3 hours between first hour & second time you turn on oven. If you do not have a rack for your roaster, put long carrots & celery in roaster and place meat on vegetables.

SEAFOOD & FISH

*CALEDONIA FISH

Make a white sauce:

    3 T butter   2 C milk
    3 T flour   ¾ C Parmesan cheese

In a small saucepan over medium heat, melt butter. Add flour & stir until the butter & flour are well combined. Pour in milk, whisking constantly as it thickens. Ade more milk depending on desired consistency. Add Parmesan cheese.

    8-12 fish fillets, any white fish   Bread crumbs
    Cherry tomatoes   Parmesan cheese
    Asparagus

Salt & pepper fish fillets. Poach fish in white wine or dry vermouth, a minute or 2 on each side. Spray or butter a 9x13 pan or glass baking dish (can be used to serve). Lay fish in pan. Trim & blanch enough asparagus to cover fish. Place asparagus on fish. Cut cherry tomatoes in half & place on asparagus. Cover with white sauce. Top with bread crumbs that have been mixed with butter & more Parmesan cheese.

If making ahead of time, cover with foil to refrigerate and hold until ready to bake. Bake uncovered at 350° for 25-35 minutes.

This is a very good company dish.

* Caledonia is a Golf & Fish Club on Pawley's Island, south of Myrtle Beach, in South Carolina.

FISH POACHED IN GALLIANO BUTTER

    2/3 C slivered almonds   Dill or oregano
    2/3 C butter   Salt & pepper
    ¼ C Galliano or Neapolitan Liqueur*   2 lb. fish
    ¼ C fresh lemon juice

In a large skillet, sauté almonds in butter until lightly toasted. Remove almonds and set aside. Allow butter to brown, then stir in Galliano, lemon juice & season. Add fish. Cover & cook over medium heat for 10-15 minutes. Spoon liquid over fish as it cooks. Place fish & sauce on a platter & top with almonds. Or use any type of licorice-flavored liqueur.

Girls getting ready to go fishing on Lake Okeechobee

FISH FILLETS with SPINACH & MUSHROOMS

Salt & pepper fish fillets and sauté. Wilt spinach in skillet with olive oil & garlic. Sauté mushrooms in butter. Have on hand some Alfredo sauce. You can use jarred or make your own. TO PLATE: Alfredo sauce, spinach, mushrooms, fish. Top with small amount of buttered crumbs. Quick & Easy! Very Good!

FISH CHOWDER

Salt pork and/or bacon – render and remove from pan.

In hot oil that remains (you may add a little butter), sauté a large chopped onion & about 1 C chopped celery and 2 or 3 cubed potatoes, until vegetables start to soften & take on color. Sauté vegetables slowly. Add liquid. You can use clam broth, chicken broth, water, the choice is yours. If you like a red chowder, try clamato juice.

Simmer about 10 minutes. Add fish, cut into 1-inch pieces. Simmer 10 minutes, and then add milk or half & half. Do not boil. Season with salt & pepper. Sometimes I use a little Old Bay Seasoning. Top with chopped parsley.

   * You may like to add 1 or 2 bay leaves while simmering liquid, but remember to remove them.

** You can, if you like, add chopped carrots and/or green peppers.

I got the fish.
Start the chowder!

Melissa loves to fish, but does not eat fish!

ROLLED STUFFED FISH

Rinse & dry fish pieces. Spoon stuffing on each piece. Roll & stand up in pan. Cover with foil & bake at 375° for about 20 minutes. Remove from oven. Cover with sauce. Return to oven for 10-12 minutes uncovered.

<u>Stove Top Stuffing:</u> Onion, celery, green pepper. Fry in butter. Add dry bread crumbs & chicken bouillon to moisten. Lemon rind optional.

<u>Sauce:</u> Sauté onion in butter. Add about 1 cup water with about 1 tsp. cornstarch. Stir over heat. Add lemon juice to taste. Salt & pepper. A little sugar optional.

BAKED SALMON with CREOLE MUSTARD SAUCE

SAUCE:

- 1 C whipping cream
- ¾ C Creole mustard
- 4 tsp. Worcestershire
- 1 T Dijon mustard
- ¾ tsp. black pepper
- ¼ tsp. cayenne pepper
- 1 C sour cream

Combine all ingredients, except sour cream, in a saucepan. Simmer until thick (about 5 min.), stirring frequently. Just before serving, add sour cream. Can make a day ahead. Reheat over low heat & add sour cream.*

FISH:

- 2 ½ lb. center cut salmon
- ¼ C melted butter (1 stick)
- 3 T brown sugar
- 3 T soy sauce
- 2 T white wine
- 2 T fresh lemon juice

Line a large baking pan with foil. Arrange fish skin-side down in single layer. Mix butter, sugar, soy sauces, lemon juice & wine in a bowl. Pour over fish. Cover & refrigerate at least 1 hour, and up to 6 hours. Preheat oven to 400°. Uncover fish and bake, basting occasionally with pan drippings, for about 18 minutes. Serve sauce with fish.

* Sauce can be kept in refrigerator & used with salads, pasta, meats, etc.

FRIED OYSTERS with PANKO*

Oysters	Panko
Cornstarch	Eggs, lightly beaten
Oil for frying	Salt & pepper

Rinse oysters. Pat dry with paper towel. Season cornstarch & egg with salt & pepper. Coat oysters with cornstarch, then in beaten egg, and finally in Panko. Shake off excess. Heat oil & fry oysters until golden brown. Do not overcook.
* Panko is a Japanese style bread crumb.

PAN-FRIED OYSTERS

Rinse & pat dry. Place oysters in a bowl with melted butter, milk & a few drops of hot sauce. Dip oysters in your choice of seasoned flour, corn meal, cracker crumbs, or any combination. Pan fry in butter with a little olive oil a few minutes until golden. Do not overcook.

CRISPY OVEN-FRIED OYSTERS

¾ C flour	2/3 C grated Parmesan cheese
¼ tsp. salt	¼ C minced parsley
¼ tsp. pepper	½ tsp. garlic salt
2 eggs	1 pt. oysters
1 C dry bread crumbs	2 T olive oil

In a shallow bowl, combine salt, pepper & flour. In another bowl, whisk eggs. In third bowl, combine bread crumbs, cheese, parsley & garlic salt. Coat oysters in flour mixture, then dip in eggs, and then coat with crumbs. Place on greased 15x10 baking sheet. Drizzle with oil. Bake at 400° for 15 minutes or until golden brown.

JALAPEÑO MAYONNAISE

¼ C mayonnaise
¼ C sour cream
2 medium jalapeños, seeded & chopped
2 T milk
1 tsp. lemon juice
¼ tsp. grated lemon peel

FRIED CALAMARI

Squid & tentacles
Beaten eggs
Flour or cornstarch
Panko, bread crumbs, or cornmeal
Salt & pepper

In a mixing bowl, beat eggs. Add salt & pepper. Dip calamari into eggs then into flour or cornstarch. You can fry at this point, or redip in egg and then your choice of Panko, bread crumbs, cornmeal, or any combination of breading you like. Fry in skillet in hot oil or a deep fryer. They only take about 2 minutes at most. I sometimes dip and bread strips of peppers in with the calamari.

MUSSELS & BREAD CRUMBS

¼ C olive oil
4-5 cloves garlic, chopped
½ C seasoned bread crumbs
Chopped parsley
Sea salt & freshly ground pepper
1 lemon, juice & zest
1 small onion, chopped
¾ C white wine
1 to 2 lbs. mussels, cleaned

In a heavy skillet, sauté garlic & bread crumbs in olive oil. Remove from heat. Add chopped parsley, chopped onion, salt & pepper. Mix & set aside.

Heat white wine in a heavy bottom pan. Bring to a boil. Add mussels, cover & cook over medium heat for 4-5 minutes until mussels open. Discard any that don't open. Add bread crumb mixture to mussels. Toss gently. Squeeze on lemon juice & add zest. Serve in shallow bowl. Good hot or cold.

PANKO-CRUSTED CRAB CAKE BITES With ROASTED PEPPER CHIVE AIOLI*

12 oz. crab	1 egg
¼ C finely diced celery	2 tsp. Dijon mustard
¼ C minced fresh chives	¼ tsp. hot sauce
¼ C mayonnaise	1 ¼ C Panko or fine bread crumbs

In a large bowl, combine celery, chives, mayonnaise, egg, mustard & hot sauce; mix well with a fork. Add crab & ¼ C Panko; stir gently to mix but not mush the crab. Put remaining 1 cup Panko in shallow bowl. Shape crab mixture into about 24 cakes, each about 2-inches wide & ½-inch thick. Coat each cake in Panko on all sides, pressing gently to make crumbs adhere. Place on lightly oiled 12x17 baking pan. Bake at 475° until golden brown, 15-18 minutes. **

FOR SAUCE:

In a small bowl, mix 1/3 C mayonnaise, ¼ cup chopped drained canned roasted red peppers, 1 tablespoon minced fresh chives, 2 tablespoons lemon juice and 1 teaspoon minced garlic. Makes about ½ cup.

* Aioli is a zesty garlic mayonnaise that's used as a sauce.

** You can make the aioli up to two days ahead and the crab 6-8 hours before you bake them. Just cover and refrigerate.

GROUPER with LEMON CAPER BUTTER

4 grouper fillets, 6-8 oz. each; can use halibut, cod, etc.
2 tsp. sea salt   ¼ C capers, drained
1 tsp. pepper   1 lemon
4 T butter (½ stick)   2-3 tsp. chopped parsley

Sprinkle all sides of fish with salt & pepper. Melt 2 tablespoons butter in skillet over medium heat. Add fish & sear until opaque halfway through, 3-4 minutes. Add remaining 2 tablespoons butter. When melted, turn fish, sear second side until cooked through, 2-3 minutes. If the butter gets too dark, drain and add fresh butter to make sauce, about 1-2 tablespoons clean butter.

Transfer fish to plate. Add capers to hot skillet with melted butter. Let them "sizzle" for 15 seconds. If they do not sizzle, raise heat until they do. Squeeze lemon juice over capers. Add parsley. Drizzle over fish.

Variation:

SHRIMP with ANCHOVY-CAPER BUTTER

Substitute 2 lbs. of shrimp for fish. Cook in 2-3 tablespoons butter about 2 minutes. Add 2-3 chopped anchovies to the pan along with capers. Omit lemon juice.

FISH & PASTA PINWHEELS

Prep time & cooking time: 15-20 minutes
Chilling time: 1-2 hours
Makes 18 hors d'oeuvres, or a nice lunch, or light supper with cheese & olives.

1 ½ lbs. cooked & flaked fish	2 tsp. Dijon mustard
½ C finely minced green onion	Salt & pepper
½ C finely minced dill pickles	¼ tsp. dried dill weed
¼ C toasted, slivered almonds	9 lasagna noodles
½ C finely minced celery	2-3 tsp. paprika
1 C mayonnaise	Lettuce for garnish

In a bowl, combine all ingredients except noodles, paprika & lettuce. Mix well. Cook noodles. Drain, pat dry. Spread filling over noodles leaving 1-inch border on short end. Roll noodles up tightly. Dip curly edges in paprika. Place noodles seam-side down on tray. Cover & chill 2-3 hours. To serve, arrange lettuce on tray. Cut each roll in half & arrange with cut-side down on lettuce.

MARYLAND CRAB CAKES

1 lb. back fin Blue crab meat, or other lump crab
8 saltine crackers   ¼ tsp. Worcestershire
1 egg, beaten   ½ tsp. Old Bay Seasoning
2 T mayonnaise   Salt to taste
1 tsp. mustard   2 T vegetable oil

Carefully check crab for any cartilage or shell. Put crab in bowl & set aside.

Crush the saltines very fine & mix with all other ingredients. Gently fold in the crab. Only mix enough to combine ingredients. You don't want to break up the crab into shreds. Shape into 6 crab cakes & refrigerate for at least 1 hour.

Heat about 2 tablespoons of vegetable oil in a non-stick pan. Sauté until golden brown on each side. This only takes about 3-5 minutes per side.

Garnish with tartar sauce, remoulade, or a squeeze of lemon.

REMOULADE SAUCE

1 ¼ C mayonnaise
¼ C mustard (Creole mustard is best)
1 T sweet paprika
1 to 2 tsp. Cajun or Creole seasoning
2 tsp. prepared horseradish
1 tsp. pickle juice (dill or sweet)*
1 tsp. hot sauce (Tabasco is best)
1 large clove garlic, minced & smashed

Mix all ingredients. Better if left to sit a few hours. Keep refrigerated.

* You can use a little lemon juice or vinegar if you don't have pickle juice.

SHRIMP IN GINGER BUTTER SAUCE

Serves 1.
Start to finish: 15 minutes.
Can be an appetizer or a main dish.

Ginger and cilantro add Southeast Asian oomph to this French-style butter sauce, which lightly coats big, meaty shrimp.

> 6 oz. large shrimp in shell, peeled
> 2 T unsalted butter
> 1 ½ tsp. grated peeled ginger
> 2 T medium-dry Sherry
> 2 T coarsely chopped cilantro

Pat shrimp dry and season with salt.

Heat butter in a heavy medium skillet over medium-high heat until foam subsides, then sauté ginger 30 seconds. Add shrimp and sauté 2 minutes. Add Sherry and sauté until shrimp are just cooked through, 1 to 2 minutes. Stir in cilantro and season with salt & pepper.

Serve with: a baguette, green beans, whatever you wish.

VEGETABLES

This section of my cookbook includes both Italian and American vegetable recipes that I like.

Most Americans tend to overcook vegetables and top with a pat of butter. OK if that is the way you like them. Most Italians, on the other hand, tend to braise or steam vegetables with olive oil, garlic, salt and pepper and never overcook.

Here are some really good Italian vegetables & some really good American vegetables.

EGGPLANT PARMIGIANA

An assembly line is a good idea when frying eggplant for parmigiana

>   1 large eggplant   Olive oil
>   2 eggs, beaten   Mozzarella, shredded
>   1 C flour   Parmesan, grated
>   Bread crumbs   Tomato sauce*
>   Salt & pepper

A few words about the way I make Eggplant Parmigiana. Every cookbook that you pick up will tell you to "salt" the slices of eggplant – Not Me! Most of the cookbooks will tell you to "peel" the eggplant – Not Me. Then they will tell you to cut the finished dish into squares to serve – Not Me.

Wipe your eggplant off and slice about ½ inch thick. Line up a shallow bowl of flour, a shallow bowl with beaten eggs and some salt, and a shallow bowl of Italian bread crumbs.

Dredge the sliced eggplant in flour, shake off excess. Dip the floured eggplant into the beaten egg, and then into the crumbs, coating well on all sides.

Fry eggplant in a skillet with olive oil until well browned. You will have to add more oil as you fry. Here again I am different. I layer the slices in a <u>round</u> casserole so that each slice can be lifted with a fork to serve.

Put a little sauce on the bottom of the casserole. Layer sliced topping each with a spoon of sauce, a sprinkle of grated Parmesan cheese, and if you like, some shredded Mozzarella cheese. Bake at 375° for about 30 minutes. You may want to cover the casserole loosely with foil, and uncover the last 10-15 minutes.

* You can use your own sauce or a good plain jarred sauce. Most restaurants will make this in a 9x13 pan and cut into squares. I like the single slices better. That's the way my grandmother and my mother did it, and the way I do it. Besides, the next day, a cold slice of eggplant on crusty Italian bread … Delicious!

** Use this as a guide – Double or triple as you wish.

RATATOUILLE
Sounds like "Rat-a-2-eee"

¼ C olive oil, more as needed
1 ½ C chopped yellow onion
5 cloves chopped garlic
1 large eggplant, cubed, skin on
Fresh thyme leaves
1 red pepper
1 green pepper
2 zucchini, thick slices or chunks
1-2 yellow squash, thick slices or chunks
1 ½ to 2 C chopped tomatoes, seeded*
Basil leaves to taste, sliced thin
Fresh parsley
Salt & pepper

In a large skillet, heat the olive oil. Add the onions and garlic & cook until onions are lightly caramelized. Add the eggplant & thyme, stirring occasionally, about 4-5 minutes. Add the peppers, zucchini, and squash. Cook about 4-5 minutes. Add the tomatoes, herbs, salt & pepper. Cook another few minutes. Serve – hot or room temperature.

This makes a good lunch with crusty bread, or a good snack anytime.

* You may or may not skin the tomatoes, but do squeeze out the seeds. To skin the tomatoes, cut an X on the bottom of the tomato and dip in hot water.

My niece Michelle lives in Arizona and does a fabulous job making Ratatouille.

Ratatouille is all vegetables and very healthy. And Michelle is the picture of health.

BROCCOLI or SQUASH CASSEROLE

2 pkgs. frozen chopped broccoli, drained
1 C mayonnaise
1 can cream of mushroom soup
1 C sharp grated cheese
1 small onion, grated fine
2 eggs, well beaten
Salt & pepper to taste

Mix all ingredients and place in a baking dish. Cover top with 1 cup of crushed Ritz crackers. Bake approximately 20 minutes at 400°.

BROCCOLI-CORN BAKE

1 can creamed corn
1 pkg. (10 oz.) chopped frozen broccoli, cooked & drained*
1 egg, beaten
¼ C finely chopped onion
½ tsp. salt
Dash of pepper
12 coarsely crumbled Ritz crackers (about ½ cup)
2 T butter, melted
7 more coarsely crumbled Ritz crackers (about ¼ cup)

Preheat oven to 350°.

Mix all ingredients except ¼ cup crackers and 1 tablespoon butter for topping. Turn into a 1 quart casserole dish. Top with cracker and butter mixture. Bake uncovered 35-40 minutes.

* Frozen cauliflower can be added with or without the corn.

BROCCOLI SUPREME

1 ½ lb. fresh broccoli*	1 T grated onion
1 can cream of chicken soup	¼ tsp. salt
1 T flour	1/8 tsp. pepper
½ C sour cream	¾ C herb stuffing mix
¼ C grated carrots	2 T melted butter

Clean broccoli. Cut into pieces. Cook stalk pieces in boiling water for 5-8 minutes. Add tops and cook for 5 minutes.

Blend soup and flour. Add sour cream, carrots, onion, salt & pepper. Stir in broccoli. Put into 2 quart casserole. Combine stuffing and butter and sprinkle around baking dish. Bake at 350° for 30-35 minutes.

* Can use frozen broccoli.

CAULIFLOWER IN VINAIGRETTE

Cook flowerets until just tender, about 5 minutes in boiling salted water. Drain and cover with sauce.

¼ C olive oil	Pinch of cayenne pepper
2 T vinegar	1 hard cooked egg, chopped
¼ tsp. salt	1 T capers
1 T minced green pepper	

Pour sauce over hot cauliflower and let marinate for several hours. Serve cold.

BROCCOLI, with PINE NUTS, GARLIC & RAISINS

- Bunch of broccoli*
- Pine nuts
- Garlic, chopped or minced
- ¼ C olive oil
- Salt & pepper
- Raisins**

Rinse broccoli in cold water. Cook broccoli in boiling salted water until tender but still firm, about 15-25 minutes. (Stems can be cut into round slices & put in boiling water first.) Drain broccoli. In a cup of hot water, plump raisins. Set aside. In a skillet with olive oil, sauté garlic and then add pine nuts just until they turn golden, being careful, they burn easily.

Drain raisins. Pour oil, garlic, pine nuts and raisins over broccoli. Season with salt & pepper. Good served hot or cold. This is my favorite broccoli recipe.

* Can use cauliflower in the same way.

** Amounts of all ingredients depend on you.

MARINATED CARROTS

Also known as "Copper Pennies"

8 carrots
2 large onions, sliced
1 can tomato soup
½ C oil
¾ C sugar
½ C vinegar

1 tsp. salt
1 tsp. pepper
1 tsp. paprika
1 tsp. dry mustard
1 T Worcestershire

Cook carrots until soft and drain. Slice.
Combine other ingredients in order given, and heat but do not boil.
Add carrots and marinate overnight.

CREAMED STEWED TOMATOES

1 large can whole peeled tomatoes
Salt & pepper to taste
Sugar to taste (2-3 T normally)
1 T cornstarch

1 ½ T Wonder flour
¼ to 1/3 C Half & Half,
    milk, or cream

Add tomatoes, including the liquid, to a pan and smash with potato masher until large chunks of tomatoes remain. Heat adding salt, pepper and sugar. In a small bowl, mix cornstarch and flour with some of the tomato liquid to make a slurry. Add the slurry to the tomatoes and bring to a boil. Once thickened, reduce heat and slowly add Half & Half, stirring constantly. This is a very good side dish, or a light lunch with a grilled cheese sandwich.

CORN PUDDING

This is the favorite dish from an old recipe my Mother gave me years ago.

2 C corn	2 T sugar
2 eggs, beaten	4-6 T flour
1 tsp. salt	2-3 C milk
1/8 tsp. pepper	Salt & pepper

Mix. Bake at 350° until set.

~~~~~~

This is the way I make Corn Pudding today and the way I have passed it on to my children.

2 cans whole corn, drained	2 T sugar
2 cans cream corn	4-6 T flour
6-8 eggs, beaten	2-3 C milk
4 T butter, melted	Salt & pepper

Preheat oven to 350°. Empty the drained whole corn & the cream corn into a mixing bowl.

In a separate bowl, mix the flour & milk, being sure there are no lumps. Add flour & milk mixture, melted butter and beaten eggs to corn. Mix well. Salt & pepper to taste along with the sugar. Bake at 350° in a well greased baking casserole 1 ½ to 2 hours or until custard is set. If your oven bakes hot, you may need to lower your oven to 325°.

CLAM STUFFED EGGPLANT

1 large eggplant
½ lb. butter
2 small onions, sliced
½ green pepper, chopped
1 C bread crumbs
1 T chopped parsley
Salt & pepper
1 can minced clams (6 oz. w/ juice)*
1 beaten egg yolk
1 slice bacon

Melt 4 tablespoons butter in skillet. Cut eggplant in half lengthwise. Fry cut-side down until soft. Cool and scrape out, leaving shell. Sauté onions, peppers, parsley and pulp in more butter. Salt & pepper. Add clams with juice and egg yolk, half the crumbs, and 1 tablespoon melted butter. Mix and stuff shell. Top with bread crumbs. Dot with butter and slice of bacon cut into small bits. Bake at 325° until brown, about 25-30 minutes until good and hot.

Wonderful Friday meal. Good both cold and next day.

* My favorite way is to replace clams with tuna & do not use bacon.

EGGPLANT & OYSTERS

1 medium eggplant
4 T chopped onion
¼ C butter
½ C bread crumbs
½ tsp. salt
1 pt. oysters
½ C light cream

Peel and cut eggplant into 1-inch cubes. Cook in boiling salted water until soft. Sauté onion in butter. Add bread crumbs and salt. Heat oysters in own juice slowly until edges curl. Put a layer of crumb mixture into buttered casserole, sprinkle with eggplant cubes, then oysters, then crumbs again. End with crumbs.

Pour cream over ingredients in casserole. Bake at 350° for about 25-30 minutes until brown on top and well heated. Also good cold.

CUBANELLES Mom's Italian Stuffed Peppers

Green peppers (your choice of amount)*
1 loaf day-old Italian bread (unsliced)
Water
1 C chopped flat leaf parsley
5 gloves garlic, chopped fine
2 cans flat anchovies
½ C grated Parmesan cheese
Black pepper to taste
½ C olive oil

Wash and cut off the tops of the green peppers and remove seeds. Take about 1 cup cold water and wet the bread to moisten. Squeeze out the water. Bread should not be soggy. To the moistened bread, add all the ingredients listed above and stuff the peppers. Do not overstuff. The bread stuffing will swell.**

On a baking sheet greased with olive oil, place the peppers, tops up, and roast at 375° for 20 minutes. Turn the peppers every 20 minutes until peppers are soft. Sprinkle with grated Parmesan cheese to serve.
* This is a guide. You figure the number of peppers and the amount of stuffing.
** If you overstuff, push the stuffing back in when they are finished. The amount of stuffing can be tricky. Go easy.

Mother, second from left, with her brothers and sisters.

FRIED ZUCCHINI SQUASH

1 medium zucchini, chopped fine*
2 eggs
Small amount of liquid
1 C flour
½ tsp. salt
1/8 tsp. pepper
½ tsp. garlic salt
1 T parsley, chopped
1 tsp. baking powder

Salt zucchini lightly. Let stand 1 hour.

Mix all other ingredients. Drain zucchini and squeeze. Add zucchini to batter. Fry in deep fat until brown on both sides. Drain on paper towels.

* You can also prepare cauliflower the same way. Cauliflower can be par-cooked in boiling salted water. Drain and cool. Ad to batter and fry.

GREEN BEAN BAKE

2 cans green beans, or large bag frozen green beans,
    Regular or French cut
1 stick butter
1 onion, chopped
2 T flour
2 C sour cream
1 C grated Swiss cheese
1 C crushed corn flakes

Melt 1 stick butter. Sauté chopped onions. Add 2 T flour to make a paste. Add 2 cups sour cream and thicken. Put green beans in casserole. Pour sour cream mixture over top. Sprinkle 2 cups grated Swiss cheese over top and then 1 cup crushed corn flakes. Bake for 1 hour at 350°.

HASH BROWN CASSEROLE POTATOES

1 pkg. (2 lb.) frozen hash browns
½ C chopped onion
2 C cheddar cheese, grated
1 can cream of chicken soup
1 pt. sour cream
½ C butter, melted
1 ½ C crushed cornflakes

Combine first five ingredients and add ¼ cup of the melted butter. Place in a greased 9x13 pan. Top with crushed cornflakes and spread the rest of the butter on top. Bake uncovered at 350° for 1 to 1 ½ hours.

ITALIAN COUNTRY BEANS

3 T olive oil
2 cloves garlic, finely chopped
1 lb. green beans, cleaned & tips removed
1 C beef broth
1 T fresh parsley, finely chopped
¼ C finely chopped ham or prosciutto

Heat oil and sauté garlic for 2-3 minutes. Add green beans and sauté 2-3 minutes until glossy. Add broth and cook until beans are just tender but crispy. Sprinkle with chopped parsley and ham and serve. Makes 4-6 servings. Best made with the big flat Roman green beans.

KLUSKI AND CABBAGE

2 C flour
1 tsp. salt
1 egg
1 8-oz. carton sour cream

* KLUSKI:

Put flour and salt in a bowl. Mix egg with sour cream and stir into flour. You will have to work in flour with hands. Roll into "pencils" between palms. Cut "pencils" into small pieces. Add dough balls to boiling salted water. Remove from top with slotted spoon. Cover with a little melted butter to keep from sticking.**

TO PREPARE CABBAGE:

In a very small amount of salted water, add cut up cabbage (cut in wedges, then crosswise). Put lid on pan and steam about 7 minutes. Add dough balls and one stick of butter. Turn over and over until butter melts. Replace lid and cook about 5 minutes. DO NOT OVERCOOK!!

Add salt & pepper to taste.

* Kluski is a generic Polish name for all kinds of soft dumplings.

** In a hurry, boil medium egg noodles, drain and use in place of dough balls.

MOM'S HOLIDAY GREENS

My Mother only made these greens at Thanksgiving and Christmas. I can't give you amounts – you go by how much you want to make. Use this recipe as a guide.

3 large heads of endive	Handful of raisins
6 cloves chopped garlic (2 cloves per head)	Handful of pine nuts
	1 can black olives, cut in half
2 cans flat anchovies, broken into pieces	Handful of grated Parmesan
	Red pepper flakes (a pinch or to taste)

Wash the endive heads in cold water and shake off most of the water. Open endive flat on a work surface and cover with the chopped garlic, anchovies, raisins, pine nuts, black olives, grated cheese and red pepper flakes. Drizzle with olive oil and carefully tie up each head with kitchen string, closing them up.

Stand heads in a pan with a little water (enough to cover heavy part of endive) and add some olive oil to water (about 2 tablespoons). Simmer covered until greens are tender. Remove from pan to a serving bowl. Cut into sections to serve. Dip Italian bread into juice.

This is a very traditional recipe and I have never seen it made outside of my family.

See next recipe to streamline this recipe. >>>>>>>>

ROSEMARY'S "STREAMLINED" GREENS

Rosemary gets everything ready and lined up. She makes large amounts to share with friends – so think big.

1. Wash and chop endive – do not shake off all the cold water.

2. Have bowls of all ingredients lined up and ready to go:

    Garlic and anchovies chopped, raisins, pine nuts, red pepper flakes, cheese, black olives halved, and olive oil

3. In a large deep pan, add a little water and a small amount of olive oil. Layer endives and remaining ingredients; repeat layers until all are used. Cover pan, simmer until greens are tender, about 20-30 minutes.

4. Rosemary jars the greens and shares with friends at Christmas. A great new twist on a great old recipe.

Thanks, Rosemary!!

My sister Rosemary and her husband Pete Caffo.

STUFFED ESCAROLE

This recipe is very much like the recipe for "My Mom's Greens". My Mother used endive. The amount of ingredients in this recipe depends on how much you make.

    1 head of escarole, rinsed
    Grated Parmesan cheese, about ¼ C
    Day-old Italian bread, cut into very small cubes
    Chopped black olives, the wrinkled ones, or calamata
    Capers, about 1 T   Golden raisins, about ¼ C
    Olive oil   (soaked in hot water to plump)
    Pine nuts (pignoli), about 2-3 T   2-3 cloves garlic, sliced

In boiling water, blanch escarole. Remove from pot and plunge into ice water. Remove large leaves and save to be stuffed. In a small dry skillet, toast pine nuts and set aside. In same skillet, toast bread crumbs lightly, 2-3 minutes.* Set aside with pine nuts. In the same skillet, add the olive oil (2-3 tablespoons) and the sliced garlic, cook about 1 minute. Do not let it brown. Add capers & chopped olives (12-18 olives).

STUFFING: In a large bowl, combine pine nuts, bread crumbs, capers, olives, chopped remaining small leaves of blanched escarole, grated cheese, drained soaked raisins, salt & pepper. Toss to combine.

Lay out the large leaves and place the stuffing on the leaf and roll. Place the stuffing near the bottom of the leaf, roll up once, fold in sides, and finish rolling. Place filled rolls in an ovenproof casserole, seam-side down. Top with any stuffing that is left over. Drizzle on a little olive oil & sprinkle with a handful of grated cheese. Bake in a preheated oven at 375° for about 20 minutes covered with foil. Uncover and bake another 15-20 minutes.

* After you toast the cubes of bread, you may like the texture better if you wet the cubes and then squeeze them dry.
** If you do not want to take the time to make rolls, you can do this in layers, but the rolls are elegant.

  You may notice many Italian greens are combined in a balance of bitter, salty & sweet.

"SLEEK" - SPINACH with BURGHUL

½ C burghul wheat*
1 bag fresh spinach, or 2-3 boxes frozen, thawed & squeezed
4 T olive oil
2 cans black eyed peas (rinsed & drained)
1 large onion, chopped
1 clove garlic, chopped or minced

Soak the burghul 15 minutes. Squeeze to remove all the water out of the soaked burghul. Sauté onion & garlic in oil for a minute or so. Add spinach & sauté for 3-5 minutes more. Add washed and drained burghul and cook for 5-10 minutes. Add black eyed peas. Salt & pepper to taste. Cook another 3-5 minutes until everything is hot. Cover and let set for 10 minutes. Eat hot or cold.

* Also called Bulgur wheat.

** This is a Syrian recipe and is good served with Syrian or Italian bread. Kale or Swiss chard can be used in place of spinach.

TATER TOT CASSEROLE

1 bag tater tots
1 ½ lb. ground meat or venison
1 large onion

1 can cream of mushroom soup
½ to 1 C milk
Velveeta cheese

Use a 9x13 casserole dish. Layer tater tots in dish. Brown meat and onion. Add salt & pepper. Mix soup with meat. Add milk to thin. Pour mixture over tater tots evenly. Slice cheese and cover casserole. Bake for 45 minutes at 350°.

STUFFED ARTICHOKES
CARCIOFI alla ROMANA

Choose heavy artichokes with tightly closed leaves.

4 artichokes	½ tsp. salt
½ small onion, chopped	½ tsp. pepper
2 T parsley, chopped	¼ C olive oil
4 T grated Parmesan	2 T water
2 cloves garlic, chopped	2 T olive oil
1 C bread crumbs	Lemon

Cut straight across with a sharp knife to cut 1 inch off the top of the artichoke. Cut off stems so that artichokes sit flat. Skin down stem and dice. Simmer stems in boiling water until tender, drain, set aside to add to stuffing. With scissors, snip thorny tips off each leaf. Remove any bottom tough leaves. Press down on artichoke to open. Remove chokes in bottom of artichoke. Rub the cut tops of the artichokes with half a lemon to keep from browning.

STUFFING:

Mix together onions, parsley, grated cheese, garlic, bread crumbs, cooked diced stems, salt, pepper, and olive oil, with enough water to moisten stuffing (about 2 tablespoons) and fill each leaf.

Place artichokes upright in baking dish or small roaster. Sprinkle each with a little olive oil. Add water about 2 inches around artichokes, or about 1/3 of the way up artichokes. Bake slowly at 325° for about 1 hour uncovered.* Uncover and bake to allow tops to brown, about 10-15 minutes.

* I prefer cooking mine on top of the stove in a pan with a tight fitting lid in a small amount of water. I also add the lemon to the water. Simmer about 1 hour. You can place in the oven to brown tops if you like.

SWEET POTATO SOUFFLÉ

SOUFFLÉ:
- 3 C mashed sweet potatoes
- 1 C sugar (½ C if using canned sweet potatoes)
- ½ tsp. salt
- 1/3 stick butter, melted
- ¼ C brandy or liqueur
- 2 eggs
- 1 tsp. vanilla

TOPPING:
- 1 C brown sugar
- 1/3 stick butter, melted
- 1/3 C flour
- 1 C chopped nuts
- 1 C coconut – optional

Mix all ingredients for soufflé together and place in a casserole dish. Mix all ingredients listed for topping together and top the soufflé. Bake at 325° for 25 minutes.

VEG-ALL CASSEROLE

- 1 large can Veg-All, drained
- ½ C celery, cut bite-sized
- ½ C onion, chopped
- ½ C cheddar cheese, grated
- 1 can water chestnuts, sliced
- ½ C mayonnaise
- Butter
- Ritz crackers

Mix all together. Melt some butter. Crush Ritz crackers for topping. Mix butter and crackers together to make crumbs. Cover top and bake at 350° for 35 minutes.

* I double and triple this recipe, depending on the number of people. Very easy and good!

ITALIAN POTATOES

14-15 large red potatoes (about 5 lb.)
½ C chopped parsley
½ C chopped green onions
3-4 large cloves garlic, sliced
1 heaping tsp. salt
½ tsp. dry mustard
1 scant T sugar
1 T Worcestershire
1 C olive oil
½ tsp. wine vinegar

Boil potatoes until tender. Peel & cut in 1 inch chunks. Sprinkle parsley & green onions over potatoes. Make the dressing by mixing the rest of the ingredients; then pour over the potatoes. Stir well. Let it stand 4-6 hours. Stir every hour. Do not refrigerate. Leftovers can be refrigerated & then brought to room temperature. Great for picnics.

MASHED POTATO BAKE

5 C water
4 C frozen hash brown potatoes
1 pkg. (7.6 oz) Butter & Herb Mashed potato mix
½ C butter (1 stick)
Small cream cheese
1 C Monterey Jack cheese
½ C sour cream
½ tsp. garlic salt
½ tsp. salt
½ tsp. pepper
2 C canned French-fried onion rings

Preheat oven to 350°. Bring water to a boil, add the hash browns & cook for 5 minutes; drain. Prepare the mashed potato mix according to package directions. Soften the butter & cream cheese together in the microwave. In a large bowl, mix together the hash browns, mashed potatoes, butter & cream cheese, Jack cheese, sour cream, garlic salt, salt & pepper. Place in a greased 2-quart casserole. Bake for 25-35 minutes or until top is golden. Sprinkle onion rings over the top & bake 5-8 minutes longer, or until onions are golden brown.

SCALLOPED POTATOES with ARTICHOKES

Serves 6-8. Prep time: 20 minutes. Cook time: 1 hour 10 minutes.

2 T olive oil
1 large onion, diced
2 C diced thawed frozen artichokes
2 garlic cloves, minced
1 T fresh thyme, minced
3 lb. russet potatoes, peeled

Salt & pepper to taste
2 C shredded Asiago cheese
2 ½ C heavy cream
½ C grated Pecorino Romano cheese

Preheat the oven to 400° and lightly butter a 13x9 casserole dish.

Heat the olive oil over medium heat and then cook the onions and artichokes until the vegetables are soft and beginning to brown, about 8 minutes, stirring often. Add the garlic, stir, and cook another minute or two until fragrant. Remove from heat and stir in the thyme.

Slice the potatoes 1/8 inch thick and layer one third of the potatoes in the baking dish. Season with salt & pepper, then top with half the artichoke mixture, and half the Asiago cheese. Repeat this layer once more, then finish with a layer of potatoes. Pour the cream over the potatoes, pushing them down gently to coat with the cream. Sprinkle the potatoes with the grated Pecorino Romano cheese.

Cover the casserole with foil, then bake on a rimmed baking sheet (to catch any drips) for 45 minutes. Remove the foil and bake another 15-20 minutes, or until the potatoes are fork tender and the casserole is bubbly and golden brown.

Let rest 5-10 minutes before serving.

SALADS

A little something about Italian salads. First of all, there are no rules. Any greens mixed with any beans, vegetables, hard boiled eggs, mushrooms, and even fruit. A little good olive oil, wine vinegar, garlic, salt and pepper and it's a salad.

As a young girl, I went into the woods with my parents and my Nana. We picked dandelions, wild mushrooms, and rapini (broccoli rabe), nothing better!

My parents and my Nana knew which mushrooms were good to eat - I think now it would be safer to buy them!

DUTCH & JENNIE'S TOMATO SALAD from THE GARDEN

When the tomatoes were ripe in my Dad's garden, my Mother would make the best salad the world has ever known. So fresh, so simple, so good. Just had to pass it on.

> Home grown tomatoes
> Sliced garlic
> Fresh Italian parsley
> Fresh basil
> Salt & pepper
>
> Onion
> Olive oil
> Good Italian bread
> Vinegar

Peel home grown tomatoes. No need to use hot water. Cut into thick slices or in wedges. Put them in a large salad bowl. Add sliced garlic, fresh Italian parsley and fresh basil. Salt & pepper to taste. Slice in a sweet onion. Drizzle with good olive oil. Toss lightly.

If you let it sit a few minutes, it makes a wonderful, flavorful juice in which we would dip Italian bread. Sometimes green peppers from the garden were cut up and tossed in. If you like, a small amount of vinegar can be used. Thanks, Mom and Dad!

Mom & Dad dressed for their 25th Wedding Anniversary in their original wedding attire.

PERFECT PASTA SALAD TOSS

8 oz. penne pasta, cooked, rinsed in cold water, & drained
4 oz. sliced salami, cut into strips
7 oz. jar roasted red peppers, drained, cut into strips
6 ½ oz. jar marinated artichoke hearts, drained & quartered
1/3 C halved kalamata olives
¼ C packed, sliced fresh basil leaves
½ C bottled Italian or Caesar dressing
1 C mixed Parmesan, Mozzarella & Romano cheeses
Romain lettuce, optional

Toss together – Cover – Refrigerate at least 30 minutes or up to 6 hours.

NO-TOSS LAYERED SALAD

1 head of lettuce, torn or chopped
Sweet onion
1 lb. bacon, fried & crumbled
1 pkg. (10 oz.) frozen peas
¼ C sugar
Salt & pepper to taste
2 C Miracle Whip
½ C Parmesan cheese

Mix salt, pepper & sugar together. Layer first four ingredients in order given, sprinkling salt, pepper & sugar between the layers. <u>Seal</u> the top of the bowl with Miracle Whip. Important no air gets in. Sprinkle cheese on top. Cover with plastic wrap. Chill 6-8 hours or overnight.

* You can use 1 C mayonnaise & 1 C of sour cream in place of Miracle Whip. You can use grated Swiss cheese in place of Parmesan.

BLUEBERRY SLAW with RASPBERRY DRESSING

This is very easy & a little different.

Mix together:

    1 bag (16 oz.) coleslaw mix
    1 small red onion, chopped
    1 pint blueberries, washed & stemmed
    1/3 – ½ C fresh cilantro, chopped
    ½ tsp. pepper

Raspberry Vinaigrette Dressing:**

¾ C olive oil	2 T sugar
¼ C cider vinegar	1 small container of raspberries

Mash half the raspberries & mix with oil, vinegar & sugar. Whisk until well blended. Drizzle over slaw mixture.* Top with remaining raspberries. Toss before serving.

* Drizzle the dressing on the slaw an hour or two before serving – then toss when you are ready to serve. You can just use a bought raspberry dressing if you want to.

** You can also try a buttermilk ranch dressing & just toss on a few raspberries, or not.

COLD ASIAN NOODLE SALAD

This can be a salad or a main dish.

> 1 lb. whole grain thin spaghetti
> ½ C vegetable oil
> 1/3 C smooth peanut butter
> ¼ C rice wine vinegar
> ¼ C soy sauce
> ¼ C dark sesame oil*
> 2 T honey
> 2 large cloves garlic
>
> ½ inch fresh ginger, pickled
> 3 T toasted sesame seeds
> ½ tsp. red pepper flakes
> 1 seedless cucumber, peeled, sliced thin
> 1 red bell pepper, sliced thin
> 6-8 green onions, sliced vertically

In a large pot, cook (al dente) the spaghetti. While the spaghetti is cooking, prepare the dressing. In a blender or food processor, blend the vegetable oil, peanut butter, rice wine vinegar, soy sauce, sesame oil, honey, garlic & ginger until smooth. Mix in the sesame seeds and red pepper flakes.

When the spaghetti is ready, toss the spaghetti with the dressing. Add the cucumbers, red bell pepper, & green onions. ** Refrigerate the pasta until cold before serving. ***

* Toasted sesame oil works great.

** You can omit any of the vegetables you want, but the green onions (cut vertically) are a must. You can, if you like, add cooked chicken, shrimp, peanuts, bean sprouts, etc.

*** My daughter Melissa loves cold noodles with peanut butter sauce. This one's for her.

MOLDED CHICKEN SALAD

20 Servings

A very special luncheon dish.

Layer 1

    3 envelopes unflavored gelatin
    ½ C cold water
    2 cans (1 lg. 4 oz. each) crushed pineapple, drained
    3 cans (1 lb. each) whole cranberry sauce
    2 C sour cream

Soften gelatin in cold water. Mash & heat pineapple & cranberry sauce. Add gelatin. Cool slightly, then add sour cream. Fill 2 large oiled molds half full.* Refrigerate. This layer should be firm before adding second layer. May be made the day before.

Layer 2

    4 envelopes unflavored gelatin
    1 C cold water
    3 (10 ¾ oz.) cream of chicken soup
    3 C cooked diced chicken
    1 C diced celery
    1 C peeled, diced cucumber
    ½ C diced onion
    4 C sour cream
    1 C slivered toasted almonds
    Salt & pepper to taste

Soften gelatin in water. Heat soup to boiling; add softened gelatin. Combine chicken, celery, cucumbers & onion. Add the soup & gelatin mixture. Cool. Add sour cream, almonds & seasoning. Pour over cranberry mixture & seal with waxed paper. Chill until firm; unmold.

* You can also make this in two 9x13 pans & cut into squares. Serve on lettuce leaf.

HEAVENLY HASH FRUIT SALAD

1 (16 oz.) Cool Whip
1 large cream cheese
2 T mayonnaise
1 large can fruit cocktail
1 can pineapple tidbits
1 can mandarin oranges
1 small jar maraschino cherries
1 ½ C miniature marshmallows

Drain all fruit. Soften cream cheese. Add mayonnaise. Fold in Cool Whip. Fold in fruit. Refrigerate.

EASY CAESAR SALAD

1 C peanut oil*
1 garlic clove, minced
1-2 C seasoned croutons
3 heads romaine
¾ C grated Parmesan
½ tsp. salt
½ tsp. pepper
¼ tsp. dry mustard
3 T lemon juice
2 eggs, slightly beaten
Dash of Worcestershire sauce
1 can (2 oz.) anchovy filets (opt.)

Pour oil in jar; add garlic. Cover & let stand 1 hour. Wash romaine; drain & tear into bite-sized pieces in a large salad bowl. Sprinkle cheese, salt, pepper & mustard over romaine. Pour oil, lemon juice & eggs over salad. Add remaining ingredients. Toss lightly until well mixed.

* I like olive oil better than peanut oil & a little more garlic.

TABOULI SALAD

1 C fine burghul wheat
1 C chopped parsley
½ C chopped spearmint leaves
3-4 chopped green onions, or
    ¼ C chopped onion
4 finely chopped tomatoes
4 finely chopped cucumbers
6-8 red radishes
Juice of 2-3 lemons
½ C olive oil
Salt & pepper to taste

Wash, soak (½ hour or more), and drain the wheat by squeezing. Add the vegetables. Combine them as you would a salad with the lemon juice and olive oil. Salt & pepper. Allowing the flavor to blend for a time before serving improves the taste. Refrigerate.

PANZANELLA – ITALIAN BREAD SALAD

My Mother would make this with the chuck roast she used to make beef broth. You need stale Italian bread cut into bite-sized pieces, diced tomatoes & onions sliced.

<u>Vinaigrette:</u> olive oil, red wine vinegar, sliced garlic, salt & pepper. (Sprinkle of oregano optional.)

Pour vinaigrette over tomatoes and bread. Add all the other vegetables.* Last, add the beef that has been cut into bite-sized pieces. Let it stand a few minutes to improve flavor. Salt & pepper to taste.**

* You can add: olives, capers, hard boiled eggs, your choice

** You may have noticed I have not given you any amounts. You work with what you have.

It's a meal – It's an appetizer – It's a salad. It is whatever you want it to be. Most of all, it's good!

SANGRIA SALAD

Has the same flavor as the popular drink.

- 3 envelopes unflavored gelatin
- 1 C orange juice
- ½ C sugar
- ¼ C lemon juice
- 2 ½ C red wine*
- ¾ C club soda
- 2 oranges, sliced
- 1 banana, sliced
- 2 peaches, sliced
- 1 C strawberry halves

Soften gelatin in orange juice. Cook over low heat until dissolved. Add sugar; stir until dissolved. Remove from heat. Stir in lemon juice, wine & club soda. Chill until slightly thickened. Fold in fruit; pour into 8-cup mold or 9-inch square dish. Chill. Make early in the day or the day before serving.

Avacodo dressing

- 2 very ripe avocadoes
- ½ C sour cream
- 1 ½ tsp. salt
- 2 T lime juice

If dressing is desired, thoroughly mash avocadoes. Mix with remaining ingredients. Dressing may also be used as a dip.

* Salad can be made with white wine if you prefer.

AUNT ELLA'S SALAD

Aunt Ella is my Dad's younger sister.

- 2 pkgs. Dream Whip
- 18 oz. cream cheese
- 2 T mayonnaise
- 1 large can fruit cocktail
- 1 can pineapple tidbits
- 1 can mandarin oranges
- 1 med. jar maraschino cherries
- 1 ½ C miniature marshmallows

Drain all fruit. Soften cheese. Add mayonnaise. Fold in Dream Whip. Fold in remaining ingredients and refrigerate. You can use Cool Whip for Dream Whip, and add coconut if you like.

BEAN & LITTLE PEA SALAD

1 can French green beans
1 can French yellow beans
1 can tiny peas (Lucerne)
2 pieces of celery, chopped
1 onion, sliced thin
1 jar pimento

Dressing:

1 C vinegar
1 C sugar
½ C oil
1 tsp. salt
1 tsp. paprika
¼ C water

Mix dressing and vegetables. Let stand overnight. Drain before serving.

BACCALA SALAD

1 lb. salt cod
2 med. Potatoes
 (Idaho or Yukon Gold)
½ lb. string beans
½ C thinly sliced red onion
1 T chopped parsley
½ C good olive oil
Fresh ground pepper
3 T red wine vinegar

Soak dried cod for 24 hours, changing water about 6 times. Boil potatoes with skins on in salted water for about 25 minutes until tender but not mushy. While potatoes are cooking, cook green beans in boiling salted water until al dente, about 6-8 minutes. Drain and rinse in cold water quickly to hold bright green color. Place salt cod in boiling water until it starts to flake, about 8 minutes. When cod is cool enough to handle, flake with hands into 1 ½ -inch bite-sized pieces, removing any bones or skin.

To assemble:

While potatoes are warm, cut into bite-sized pieces. Add green beans, red onion, chopped parsley and salt cod. Mix olive oil, vinegar and pepper. Drizzle over salad. Toss gently, being careful not to mash potatoes and cod.

Serve warm or room temperature. Good the next day cold, if any is left over. Very Italian, very good. Can be a salad, appetizer, or light lunch.

CALICO POTATO SALAD LOAF

I must tell you before you try this recipe, that most members of my family did not care for it. But having said that, I always liked the way it looked on a buffet, and I liked the taste. They say, "You eat with your eyes first."

    8 oz. sliced ham (cold cuts)   1/3 C chopped celery
    1 envelope (1 T) unflavored gelatin   2 T chopped onion
    ½ C cold water   1 T snipped parsley
    1 C mayo or salad dressing   1 T chopped pimento
    1 tsp. prepared mustard   6 C diced cooked potatoes
    1 tsp. salt   8 oz. pickle & pimento loaf

Line a 9x5x3 loaf pan with waxed paper, extending paper up over the sides. Line bottom and sides of pan with sliced ham. Soften gelatin in ½ cup cold water in cup. Place cup in a pan or bowl of hot water to dissolve. Combine mayo, mustard, salt, celery, onion & pimento. Add dissolved gelatin and mix well. Stir in diced potatoes and pickle & pimento loaf. Spoon into lined pan. Press down gently. Chill 3-4 hours. Turn out onto serving platter.

CAULIFLOWER IN VINAIGRETTE

Cook flowerets until just tender, about 5 min. in boiling salted water. Drain and cover with sauce.

    ¼ C olive oil   Pinch of cayenne pepper
    2 T vinegar   1 hard cooked egg, chopped
    ¼ tsp. salt   1 T capers
    1 T minced green pepper

Pour sauce over hot cauliflower and let marinate for several hours. Serve cold.

CHICKEN SALADS

Both of these chicken salads have seen me through many buffets, bridal showers & baby showers.

HOT CHICKEN SALAD

- 2 ½ C cooked diced chicken
- 2 C chopped celery
- 1 C sliced or slivered almonds, toasted
- ½ tsp. salt
- 1 C mayonnaise (not salad dressing)
- 1 grated lemon peel
- Juice of 1 lemon (2-3 tsp.)
- ½ small onion, grated
- 1 C crushed potato chips
- 1 C sharp cheddar, grated

Blend mayo with lemon peel, juice, onion & salt. Mix lightly with chicken, celery & almonds. Mix in half the cheese & top with remaining cheese. Top off with crushed chips. Bake at 400° for 15-20 minutes or until piping hot.

CHINESE CHICKEN SALAD

- 4 C chopped cooked chicken
- 1 (5 oz.) can bamboo shoots
- 1 (5 oz.) can water chestnuts
- 1 C slivered almonds
- 2 (11 oz.) cans mandarin oranges, drained
- 2 C mayonnaise
- 2 T diced onions

Mix together and chill about 3 hours or overnight. Just before serving, mix in 2 medium cans of Chinese noodles.

COLE SLAW with CLEAR DRESSING

SLAW:
- 8 C or 2 small heads of red and/or green cabbage
- 2 carrots, shredded
- 1 green pepper, cut small
- ½ C chopped onion

DRESSING:
- 2/3 C vinegar
- 1 ½ tsp. salt
- 2 tsp. celery seed
- 2/3 C sugar
- ¼ tsp. pepper
- 1 pkg. clear gelatin
- 1/3 C water
- 2/3 C oil

Put 1 cup cold water over vegetables. Refrigerate to keep crisp. Drain before adding dressing.

Cook all ingredients for dressing until just before boiling point. Cool cooked mixture. Mix 1 package of clear gelatin with 1/3 cup cold water. Mix cooked dressing and gelatin together with 2/3 cup oil. Beat with mixture.

CONFETTI SWEET & SOUR SLAW

- 3 C shredded red cabbage
- 1 C shredded carrots
- ¼ C green onion, chopped fine
- 3 T chopped onions
- 3 T chopped celery
- 2 T raisins, plumped
- 2 tsp. vegetable oil
- 1 tsp. each sugar, vinegar, and honey
- Salt & pepper to taste

Combine all ingredients. Refrigerate at least 1 hour or overnight before serving.

SPECIAL COLE SLAW

SLAW:
- 2 (1 lb.) bags cole slaw mix
- 2 pkgs. Roman chicken noodles
- 1 bunch green onions, sliced thin
- 1 C slivered almonds, toasted
- 1 C sunflower kernels

DRESSING:
- 1 C oil
- 6 T wine vinegar
- 2 pkgs. Roman seasoning mix
- 4 T sugar

Pour dressing over slaw mix a few hours before serving. You can use a head of cabbage cut up. You can also add 2-4 tablespoons toasted sesame seeds. Refrigerate.

THREE CABBAGE SALAD

SLAW:
- 3 C each green & savory cabbage
- 2 C red cabbage
- 1 ½ C grated carrot
- ½ C chopped onion

DRESSING:
- 1/3 C cream
- 6 slices crisp bacon, crumbled
- 3 T mayo
- 2 T chopped dill
- 1 T Dijon mustard
- 2 T lemon juice
- Salt & pepper

Mix slaw together in large salad bowl. Mix dressing ingredients together and pour over cabbage mixture. Refrigerate at least 1 hour before serving.

COOKED VEGETABLE SALAD

2-3 potatoes, cooked & peeled
1 C green beans, cooked
3 carrots, cooked & quartered
1 pkg. artichoke hearts, cooked
1-2 zucchinis, sliced & cooked
¼ C vinegar
1 tsp. salt, or to taste
Black pepper
2 T grated onion
2 cloves garlic, crushed
Parsley
Capers

All vegetables should be cooked separately until just tender crisp. Drain and let cool. Combine olive oil, vinegar, salt, pepper, grated onion and garlic. Divide dressing among vegetables, marinating each separately. Before serving, arrange vegetables on platter. Garnish with parsley and capers. You can grill vegetables if you like.

CREAMY WALDORF SALAD

2 pkgs. (3 oz.) lemon Jello
   (or one 6 oz. pkg.)
2 C boiling water
1 C cold water
1 (10 oz.) can vanilla pudding
2 unpeeled apples, cored & diced
½ C chopped celery
½ C chopped walnuts

Dissolve Jello in boiling water. Stir in cold water. Chill until partially set. In mixer, combine chilled Jello and pudding. Beat 2 minutes at medium speed. Chill until mixture mounds when spooned. Fold in apples, celery and nuts. Pour into a 7- or 8-cup mold. Chill until firm, about 6 hours or overnight. Unmold.

Cucumbers with Oregano, Feta & Pine Nuts

- 1 shallot, minced
- ¼ C red wine vinegar
- ¼ C extra virgin olive oil
- ¼ tsp. salt
- 3 English cucumbers, peeled & sliced
- 3 sprigs fresh oregano, stems removed
- ½ C crumbled feta cheese
- ¼ C pine nuts, toasted
- Coarsely ground black pepper

Combine shallot & vinegar in a small bowl. Let stand about 10 minutes. Add olive oil & salt, whisking well. Pour vinaigrette over cucumbers and toss well. Sprinkle with oregano, cheese & pine nuts. Season with black pepper.

Cucumber Salad

- ¼ C yogurt
- 2 T coarsely chopped dill
- 1 T coarsely chopped parsley
- 2 T fresh lemon juice
- 1 T olive oil
- 1 ½ tsp. chopped mint
- 2 tsp. Dijon mustard
- ¼ tsp. each sugar, salt and pepper
- 5 ½ C thinly sliced cucumbers (about 2 large)
- 2 ½ C thinly sliced red onion

Combine first 8 ingredients in food processor or blender, and pour over cucumbers and onions. Takes about 10 minutes to make.

DO NOT MAKE AHEAD OF TIME - gets watery.

When you buy cucumbers, pick the skinny ones with less seeds.

GRILLED ROMAINE

Drizzle olive oil over romaine hearts. Grill on outdoor grill or grill in pan on stove top. Turn romaine hearts to grill on all sides. Salt & pepper romaine hearts, then spoon over a dressing of olive oil, garlic chopped fine, diced tomatoes, green onions (or chopped sweet onion), and a little vinegar.

If romaine hearts are too large for a serving, they can be cut in half and then grilled.

This salad is very impressive – be careful when you grill the romaine – Do Not Burn!

INSALATA di POTATE
My Mother's Italian Potato Salad

Cook potatoes on the firm side. While potatoes are cooking, steam green beans until just tender (Roman beans are best, but string beans work). Do not overcook potatoes or green beans. Peel potatoes and slice. In a large shallow bowl, gently mix potatoes and green beans with sliced red onion or a sweet onion, parsley, vinegar, olive oil, salt, pepper and garlic. Best if served warm or room temperature.

The amounts of ingredients depend on how much you want to make. To my Mother's salad, I sometimes add some or all of the following:
- 1 can drained chick peas
- 1 can of good Italian tuna fish in oil
- ½ C pitted black olives, sliced
- ½ C pitted green olives, sliced
- ½ C shredded Provolone cheese

Toss together well. Makes a wonderful light meal, or serve on a bed of your favorite greens for an excellent antipasto. Top with some capers.

MACARONI SALADS: PLAIN MACARONI SALAD

Cook elbow macaroni. Add chopped onion, chopped celery, chopped hard boiled eggs, salt, pepper and mayonnaise. Add a little sweet relish.

MACARONI SALAD PLUS

- 8 oz. macaroni, cooked
- ¼ C chilled French dressing
- ¼ C sliced green onion
- ¼ C chopped pimentos
- ½ C shredded carrots
- 2 T mustard
- ¼ to ½ C salad dressing
- ½ C celery

MACARONI SALAD with SHRIMP

- 8 oz. macaroni, cooked
- ½ C diced celery
- ¼ C green pepper, diced
- ¼ C onion, chopped
- Juice of ½ lemon
- Salt & pepper
- Mayonnaise
- 2 cans of small shrimp, drained; or ½ lb. salad shrimp

To give this shrimp salad an extra kick, you can use ¼ cup French dressing, and add ¼ cup chopped pimentos, 2 tablespoons mustard, ½ cup sweet relish, and ½ cup shredded carrots to the basic recipe.

This can be made with shrimp, crab, tuna, etc. Whatever you like. To give the shrimp an added flavor, you can marinate them for 2 hours in 1/3 cup oil, ¼ cup vinegar, 2 T soy sauce, 1 T sugar, 1 tsp. hot mustard, ½ tsp. ground ginger, and ½ tsp. garlic. Drain and add shrimp to salad. The marinade is up to you.

I am not thrilled with pasta salads, but these are not bad, and they are crowd pleasers.

PASTA, BEANS & VEGETABLE SALAD

Bow-tie pasta, cooked & drained
Kidney beans, drained
Peas, drained
Cheese, in chunks
Broccoli
Olives
Italian dressing
Celery
Onions
Garlic
Cherry tomatoes

You can also add Italian meats: salami, pepperoni, etc. Mix and chill before serving.

PAPAYA, JÍCAMA & AVOCADO SALAD

This salad is served more as a condiment rather than a separate course.

¼ C fresh lime juice
2 T olive oil
1 tsp. salt
1/8 tsp. ground black pepper
1 ripe papaya (about 1 ½ lb.), peeled, seeded, and cut into ½-inch cubes
1 jícama (about 1 lb.), skinned and cut into ½-inch cubes
1 avocado, ripe but firm
¼ C cilantro leaves, coarsely chopped

Combine papaya and jícama. Cut avocado in half; remove pit and skin. Cut into ½-inch cubes and add papaya and jícama. Add lime vinaigrette and toss well to combine. Add cilantro, adjust seasoning and toss again.

SCUNGILLI SALAD

Scungilli is a conch or a large sea snail. You can find it frozen or in a can fresh, if you live in Florida.

- 2 large cans of scungilli
- ¼ C chopped Italian parsley
- 2 C celery, chopped
- 1 C black olives, pitted and sliced
- 6 T olive oil
- 4 T lemon juice
- ½ tsp. pepper
- Salt to taste

Drain scungilli – clean by running under cold water. Check for cartilage. Cut into bite-sized pieces. Mix all together. Refrigerate about 30 minutes. Good at room temperature.

BROCCOLI SALAD

- 4 stalks of broccoli, cut in bite-sized pieces
    - (4 stalks = 1 large bundle)
- 8 slices of cooked bacon
- 4 oz. of grated cheddar cheese
- 1 small onion, diced fine

DRESSING: Mix and pour over all.

- 3 T vinegar
- ½ C sugar
- 1 C mayonnaise (not Miracle Whip)

Make several hours ahead of time, or overnight. Chill until ready to serve.

CANDY, DESSERTS, & PIES

MARY LESTER'S PEACH COBBLER

When I first met Mary Lester in Okeechobee, Florida, she introduced herself by telling me,"Buck and I are alcoholics, but we are the nicest people you will ever meet." She wasn't far off.

Batter:
    1 C milk   1 C self-rising flour
    1 C sugar

    1 stick butter, melted slowly in pan
    1 qt. of fruit (peaches, cherries, berries, apples)
        Sugar to sweeten if needed, depending on fresh or canned fruit

Pour batter over melted butter in pan. Pour fruit over batter. Bake at 350°. Start with 35 minutes, and add time up to an hour, until you see it is done and the juice has set.

I thought about not including this story, but I just could not help myself.

My parents were well up in age, in their 90s. We were living in Lower Burrell, PA, and I would go every day to help them in Arnold, PA, and stayed with them until I got them in bed. Buck &Mary were coming from Florida for a visit, so in trying to help my parents and in getting ready for their visit to my home, I would get my parents up, washed & fed breakfast – run home – do a little – then run back to my parents'. I was rushing because Buck & Mary were coming. This went on for a week. Finally my Mother said, "Amelia, why are you killing yourself running back & forth when you don't even like that lady." I asked what she was talking about, and her answer was, "Well, for a week you have been saying 'F_ _ _ in Mary' was coming." I had to tell her it was a **B** for **Buck** & Mary! And that from my mother who never swore!

PIE CRUST

There are many different pie crust recipes, but what you must know about all of them is to work fast, use a light hand, and don't over work.

I have heard this recipe called:

No Fail Pie Crust

3 C flour
1 ¼ C shortening
1 tsp. salt

1 egg, beaten
1 tsp. vinegar
6 T ice water

Cut shortening into flour & remaining ingredients. Shape into a disk and wrap in clear plastic. Let rest in refrigerator for 20 minutes or so. Roll out on a little flour.

Ready-to-Make Pie Crust

Cut together: 6 C flour and 2 C shortening

Keep in tight container in cupboard. Add ice water to mix to form crust in the amount needed.
    3-4 T water & pinch of salt per crust.

Perfect Pie Crust

1 ½ C flour
¾ tsp. salt

¾ C shortening
4-5 T ice water

Mix flour & salt. Cut in shortening using knives or pastry blender until crumbs are the size of peas. Add ice water slowly, blending with fork. Shape into a ball. Chill. Roll out on lightly floured surface. This recipe is enough for one 9-inch single pie. Prick thoroughly with a fork & bake on top rack in oven at 450° for 12-15 minutes.

APPLE PIE

Because everyone thinks everyone knows how to make an apple pie, it is very hard to find a recipe for apple pie. If you are the one person who does not know how to make a plain old-fashioned American Pie – Here it is!

    4-6 tart, juicy apples,   1 tsp. lemon juice
        Granny Smiths are great   1 tsp. cinnamon or nutmeg,
    1 C sugar   if desired
    1-2 T butter

Preheat oven to either 425° or 450°.

Line a pie pan with any plain crust. Slice apples thinly, mix with sugar, lemon juice, spices & flour. Fill crust, dot with butter. Cover with top crust. Cut a few slits in top crust to allow steam to escape.

<u>Depending on your oven</u>, bake for 40-45 minutes:
       10 minutes at 450°. Reduce to 425° for 30-35 minutes.
          OR
       10 minutes at 425°. Reduce to 375° for 30-35 minutes.

Stephanie ... Wow!

Beautiful crust!

EASY SKILLET APPLE PIE

2 lbs. Granny Smith apples
2 lbs. Braeburn apples
1 tsp. ground cinnamon
¾ C granulated sugar
½ C butter
1 C firmly packed light
    brown sugar (or dark)
1 pkg. (14.1 oz.) refrigerated pie crusts
1 egg white
2 T granulated sugar

Skillet Apple Pie

Preheat oven to 350°. Peel ales and cut into ½ inch thick wedges. Toss apples with cinnamon and ¾ cup sugar.

Melt butter in a 10-inch cast iron skillet over medium heat; add brown sugar and cook, stirring constantly 1 to 2 minutes or until sugar is dissolved. Remove from heat and place 1 pie crust in skillet over brown sugar mixture. Spoon apple mixture over pie crust and top with the remaining pie crust. Whisk egg white until foamy. Brush top of pie crust with egg white; sprinkle with 2 tablespoons of sugar. Cut 4 or 5 slits in top for steam to escape.

Bake at 350° for 1 hour to 1 hour 10 minutes, or until golden brown and bubbly. (Shield with aluminum foil the last 10 minutes to prevent over-browning if necessary.) Cool on wire rack 30 minutes before serving.

Good with ice cream.

I don't know how the butter & sugar gets from the skillet into the pie, but it does. If you don't have a cast iron skillet, it is worth getting one. This recipe was given to me by my good friend, & a wonderful cook, Ed Wright.

MOCK APPLE PIE

Pastry for 2-crust 9-inch pie
36 Ritz crackers, coarsely broken
    (about 1 ¾ Cup)
1 ¾ C water
2 C sugar
2 tsp. cream of tartar
2 T lemon juice
Grated peel of 1 lemon
2 T butter
½ tsp. cinnamon

Place broken crackers in bottom crust. Set aside. Heat water, sugar & cream of tartar to a boil over high heat; simmer 15 minutes. Add lemon juice & peel. Cool. Pour syrup over crackers. Dot with butter. Sprinkle with cinnamon. Place on top crust. Slit crust to allow steam to escape. Bake at 425° for 30-35 minutes. Cool completely.

This is a fun pie – People don't believe it is crackers. I like to have people guess what they are eating. This can also be made with saltines.

NORWEGIAN PIE
Very Good & Easy

2 C sliced apples
1 C nuts (or more)
1 C flour
1 ½ C sugar
2 tsp. baking powder
1 tsp. vanilla
½ tsp. salt
2 well beaten eggs

Mix together all ingredients. Press into two 8" or 9" pie pans that have been well greased. Bake at 350° for 30 minutes.

NO-BAKE TURTLE PUMPKIN PIE

This is Easy – Good – Fast. Can be made ahead. I thank my daughter Melissa for this one.

    1 (10") graham cracker crust   1 (8 oz.) Cool Whip*
    ½ C pecan pieces + 2 T for topping   Caramel topping
    1 C milk
    1 large pkg. <u>instant</u> vanilla pudding
    2 C canned pumpkin
    2-2 ½ tsp. pumpkin pie spice
        OR: 1 tsp. cinnamon, ½ tsp. each of nutmeg, ginger, & cloves

1. Pour ¼ cup caramel topping into crust. Sprinkle with ½ cup pecan pieces.
2. Whisk milk, pudding mix, pumpkin & spices.
3. Stir in ½ cup Cool Whip.
4. Spread into crust.
5. Refrigerate at least 1 hour or overnight.
6. Top with remaining Cool Whip, caramel and pecans.

* You can cut down on Cool Whip in filling & add a little more pumpkin for a heavier pie filling.

EASY TO MAKE PIE

    Graham cracker crust
    Small Cool Whip
    Small Jello & 8 oz. yogurt: both of the same flavor

Dissolve Jello in ¼ cup hot water. Cool. Mix Cool Whip, Jello & yogurt. Pour into crust. Sets up in 2 hours in the refrigerator.

PEACHES & CREAM SUPREME PIE

Prepare filling first.

FILLING:

    1/3 C sugar   ¼ C sour cream
    ¼ tsp. salt   3 oz. cream cheese, softened

Combine in small mixer bowl & blend for 3 minutes. Set aside.

CRUST:

    1 C flour   ½ C butter, softened
    2/3 C sugar   1 T reserved peach syrup
    1 tsp. baking powder   1 tsp. vanilla
    ¼ tsp. salt   2 eggs

Grease bottom & sides of a 9 or 10-inch pie pan. In large mixer bowl, combine all the ingredients for the crust. Spread crust batter over bottom & sides of pie pan. Pour filling into unbaked crust. Bake at 350° for 25-30 minutes, until crust is golden brown.

Top with 1 can (1 lb. 13 oz.) sliced peaches, drained. Prepare topping.

TOPPING:

    1 C sour cream
    ¼ C brown sugar

Combine sour cream & brown sugar and spoon over peaches.

Return pie to 350° oven for 5 minutes to set topping. Refrigerate at least 2 hours before serving.

STRAWBERRY GLAZE PIE

3 ½ C fresh strawberries (1 qt.)
¾ C sugar
1 T cornstarch
1 C water
¼ tsp. salt

Line baked shell with berries. Combine sugar, cornstarch, salt & water. Cook over low heat slowly until thickened and clear (about 5 minutes). Pour glaze over berries. Chill. Just before serving, garnish with whipped cream & whole berries. Can substitute: fresh sliced peaches or raspberries.

FRUIT STRUESEL PIE

2 C (½ lb.) cranberries
2 C sliced apples
1 ½ C sugar
3 T quick cooking tapioca
1 tsp. grated orange peel
1 uncooked 9" pie crust
1 C flour
1/3 C grated sharp cheese
¼ C butter, softened

Combine cranberries, apples, sugar, tapioca & orange peel. Pour into pie crust. Combine remaining ingredients & crumble over pie filling. Bake at 400° for 30 minutes. Cover top with foil & bake 15 minutes longer.

EASTER RICE PIE

This recipe has been handed down in my family for many, many years. From my grandmother Amelia DeMao to my mother Jennie Landi, and then to me. Now with much love, I pass it on to my children & family. I have seen other Rice Pie recipes, but they all have ricotta cheese in them. In my family Easter Rice Pie is made on Good Friday. Sometimes we are still making them on Holy Saturday. I hope you will keep the tradition going for many more years.

CRUST:

- 2 C flour
- 1 C sugar
- ¼ tsp. salt
- ½ C butter, room temp.
- 2 eggs, beaten*

Sift flour, sugar & salt. Cut in butter as you would for pie crust. Make a well in the flour mixture & add 2 beaten eggs. Work dough with hands quickly. <u>Do Not Add Water</u>. When smooth, shape into a ball, wrap in plastic wrap, & chill for 30 minutes. **

FILLING:

1 C of rice cooked for 10-15 min. in 3 C water & 1 T butter.

Arborio Italian rice is best, but you can use long grain rice.

To the cooled rice add:
- 1 ½ tsp. salt
- ½ C butter, melted
- 10 eggs
- 4-5 C milk
- 2 ½ C sugar
- 2 tsp. vanilla
- 1 tsp. lemon extract
- Grated rind & juice of 1 lemon
- Grated rind & juice of 1 orange

Bake at 350° for 1 hour, or until custard is set. Makes two 10-inch-deep pies. Dust top of pies with cinnamon before putting them in the oven.

* If you think you need it, you can add a third beaten egg to crust.
** Do not crimp crust over rim of pie pan – Crimp inside rim.

EASTER RICE PIE, continued

Things change: I now use a food processor for the crust. Put in the flour, sugar & salt – pulse a few times to mix. Next add the butter & peels until blended. With processor running, add the beaten eggs. Pulse a few more times. Turn out the dough onto your work surface & work with hands quickly until you can form a smooth ball. Wrap with plastic wrap & chill at least 30 minutes. Roll out crust, fill with rice filling, and bake at 350° for 1 hour, or until custard is set. Makes two 10-inch deep pies.

This is a good place to tell you how to cook rice.

In a saucepan, bring water to a boil. Stir in rice, add salt & butter. Cover pan – reduce heat, simmer for 15-20 minutes until water is absorbed.

Rice	1 C	2 C	3 C
Water	2 C	4 C	6 C
Yield	3 C	6 C	9 C
Servings ¾ C cooked	4	8	12

NOTE: For Rice Pie I use Italian Arborio rice – but any rice works – just do not cook it the full 20 minutes as you would for cooking rice.

Happy Easter!

DELICIOUS CAKE BITES

I think of these more as a dessert than a cake.

Start with any box cake mix you like. Bake according to directions on the box. While the cake is in the oven, you can mix together a cream cheese frosting or you can use a bought cream cheese frosting. For the frosting you will mix:

    ¼ C butter   1 tsp. vanilla
    6 oz. cream cheese   Enough milk to make a frosting
    2 ½ C powdered sugar

When the cake is done, dump it into a large bowl. Add the cream cheese frosting. Mix it all together with a wooden spoon. (It will be mushy.) Refrigerate 4-6 hours or overnight.

Roll into balls and dip in melted chocolate. If balls are sticky, put them in a plastic bag & flash freeze them until ready to dip. Do not try to dip the balls until they are well chilled (about 2 hours in the freezer). If you add nuts, candy, etc., be sure to chop them very fine in a food processor or electric chopper.

Everyone loves chocolate, but my favorite is:

BIRTHDAY CAKE BITES

    1 vanilla cake mix
    ½ to ¾ C cream cheese frosting
    White chocolate for coating (about 24 oz.)
    Rainbow sprinkles for decoration

PUMPKIN PITA (Pumpkin Sheet Pie)

    1 qt. milk   2 C sugar
    ½ C cream of rice   2 T butter

Cook milk, cream of rice, sugar & butter until thick, stirring constantly. Remove from heat & let cool slightly. <u>Fold in</u>:

    1 (15 oz.) can of pumpkin
    4 eggs, beaten
    2 tsp. pumpkin pie spice.

Also needed:
    1 C (2 sticks) butter, melted
    1 lb. phyllo dough

Preheat oven to 350°. In a 9x13 pan, layer a half pound of phyllo, buttering each sheet well, according to package directions. Pour pumpkin mixture over phyllo. Layer the remaining half pound of phyllo, making sure to butter each sheet well. Score the top into 16-20 pieces. Bake 1 hour until top is golden. Dust top with confectioner's sugar before serving.

CANDY EASTER EGGS

    3 C sugar   1 C water
    1 C Karo   1 tsp. vanilla

Cook to 238° on candy thermometer.

Beat 1 egg white – Beat 1 C cooked syrup into egg white. Let remaining syrup cook until it reaches 254° on candy thermometer. Pour into egg white mixture. Beat until it loses its gloss. Add fruit, nuts & vanilla. Shape into eggs. Cover with chocolate.

FRIDGE NUT EASTER EGGS

    3-4 C sugar   ¼ lb. Butter
    1 C milk

Cook to soft ball stage over low heat. Takes about ½ hour. Keep stirring.

In a large bowl, combine 1 large bag chocolate chips, 1 pint marshmallow cream, 1 tsp. vanilla, & nuts. Pour soft ball syrup over ingredients. Beat by hand until smooth. Pour on cookie sheets & refrigerate until cool enough to shape into eggs. Melt 1 pound chocolate in double boiler or microwave. Dip eggs. Makes one 5-pound egg, or five 1-pound eggs.

QUICK BITTERSWEET CHOCOLATE MOUSSE

1 ½ C bittersweet chocolate morsels
1 oz. unsweetened chocolate
1 egg
1 splash brandy or creme de cacao*
¾ C scalded milk

If using unsweetened chocolate, whirl in blender to grate. Combine all ingredients in blender or electric mixer, adding scalded milk last. Mix at low speed. Pour into dessert dishes or a crumb crust. Chill until firm. Garnish with whipped cream & chocolate shavings.

* Can use vanilla in place of liqueurs.

MAKE AHEAD CHOCOLATE MOUSSE

½ C butter
1 C powdered sugar, sifted
2 squares bitter chocolate, melted
2 eggs
1 ½ tsp. vanilla

Mix butter & sugar with electric mixer until fluffy. Add melted chocolate. Add eggs, beating constantly. Add vanilla. Pour into dessert dishes, cover with waxed paper & freeze.

To serve, remove from freezer, top with whipped cream & crushed pecans. Does not freeze hard. No need to thaw.

ZEPPOLE ST. JOSEPH'S DAY CREAM PUFFS *(Fillings on next page)*

St. Joseph's Day is celebrated every year on March 19th. The feast of San Giuseppe is a time for zeppole. Italian cream puffs are served in every Italian home in one form or another.

CREAM PUFF SHELLS – Zeppole

- 1 C water
- 4 T butter
- 1 T sugar
- ½ tsp. salt
- 1 C flour, sifted
- 4 large eggs
- 1 tsp. orange peel, grated
- 1 tsp. lemon peel, grated
- 6 C vegetable oil (if frying the zeppole)
- Confectioner's sugar

In a heavy saucepan, bring the water, butter, sugar and salt to a boil. Add the flour all at once and beat vigorously with a wooden spoon over medium heat until dough leaves the sides of the pan and forms a ball around the wooden spoon. Remove from heat and quickly beat in eggs ONE at a time, beating until batter is smooth after each egg. Add the orange & lemon zest & continue beating until mixture is smooth & glossy. (You may want to use a hand mixer when adding the eggs. Batter will be lighter.)

For the fried version:
In a heavy 3 quart pan, heat the oil to 350°. Drop rounded tablespoonfuls of batter into the oil. Fry, turning, about 6 minutes, until golden brown. Remove with a skimmer to paper towels.

For the baked version:
Preheat oven to 425°. Drop the batter by rounded tablespoonfuls onto a lightly greased or non-stick baking pan. Bake until lightly golden brown, about 20 minutes. Reduce the oven temperature to 350° and continue baking until medium golden brown, about 15 minutes. Cool & fill. To fill, cut off top; fill and replace top.

ZEPPOLE CREAM PUFFS, Continued

FILLING #1: RICOTTA

    3 C ricotta
    ½ C confectioner's sugar
    ¼ C candied orange peel, finely chopped
    ¼ C candied lemon peel, finely chopped
    ¼ C small chocolate chips, or chopped bittersweet chocolate
    2 T orange flavored liqueur, or 1 ½ tsp. vanilla extract

A day before, line a sieve with cheesecloth & drain ricotta. Cover the sieve with plastic wrap & drain ricotta in the refrigerator overnight. Discard the drained liquid. Combine the drained ricotta & confectioner's sugar in a food processor. Process until creamy. Add flavoring, candied fruits & chocolate. Store covered in refrigerator until needed. Keeps 2 days.

FILLING #2: CREAM

    ¼ C cornstarch   ¾ C sugar
    2 C milk   2 large egg yolks
    2 T butter (¼ stick)
    1 ½ tsp. vanilla or orange or lemon or almond extract

In a small bowl, mix the cornstarch & sugar & set aside. In a saucepan, heat the milk & butter until butter is melted. Add the cornstarch & sugar. Cook over medium heat until it starts to thicken, about 2 minutes. Remove from heat & slowly add the eggs, beating well. Return to heat for a few seconds to cook, but not scramble the eggs. Add flavoring. Cover & refrigerate until ready to use. Place plastic wrap on mixture not to form a skin.

PINE BARK CANDY

Line a jelly roll pan with foil. Place one package of saltine crackers in a single layer over foil. In a sauce pan, melt 1 cup brown sugar & 2 sticks of butter. Let cool & thicken, then pour over crackers. Bake at 400° for 7 minutes (until bubbly). Remove from oven & pour a 12 oz. package of milk chocolate (or dark chocolate) morsels over the top. Place back in the oven for 1 or 2 minutes, and then spread the chocolate over the top like icing. Cool in freezer 30-60 minutes, then bread into pieces. Store in refrigerator.

KENTUCKY KERNELS

Mix & refrigerate:
- ¼ lb. butter
- 1 lb. confectioner's sugar
- ½ C bourbon

Melt in double boiler:
- 1 lb. semi-sweet chocolate
- 2 T melted paraffin
- 1 T butter

Roll into balls. Dip in chocolate. You can substitute cream de mint or rum for the bourbon. Place a piece of nut on top to hide imperfections.

I made hundreds of Kentucky Kernels and used them for a fundraiser. They look good, they taste good, they are not hard to make, and I made a lot of money for the fundraiser.

LEMON MERINGUE PIE with FRESH LEMONS

My Uncle William DeMao (*Uncle Willie* as he was known to everyone) was the Mayor of Arnold, PA, for 40 years.* He loved lemon pie, so every year on his birthday, I made him this fresh lemon pie.

CRUST:
    2 ½ C flour   ½ C cold butter
    1 ½ tsp. salt   ½ C cold shortening

Do not overwork, & allow to rest in refrigerator for 30 minutes. Bake crust at 425° for 10-15 minutes, then turn down to finish baking.

FILLING:
    In a saucepan mix 1 cup sugar & 6 T cornstarch. Add ½ cup lemon juice & 4 egg yolks. Mix well, then add 1 ½ C boiling water. Cook over medium heat until bubbles form. Remove from heat and add 2 T butter. Let cool.

MERINGUE:
    4 egg whites, room temp. Beat, adding 1/3 cup sugar, slowly.

Fill baked crust with filling & meringue and bake meringue. Bake meringue at 400° for 10-12 minutes.

This recipe makes 2 pies.

****

* Uncle Willie was the longest serving Mayor in the state of Pennsylvania, and the longest serving Mayor of a 3rd class city in the United States. For 13 years before becoming Mayor of Arnold, PA, he served as Alderman. City Hall in Arnold, PA, was named for my Uncle Willie.

BANANA SPLIT DESSERT

Mix 2 C graham cracker crumbs with 1 stick of melted butter. Press into bottom of a 9x13 pan. Bake at 350° for 5 minutes.

    1 (1 lb.) box powdered sugar   2 tsp. vanilla
    2 sticks butter   2 eggs

Mix 15 minutes in mixer until light & fluffy. Spread on baked crumbs by the spoonfuls.

Next, add 6 bananas cut in half length wise. Spread 1 or 2 cans crushed pineapple, well drained, over the bananas. Cover with Cool Whip.

Very good, but because of the bananas it does not keep well – 1 or 2 days at most.

PRETZEL SALAD DESSERT

    2 C coarse broken pretzels   3 tsp. sugar
    ¾ C melted butter
Mix. Bake in 9x13 pan at 400° for 8 minutes.

    1 (8 oz.) cream cheese   1 large Cool Whip
    1 C sugar
Beat sugar into cheese. Fold in Cool Whip. Spread over pretzels.

    1 large strawberry Jello
    1 ½ C boiling water
    2 (10 oz.) frozen strawberries with juice
Let start to gel, then pour over cream cheese. Top with more Cool Whip.

FRESH FRUIT TART DESSERT

½ stick butter
1 C sugar
1 C flour
1 jar apricot *jam*, not preserves

1 egg
1 tsp. vanilla
1 tsp. baking powder
2 T lemon juice

Cream butter & sugar together. Add egg, then flour, baking powder & vanilla. Mix well. Dough will be moist. Set aside.

Butter & flour a 10" spring form pan or tart pan. (Tart pan works best.) Flour hands & pat dough on bottom & up sides a bit.

Peel fruits, also can use bit fresh strawberries & berries. Fruits used: apples, peaches & plums.* Slice fruits, then starting on outer edge, push fruit into dough, standing on edge. Sprinkle with cinnamon & bake at 350° for 50-60 minutes.

Melt ½ jar apricot jam & lemon juice. Brush on hot cake & bake 10 minutes longer.

* As a guide, you can start with 3-4 Granny Smith apples, 4-5 peaches, 6-8 Italian plums, and any berries you like.

TRUFFLES: CHOCOLATE TRUFFLES

1 C heavy cream
8 oz. bittersweet chocolate, chopped
8 oz. semisweet chocolate, chopped
2 T coffee, hazelnut, or orange liqueur
2 tsp. vanilla
½ tsp. salt
1 C unsweetened cocoa powder

In a medium saucepan, bring cream to a simmer. Remove from heat. Add the chocolates & stir until melted & mixture is smooth. Stir in liqueur of your choice, vanilla & salt. Pour into a shallow container and let stand for 15 minutes. Cover with plastic & refrigerate until firm, at least 2 hours.

Place cocoa in a small bowl. Scoop enough chocolate mixture to make 1" balls. Roll in cocoa, shaking off excess. Store in airtight container, placing waxed paper between layers. Refrigerate up to 3 days.

VARIETY: Roll in finely chopped nuts, coconut, crushed toffee, or confectioner's sugar.

TO GIVE: Set in bonbon liners & place in a shallow tissue lined box and tie with a ribbon.

OREO TRUFFLES

16 oz. Oreos
1 (8 oz.) cream cheese

Crush all but 9 Oreos in a food processor or blender. In a mixer, cream cheese & add cookies that have been crushed. Shape into balls after you chill the mixture. Crush remaining 9 Oreos & roll balls to coat.

CREAM CHEESE BASIC TRUFFLES

    1 pkg. (8 oz.) cream cheese
    3 C confectioner's sugar
    3 C melted any flavored chips
        OR 2-3 T any flavored liqueur you wish
    1 - 1 ½ tsp. vanilla

OREO CREAM CHEESE BALLS*

No cooking required!

Crush a package of chocolate cream Oreos. Toss in a package of cream cheese. Mix well. Make balls & coat with melted chocolate. **

* This is a recipe that my daughter Jeannine got from one of the Montessori parents at the school where she works. She gets lots of treats and hugs from the little ones!

** You can either dip the balls in melted chocolate, or drizzle the chocolate over the balls.

TEQUILA-SPIKED CARAMEL CORN

16 C air-popped popcorn
½ C salted roasted peanuts
1 C light brown sugar
1 stick unsalted butter
3 T agave nectar (liquid sweetener; found at health food stores)
2 T light corn syrup
½ tsp. salt
¼ tsp. baking soda
1 ½ T tequila

1. Preheat oven to 250°. Racks in the upper to middle thirds. Toss popcorn with roasted peanuts in large pan

2. In large sauce pan, combine butter, brown sugar, agave nectar, corn syrup & salt. Bring to a boil, stirring until sugar dissolves. Boil over medium heat for 3 minutes. Stir in baking soda & tequila. The syrup will foam. Immediately pour hot syrup over popcorn. Using 2 spoons, toss to coat thoroughly.

3. Spread the popcorn on 2 foil-covered baking sheets. Bake for 1 hour, stirring occasionally, switching sheets in oven half way through. Turn off oven, open door completely. Let popcorn cool in the oven.

MELON CARPACCIO with LIME
Dessert

½ C sugar
¾ C water
4 sprigs mint + small leaves for garnish
½ tsp. finely sliced fresh red chili (jalapeño or fresno)
½ vanilla bean, split lengthwise
½ C fresh lime juice

Bring sugar & water to a boil. Add mint & chili. Add vanilla bean. Remove from heat. Let steep for 15 minutes. Strain syrup. Add lime juice. Can be made 1 week ahead.

Arrange melon in a 9x13 glass dish. Pour on syrup. Cover. Chill 2 hours or more. Can use any firm fruit: pineapple, peaches, etc.

FRUIT with LIME JUICE & RUM

¼ watermelon
1 cantaloupe
1 honeydew
1 C blueberries

2/3 C sugar
1/3 C water
½ C rum
1 T lime zest + 6 T lime juice

Use melon scoop or cut melons into chunks. Add berries. Chill. Boil water & sugar for 5 minutes. Let cool to room temperature. Add zest & lime juice. Add rum. Pour over chilled fruit. Cover & refrigerate. Marinate a few hours.

RICHARD III HOMEMADE ICE CREAM

1 qt. size Ziploc bag
1 gallon size Ziploc bag
¼ C sugar
½ C heavy cream
½ C milk
¼ tsp. vanilla
½ C salt
Lots of ice

In the small bag, mix sugar, heavy cream, milk and vanilla. Seal small bag tightly and place in large bag.

In large bag, surround the small bag with salt and ice. Knead constantly until frozen.

Top with favorite toppings. Richard loves Reese's peanut butter cups broken up on his.

My grandson Richard III is an Eagle Scout – This is his recipe. Lots of fun for kids to make.

CAKES

TIRAMISU CAKE

(tee-rah-mee-su) It means "Pick me up"

1 (8 oz.) container of mascarpone cheese*
    or 1 (8 oz.) cream cheese, softened
½ C powdered sugar
3 T coffee liqueur
2 C whipping cream
¼ C sifted powdered sugar
2 T coffee liqueur

1 round angel food cake**
    (8-10 inches)
¾ C strong black coffee
¼ C coffee liqueur

Chill a medium bowl & beaters.

FOR FILLING:
In a large bowl, combine mascarpone or cream cheese, ½ C powdered sugar & 3 T coffee liqueur; beat with mixer on medium speed until blended & smooth.

In chilled bowl, combine whipping cream, ¼ C powdered sugar, 2 T coffee liqueur; beat until stiff peaks form. Fold ½ C whipping cream into cheese mixture.

Cut angel food cake into 3 layers. Place first layer on serving plate. With a long tined fork or skewer, poke holes in each layer.

In small bowl, combine coffee & ¼ C liqueur; drizzle over layer. Spread first layer with half of cheese filling. Add second layer & remaining filling. Add third layer. Frost with remaining whipped cream. Top cake with Mocha Fudge Sauce.

MOCHA FUDGE SAUCE:
In a small saucepan, heat ¼ C fudge ice cream topping just until warm. Stir in coffee liqueur (1-2 tablespoons). Drizzle over top of cake.

* Mascarpone is a rich Italian creamed cheese

** You can use ladyfingers in place of angel food cake. Dip each one in a coffee & liqueur mixture.

CHOCOLATE CARAMEL POKE CAKE

1 box chocolate or chocolate fudge cake mix*
1 (14 oz.) can sweetened condensed milk
1 jar caramel or butterscotch topping*
Cool Whip
Heath bars broken into small pieces, or Heath Toffee Bits

Bake cake according to package directions using a 9x13 pan.* Let cake cool for 5-10 minutes. "Poke" holes in the cake using the end of a wooden spoon. The more holes the better. Pour the can of condensed milk over the top of the cake & into all the holes. Let cool another 5-10 minutes. Pour the caramel or butterscotch topping over the top of the cake. Let cake cool completely. Spread Cool Whip over the top of the cake. Sprinkle Heath bar pieces over the Cool Whip. Chill until served.

* You can use different flavored cake mixes and different toppings.

** Use parchment paper & baking spray if you want to turn the cake onto a serving plate; then make the holes. If you use a glass 9x13 baking dish, you can serve it in the baking dish.

PINEAPPLE POKE BUNDT CAKE

1 can (20 oz.) crushed pineapple
1 box yellow cake mix
1 pkg. instant vanilla pudding
    (4-serving size)
¾ C vegetable oil
4 eggs
2 T vanilla extract, divided
1 C powdered sugar
1 T butter, melted

Preheat oven to 350°. Spray 12-cup Bundt pan with cooking spray. Drain pineapple; measure ¾ C juice to use with cake mix. Reserve remaining juice for soaking mixture. Beat cake mix, pudding, eggs, oil & ¾ C pineapple juice in a large bowl of an electric mixer & mix for 2 minutes. Add 1 T vanilla extract. Fold in crushed pineapple. Pour into prepared pan. Bake for 38-42 minutes.

Soaking Mixture: Combine remaining pineapple juice, powdered sugar, melted butter & remaining 1 T vanilla extract.

Remove cake from oven. Poke holes in cake. Pour soaking mixture over cake. Allow cake to cool for 30-40 minutes, then flip cake upside down onto serving platter. Remove pan. Cool completely. Drizzle with glaze.

Confectioner's glaze: Combine ½ C powdered sugar & 1 T cold milk.

HEAVENLY PINEAPPLE CAKE
Not a sweet cake

1 can (20 oz.) crushed pineapple
1 box angel food cake
Cool Whip

Mix pineapple and dry cake mix together. Spread in a 9x13 pan or round baking dish. (If using a Pyrex casserole, you can mix and bake in the same dish.)

Bake uncovered according to cake mix directions (about 45 minutes). Spoon onto plate and serve with Cool Whip.

WHITE TEXAS CAKE

½ C Crisco
2 C sugar
2 egg whites
1 tsp. baking soda
2 C flour

½ tsp. salt
1 ¾ buttermilk
1 tsp. vanilla
½ tsp. almond extract

Beat Crisco, sugar & egg whites until fluffy. Add baking soda, salt & flour. Mix together buttermilk, vanilla & almond flavoring. Add to other mixture. Bake in greased & floured cookie sheet pan (11x17x1). Bake at 350° for 25-30 minutes.

Ice the cake while hot with:
 1 stick butter, melted
 1/3 C buttermilk
 1 lb. powdered sugar

Optional: ½ C coconut and/or 1 C chopped pecans

TEXAS CAKE – CHOCOLATE

2 C flour
2 C sugar
2 eggs

½ C sour cream
½ tsp. salt
1 tsp. baking soda

Put in pan and boil: 2 sticks butter, 4 T cocoa & 1 C water.
Mix with flour mixture and blend well. Pour into greased cookie sheet (11x17x1). Bake at 350° for 20 minutes.

ICING:
 1 box powdered sugar
 1 C chopped nuts, if desired
 1 tsp. vanilla

Bring to a boil: 4 T cocoa, 1 stick butter & 6 T milk. Mix in powdered sugar mixture. Before cake cools, pour icing on cake.

COOKIE SHEET CAKE with PIE FILLING TOPPING

1 yellow cake mix: Bake cake as directed in a jelly roll pan.

Cook 3 oz. box vanilla pudding & allow to cool.

While the cake is baking, mix together:
Cool pudding & 1 C milk

In another bowl beat together:
½ C sugar   ½ C Crisco   ½ C butter

Combine the sugar, Crisco and oleo with the cooled pudding mixture. Spread this mixture over the cool cake. Top with pie filling of your choice (apricot, pineapple, peach, cherry, etc.) Sprinkle a cup of nuts on top (optional).

AUNT MADDY'S ALMOND POUND CAKE

1 stick butter   3 C sugar
¾ C Crisco

Cream the above ingredients. Cream well.

Add 5 eggs, 1 at a time. Beat well. Add 1 tsp. vanilla and 2 T almond extract. Add 3 C flour alternately with 1 C milk.

Grease bottom of tube pan. Pour in batter. Bake at 350° for 1 hour 10 minutes (may need to bake a little longer). Let cool, remove from pan. Dust with powdered sugar.

Good cake!

PEANUT BUTTER SHEET CAKE

2 C all purpose flour
2 C white sugar
½ tsp. baking soda
¼ tsp. salt
1 C water
¾ C butter, softened

½ C peanut butter
¼ C vegetable oil
2 eggs
½ C buttermilk
1 tsp. vanilla extract

Preheat oven to 350°. Grease a 10x15x1 jellyroll pan. In a large bowl, stir together the flour, sugar, baking soda and salt. Set aside. Combine the water and butter in a saucepan and bring to a boil. Remove from the heat and stir in peanut butter and vegetable oil until well blended. Stir this mixture into the dry ingredients. Combine the eggs, buttermilk and vanilla; stir into the peanut butter mixture until well blended. Spread the batter evenly in the prepared pan. Bake for 18 to 26 minutes in the preheated oven, or until a toothpick inserted near the center comes out clean.

FROSTING:

2/3 C white sugar
1/3 C evaporated milk
1 T butter

1/3 C chunky peanut butter
1/3 C miniature marshmallows
½ tsp. vanilla extract

While the cake bakes, place sugar, evaporated milk and butter in a saucepan. Bring to a boil, stirring constantly. Cook stirring for 2 minutes. Remove from heat and stir in the peanut butter, marshmallows and vanilla until marshmallows are melted and the mixture is smooth. Spoon the frosting over the warm cake and spread in an even layer. Allow to cool before cutting and serving.

Makes 20 servings.

FRESH APPLE CAKE
with CHOICE OF 2 FROSTINGS

CAKE:

- 1 ½ C oil
- 3 C sugar
- 4 eggs
- 4 C diced apples
- 3 ½ C flour
- 2 tsp. baking soda
- 2 tsp. cinnamon
- 1 tsp. salt
- 2 tsp. vanilla
- ½ C chopped nuts
- ½ C raisins (optional)

Beat eggs. Add sugar & oil. While mixing, add dry ingredients. When blended, add apples, vanilla, nuts & raisins. Grease & flour 2 bread pans for loaf cakes, or a large tube or Bundt pan.

TOPPING #1: To pour over hot cake.

- ½ C brown sugar
- ½ C white sugar
- 2 T flour
- 1 C water
- ½ C butter
- 1 tsp. vanilla
- ½ C chopped nuts
- ½ C raisins (optional)

In a saucepan, combine brown sugar, white sugar & flour. Stir in water. Cook over medium heat, stirring until mixture boils & thickens. Remove from heat & stir in butter, vanilla, nuts & raisins. Stir until butter melts, then pour over cake

TOPPING #2: Frosting for a cooled cake.

- 8 oz. cream cheese
- 1 stick butter
- 2 C powdered sugar
- 1 tsp. vanilla

Cream cheese and butter. Add powdered sugar & vanilla. Frost cold cake.

COCONUT CAKE*

This cake is very good and very easy!

- 1 box yellow cake mix
- 2 C sugar
- 1 C sour cream
- 10-14 oz. flaked coconut
- 8 oz. Cool Whip

Bake cake in 2 layers as directed on the package. When baked, split into 4 layers.

Mix the sugar, sour cream & coconut. Remove 1 cup of the mixture for icing. Put the coconut mixture between the layers. Mix 1 cup of the reserved mixture with Cool Whip, then spread on the top and sides of the cake to frost.

Refrigerate for 3 days in an air tight container to ripen before serving. Keep the cake in the refrigerator.

* I became famous for this cake, and when I first made it, I did it from scratch. But I found that a box cake mix works just as well. Who's to know!

ICEBOX CAKE with ORANGE CARAMEL CREAM

3 oranges
1/3 C sugar
3 C cream, divided
1 ½ tsp. vanilla extract
2 (9 oz.) pkgs. chocolate wafers
(about 50 wafer cookies)

Remove the zest from 2 oranges in strips with a vegetable peeler, & finely grate 1 tsp. zest from 3rd orange. Juice all 3 oranges. Combine sugar & orange strips in a skillet & cook over medium heat, undisturbed, until sugar is melted. Swirl the pan and continue swirling until dark amber color, about 4 minutes. Immediately stir in orange juice & cook at a rapid simmer until reduced by half, about 15 minutes.

Add ½ cup of cream; simmer until incorporated, about 5 minutes. Remove from heat, stir in vanilla. Remove strips & set aside for topping. Let caramel sauce cool to room temperature, about 45 minutes.

Put 2/3 of the cooled caramel sauce in a medium bowl. In a separate bowl, beat the remaining 2 ½ C of cream with a mixer until very soft peaks form. (Do Not Over Beat.) Stir the grated orange zest & 1 C of the whipped cream into the bowl with the caramel sauce, and then fold in remaining whipped cream.

Line an 8-inch springform pan with plastic wrap. Lay 6 cookies in the pan. Spread ½ cup caramel whipped cream on top, then drizzle with 2 tsp. reserved caramel sauce. Repeat to make about 6 or 7 more layers of cookies, caramel whipped cream, & caramel sauce, ending with a layer of caramel whipped cream.

Cover the cake with plastic wrap. Chill 6 hours or overnight. Uncover, invert onto plate, & remove pan & plastic wrap. Top with candied orange zest.

OREO ICEBOX CAKE

Same idea as Icebox Orange Caramel Cream Cake, but much simpler & faster, and just about as good.*

    90 Oreos
    3 (12 oz.) tubs Cool Whip
    1 ½ C milk
    Chocolate sauce

Dip 30 cookies in milk – just in & out, do not soak. Lay 30 dipped cookies in a 9x13 serving dish. Spread 1 tub of Cool Whip. Repeat 2 more times: dip next 30 cookies, place layer in dish, add Cool Whip. Ending with Cool Whip. Drizzle with chocolate sauce. Cover & chill 6 hours or overnight.

* Have fun with this – any cookie, any topping. Ex. Peanut butter Oreo with Cool Whip & caramel sauce.

BOX CAKE DELIGHT

    1 large cake mix
    1 C water
    ½ C oil
    4 eggs
    1 pkg. instant pudding

Beat all ingredients together for 4 minutes. Bake at 350° for 45 minutes.

This works with any flavor cake mix & any instant pudding flavor you may like. I have used both the large & small instant pudding.

LAYERED CHOCOLATE CAKE & PEANUT BUTTER CHEESECAKE

For my beautiful granddaughter, Stephanie Lednak's, Sweet 16 Birthday, this is the cake I made, and it will always be hers.

Peanut butter cheesecake

Peanut Butter Cheesecake:

2 (8 oz.) cream cheese, softened
1 C white sugar
½ C creamy peanut butter
3 T flour
4 eggs
½ C milk

1. Bake the cheesecake one day in advance so that it has plenty of time to chill in the fridge.
2. Preheat oven to 325°.
3. Beat together the cream cheese, peanut butter, sugar & flour until light & smooth & creamy. Beat in the eggs one at a time. Stir in the milk.
4. Grease a 9" round springform pan very well. There is no crust to this cheesecake, so it is imperative that you really grease the pan so the cake will release.
5. Pour batter into greased pan.
6. Bake for 10 minutes at 325°.
7. Reduce heat to 260° & bake for 50 minutes, or until center is slightly jiggly.
8. Cool on the counter for 2 hours. Refrigerate overnight.

LAYERED CHOCOLATE CAKE & PEANUT BUTTER CHEESECAKE ... Continued

Chocolate Cake:
    1 box chocolate cake mix

9. Prepare cake mix according to package directions.
10. Bake in two 9" round, well-greased cake pans. Cool completely.

Peanut Butter Frosting:
    ½ C butter, softened   4 C powdered sugar
    1 C creamy peanut butter   1/3 C heavy whipping cream

11. Cream together the butter & peanut butter until light & fluffy. Add half the powdered sugar & mix well. Beat in half of the cream. Add remaining powdered sugar & continue mixing until combined. Beat in remaining cream.

Chocolate Peanut Butter Glaze:
    8 oz. semi sweet chocolate chips   2 T light corn syrup
    3 T creamy peanut butter   ½ C heavy whipping cream

12. In a double boiler, or a bowl set over a pot of simmering water, melt chocolate, peanut butter & corn syrup. Remove from heat and whisk in the cream until it is a smooth creamy consistency.

SEE NEXT PAGE FOR ASSEMBLY ...

LAYERED CHOCOLATE CAKE & PEANUT BUTTER CHEESECAKE ... Continued

TO ASSEMBLE:

13. Place one layer of chocolate cake on your cake stand or cake plate, and top with ¼ of the chocolate peanut butter glaze. Spread to the edges.
14. Very carefully remove the sides of your springform and place the entire cheesecake upside down on the chocolate cake layer. The bottom of the springform pan should now be on top of the cheesecake. Carefully slide a knife in between the cheesecake & the pan bottom to loosen & remove the pan bottom.

15. Pour another ¼ of the chocolate glaze over the cheesecake & spread to the edges.

16. Top this with the second layer of chocolate cake.

17. Place the whole cake in the refrigerator for 15-30 minutes to harden up a bit.

18. Remove from fridge & cover the top & sides of the cake with peanut butter frosting. Smooth it out as best you can.

19. Microwave the chocolate glaze about 5-10 seconds to soften it back up. Whisk well & then pour over the top center of the cake. Use an offset spatula to spread the glaze to the edges, letting it drip down in some areas.
20. Store in the refrigerator.

ZUPPA INGLESE

Zuppa Inglese translates into "English Soup". There are many stories about how this cake got its name. The *zuppa* or soup comes from *inzuppare* which means "to soak". That is just what this cake does: soaks up the liqueur-flavored syrup, or the "soup". The English part comes from the fact that the English love their rum. Another theory refers to the way this cake is sometimes put together in a floated glass container that looks like an English trifle.

The next thing you should know about Zuppa Inglese is that there are many ways of making it. The classic is made from a sponge cake base. I have seen it made using lady fingers, an angel food cake, and even a box cake mix. The container must be given some thought. Whatever you choose, it must have a lip or a rim to hold in the liqueur-flavored syrup.

It can be made in a rectilinear glass baking dish and put together and served in the same. A trifle bowl can be used, or any serving platter with a rim.

SPONGE CAKE LAYERS:
    5 eggs, separated   1 ½ tsp. lemon rind
    1 ½ C sugar, divided   1 tsp. vanilla
    2 T lemon juice   1 C cake flour

I double the amounts of this cake & bake it in a jelly roll pan. I cut the cake into 3 sections. This amount will make two 8" or 9" cakes.

Beat together the 5 egg yolks & ½ cup sugar using a hand held mixer until egg yolks are a pale yellow. Beat the lemon juice, lemon rind & vanilla into the egg yolks. Set aside.

With an electric mixer, beat 5 egg whites until stiff peaks, but not dry. Sifting, fold in flour about ¼ cup at a time. Bake at 325° for 30 minutes in a greased pan lined with greased parchment paper.*

* Time & temperature depend on the size pan. Test cake with toothpick. Do not overcook.

ZUPPA INGLESE... Continued

Cool cake on a wire rack about 15 minutes. Invert pans by hanging between two other pans. Cool completely before removing from pans. Remove parchment paper when cake is completely cooled.

RUM & CREAM FILLINGS:

Mix ½ cup rum with ½ cup simple syrup. Make simple syrup by boiling equal parts sugar & water (½ cup sugar with ½ cup water). Boil until sugar is dissolved, about 1 minute. Cool before using.

Next you will need a cream filling. This is where I cheat. I use a box of vanilla pudding and a box of chocolate pudding. Just cut down on the milk just a little. I drain a can of crushed pineapple (drain it well) & add to the vanilla.

TO ASSEMBLE:

Depending on your pans. Cut round cakes by splitting the layers. You need 3 layers. Use the fourth for decoration. If you use a jellyroll pan, cut into 3 sections.

Place first layer, cut-side up, on serving platter and brush or spoon rum mixture onto cake layer. Spread on chocolate pudding. Top with second cake layer. Brush or spoon with rum mixture. Spread on pineapple cream. Top with last cake layer. Brush or spoon with remaining rum syrup. At this point, it's a good idea to wrap the cake in waxed paper and refrigerate to help set up. You can do this overnight or at least 4 hours.

Frost cake with whipped cream or Cool Whip. Decorate with maraschino cherries** & sliced or chopped almonds.

** I use a toothpick dipped in green food dye to draw stems & leaves from cherries. Cut up extra layer or extra cake pieces into diamond shape, dip in rum & use to decorate cake. Top decorations with whipped cream or Cool Whip.

OLIVE OIL CAKE

1 T butter
3 C plus 2 T flour
4 eggs
1 C sugar
½ tsp. lemon zest

¾ C quality extra virgin olive oil
2/3 C milk
3 T Grand Marnier
1 T baking powder

Preheat oven to 325°. Grease an 11-cup Bundt pan with butter & dust with 2 tablespoons flour. Set pan aside.

Beat eggs & sugar together on medium speed in mixer until pale yellow, about 1 minute. Add remaining 3 cups flour, lemon zest, oil, milk & liqueur. Mix until blended. Add baking powder & combine – Do not over mix.

Spoon batter into prepared pan. Smooth top with back of spoon. Bake until cake is a deep golden brown & a toothpick comes out clean, about 40 minutes.

Some variations:

1. Add orange zest & orange juice.
2. Add fresh chopped (fine) rosemary or thyme.
3. Add sliced toasted almonds to batter.
4. Serve cake topped with figs that have been warmed in a little olive oil & sugar to taste, fine diced rosemary or thyme, a pinch of salt & a little ground pepper. (You can heat fig jam in place of figs.)

GLAZE FOR CAKE if you wish:

1 ¼ C confectioner's sugar
1 T + 1 tsp. freshly squeezed orange juice

GINGER CARROT CAKE

My granddaughter Stephanie taught me a new meaning for the word "Ginger".* So how do you make a better carrot cake? – Add Ginger.

2 C flour
2 C sugar
2 tsp. baking powder
½ tsp. baking soda
4 eggs
3 C finely shredded carrots
¾ C cooking oil

¾ C mixed dried fruit bits
2 tsp. grated fresh ginger
   OR ¾ tsp. ground ginger
Orange-cream cheese frosting
1 C finely chopped toasted pecans
   (optional)

1. Preheat oven to 350°. Grease & flour two 9" pans.
2. In a large bowl, stir together flour, sugar, baking powder & baking soda. Set aside.
3. In a medium bowl, beat eggs; stir in carrots, oil, dried fruit bits & ginger. Stir egg mixture into flour mixture. Pour batter into prepared pans.
4. Bake for 30-35 minutes. Cool in pans on wire rack for 10 minutes. Remove from pans. Cool completely on wire rack. Fill & frost cake.

ORANGE-CREAM CHEESE FROSTING

2 (3 oz.) pkgs. cream cheese, softened
½ C butter, softened
1 T apricot brandy or orange juice

2 C powdered sugar plus
   2 ½ to 2 ¾ C
½ -1 tsp. finely shredded
   orange peel

In an electric mixer, combine cream cheese, butter, & brandy or orange juice. Beat until smooth. Gradually add 2 cups powdered sugar, beating until mixed. Gradually beat in enough of the additional 2 ½ to 2 ¾ cups powdered sugar to make a spreading consistency. Stir in orange peel.** If desired, press toasted pecans onto sides of cake.

  * Ginger: You're a redhead. That's a new one on me.

** You may also like to add about ½ cup well drained crushed pineapple to batter.

PUMPKIN SURPRISE CAKE

1 box yellow cake mix – Save 1 cup mix

Put the rest in a bowl and add:
- ½ C melted butter
- 1 egg

Mix and press in the bottom of a greased 9x13 pan.

Mix 1 large can of pumpkin with:
- 2 tsp. cinnamon
- 3 eggs
- 2/3 C milk
- ½ C brown sugar
  (can use white or both)

Beat well and spread over cake batter.

TOPPING:
- 1 C cake mix
- ½ C sugar
- ¼ C butter

Mix crumble. Sprinkle over pumpkin. Add ½ cup nuts. Bake at 350° for 50-60 minutes.

PUMPKIN GOOEY BUTTER CAKE

Preheat oven to 350°.

CRUST:
- 1 yellow cake mix
- 1 egg
- 8 T butter, melted

Combine cake mix, egg & butter. Mix well with electric mixer. Pat the mixture into the bottom of a lightly greased 9x13 pan.

FILLING:
- 1 (8 oz.) cream cheese, softened
- 1 (15 oz.) can pumpkin
- 3 eggs
- 1 tsp. vanilla
- 8 T butter, melted
- 1 lb. box powdered sugar
- 1 tsp. each cinnamon & nutmeg
- Whipped cream or ice cream

In a large bowl, beat the cream cheese & pumpkin until smooth. Add the eggs, vanilla & butter. Beat together until thoroughly incorporated. Next add the powdered sugar, cinnamon & nutmeg. Mix well. Spread filling mixture over crust & bake for 40-50 minutes. Make sure not to over bake as the center should be a little gooey.

PRALINE PUMPKIN CHEESE CAKE

CRUST:
    2 C crushed gingersnaps   4 T melted butter

Mix and bake crust in bottom of springform pan for at 350° for 9 minutes.

FILLING:
- 3 (8 oz.) cream cheese (room temp)
- 1 C sugar
- ½ C brown sugar, packed firm (light or dark)
- 4 eggs, large
- 1 (15 oz.) pumpkin (not pie filling)
- 1 tsp. cinnamon
- ½ tsp. ginger
- ¼ tsp. cloves
- 2 tsp. vanilla

Beat cream cheese and both sugars on low until well blended. Scrape bowl well. Add eggs one at a time. Add pumpkin, spices and vanilla. Do Not Over Beat!! Just mix by hand.

Pour into cake pan over ginger crust bottom. Pour water into roasting pan about 1 inch deep. Be sure the bottom & sides of the cake pan are well covered with 3 layers of foil so that no water seeps into the cake pan. Place in the oven.

Bake about 1 hour and 45 minutes to 2 hours until the center of the cake no longer trembles. Remove from oven. Cool on rack at room temperature for 30 to 60 minutes. Refrigerate.

TOPPING:
- ½ C light or dark brown sugar
- ¾ C whipping cream
- 4 T butter
- ¼ tsp. salt
- 1 T vanilla
- 1 ½ C pecans

An hour before serving, remove from refrigerator and bring to room temperature. Toast pecans for 8 minutes in a 350° oven. Bring topping ingredients to a boil – excluding pecans – and boil for 3 minutes. Remove from heat and add the pecans. Cool for 15 minutes, then spread on the cake. Remove from pan.

BLACK-BOTTOM PECAN CHEESECAKE

This decadent pie has three irresistible layers. A rich chocolate ganache on the bottom, a creamy cheesecake filling in the middle, and a traditional pecan pie topping. The pie plate will be very full, so carefully transfer it to the oven.

½ (15 oz.) package refrigerated pie crusts
1 C semisweet chocolate morsels
3 T whipping cream
1 (8 oz.) pkg. cream cheese, softened
4 large eggs
¾ C sugar, divided
2 tsp. vanilla, divided
¼ tsp. salt
1 C light corn syrup
3 T butter, melted
1 ½ C pecan halves
Chocolate syrup (optional)

Preheat oven to 350°. Unroll pie crust; fit into a 9" pie plate according to package directions. Fold edges under and crimp. Microwave chocolate morsels and whipping cream in a small glass bowl at medium power for 1-1 ½ minutes, or until morsels begin to melt. Whisk until smooth. Set aside.

Beat cream cheese, 1 egg, ½ cup sugar, 1 tsp. vanilla and salt at medium speed with an electric mixer until smooth. Pour chocolate mixture into pie crust, spreading evenly. Pour cream cheese mixture over chocolate layer.

Whisk together corn syrup, melted butter, remaining 3 eggs, remaining ¼ cup sugar, and remaining 1 tsp. vanilla. Stir in pecans. Pour over cream cheese layer.

Bake at 350° for 55 minutes or until set, shielding pie after about 45 minutes to prevent excessive browning. Cool completely on a wire rack. Drizzle each slice with chocolate syrup if desired.

CHEESECAKE

CRUST:

    1 ½ c graham crackers   ¼ lb. butter, melted
    ¼ C sugar

Mix all of the above and work into a baking pan halfway up sides.* Chill.

FILLING:

    3 (8 oz.) cream cheese   4 eggs
    1 ½ C sugar   2 tsp. vanilla

With mixer at low speed, soften cream cheese. Mix in sugar, then eggs, one at a time. Add vanilla. Bake at 350° for 1 hour. Remove cake and let stand for 15 minutes.

TOPPING:

    1 pt. sour cream   2 tsp. vanilla
    ¼ C sugar

Mix sour cream, sugar & vanilla. Pour mixture over cheesecake. Place cake in oven at 400° for 10 minutes. Handle carefully. Cake can fall.

* I use a springform pan and cover the bottom & sides with foil. Place the springform pan in a 9x13 pan with a little water & bake. Helps to keep the top from cracking. Sour cream covers any cracks.

CHOCOLATE ÉCLAIR CAKE

1 box graham crackers
2 small boxes instant French vanilla pudding
1 (8 oz.) container Cool Whip
1 can Duncan Hines fudge icing
3 C milk

Mix pudding with milk then add the Cool Whip. Place a layer of crackers in a 9x13 cake pan. Add ½ the pudding mixture, and then add another layer of the crackers, a layer of the pudding mixture and a layer of the crackers. Frost with icing & refrigerate.

CHOP SUEY CAKE

CAKE:

2 C flour
2 C sugar
1 C chopped nuts
2 eggs
2 tsp. baking soda
1 large can pineapple with juice
1 C coconut

Mix all ingredients together until well blended. Pour into a greased and floured 9x13 pan. Bake at 350° for 35-45 minutes.

FROSTING:

1 (8 oz.) cream cheese
1 Stick butter (or less)
2 C powdered sugar
1 tsp. vanilla

Mix all ingredients together until smooth. Frost cake while it is warm. Refrigerate cake.

CREAM PUFF CAKE

CAKE:
    C water   4 eggs
     stick butter   1 C flour

Boil together water & butter until butter is melted. Pour into a bowl. Using an electric mixer, add eggs one at a time. Add flour and beat until smooth. Pour into a greased 9x13 pan. Bake at 375° for 30-35 minutes.

FILLING:
    4 C milk
    3 small pkgs. instant pudding

Mix well and pour over shell. Top with 1 tub of Cool Whip. Sprinkle with nuts. Chill 1 hour.

CREAMY SOUTHERN POUND CAKE

    3 sticks butter   1 ½ tsp. vanilla
    3 oz. cream cheese   3 C sifted cake flour
    3 C sugar   (sift before measuring)
    6 eggs

Cream together butter, cream cheese & sugar. Add eggs one at a time at room temperature. Add vanilla & sifted flour.

Spoon into a 10-inch angel food pan. Bake at 325° for about 1 ½ hours.

DEER CAKE* – SPICY RAISIN SAUSAGE CAKE

CAKE:

    2 C raisins   1 tsp. baking soda
    1 C hot water   1 tsp. cloves, ground
    2 C sugar   1 tsp. cinnamon
    1 lb. bulk sausage   1 tsp. nutmeg
    3 C flour   1 C chopped walnuts

In a small bowl pour hot water over raisins to plump them. Let stand 5 minutes. Drain, reserving ¾ cup of water. Combine raisins, sugar and sausage. Mix well. Break up sausage with back of spoon. Stir in reserved liquid.

Combine flour soda and spices. Add to raisin mixture and mix well. Stir in nuts. Batter will be stiff. Spoon into greased pans, filling them 2/3 full. Use two 8x4 loaf pans.

Bake at 350° for 55-65 minutes, or for 12 small mini loaves bake at 350° for 30-35 minutes. Test with toothpick.

GLAZE:

    1 C confectioner's sugar   Milk
    1/8 tsp. Vanilla

Mix confectioner's sugar and vanilla. Mix in enough milk to make a smooth pouring mixture.

* This is "Deer Cake" because we make our own sausage when we put down a deer. You can use any bulk sausage. Up until now I never shared this recipe. It was always something I wowed everybody with when they found out they were eating a cake with meat. Buck season starts the Monday after Thanksgiving in Pennsylvania.

FRUIT CAKE

You might want to make this a week or so before the Holidays to allow the flavors to mingle.

1 lb. crushed graham crackers	1 ½ lbs. pecans
2 lb. large marshmallows	1 ½ lbs. walnuts
1 lb. butter	1 lb. raisins
2 (8 oz.) candied red cherries	½ lb. toasted almonds
2 (8 oz.) candied green cherries	½ C rum
2 (6 oz.) candied pineapple	¼ C Cream di Cacao

Melt marshmallows and butter together. Mix all other ingredients. Use half nuts or a very rough chop. Pour marshmallow mixture over all other ingredients and mix well. Mix in a very large pot. Press into loaf pans. Let stay in refrigerator for a few days before serving. You can also freeze it.

HALLOWEEN CAKE

3 C flour	1 tsp. vanilla
2 T baking powder	½ C milk
¼ tsp. salt	½ C water
1 ½ C sugar	3 beaten egg whites
½ C shortening	

Sift dry ingredients together (flour, baking powder & salt). Cream shortening and sugar & add vanilla. Combine milk & water. Alternately add dry & wet ingredients to creamed mixture, starting and ending with dry ingredients. Fold in egg whites. Bake at 375° for 35-40 minutes. Allow to cool. Cut into squares.

Dip tops in powdered sugar and milk that has been missed to a runny consistency. Dip in crushed peanuts.

ITALIAN LOVE CAKE

This is a beautiful cake – very good and very easy. It takes longer than 1 hour, about 1 ½ hours. You can use less sugar. Enjoy!!

Mix up 1 marble cake mix – DO NOT BAKE.

    2 lb. ricotta   1 C sugar
    4 eggs   1 tsp. vanilla

Mix all the ingredients and drop by spoon on top of the cake mix. Bake at 350° for 1 hour.

HOLIDAY RUM CAKE

CAKE:

    1 C chopped pecans or walnuts   ½ C water
    1 yellow cake mix   ½ C vegetable oil
    1 (3 oz.) pkg. instant vanilla pudding   ½ C rum, 80 proof
    4 eggs

Heat oven to 325°. Grease and flour a tube or Bundt pan. Sprinkle nuts over bottom of pan. Combine all ingredients. Pour over nuts and bake 1 hour. Cool and invert cake onto plate. Prick cake with fork.

GLAZE:

    ¼ lb. butter   ¼ C water
    1 C sugar

Melt butter. Add water and sugar. Boil for 5 minutes. Remove from heat and stir in rum. Drizzle over cake until all is used.

KEY LIME CAKE

CAKE:
>1 pkg. Duncan Hines lemon supreme cake mix
>½ C water
>½ C key lime juice   ½ C vegetable oil
>Zest of 3 key limes, or can   4 eggs, slightly beaten
>>use regular limes

Using an electric mixer, blend ingredients together until well mixed (about 3 minutes). Pour into a greased 9x13 pan. Bake at 350° for 45 minutes (35-40 minutes, depending on your oven) in disposable pan.

FROSTING:
>¼ lb. butter, softened   2-3 C confectioner's sugar
>1 (8 oz.) cream cheese, softened 1-2 T milk
>1 tsp. vanilla

Use electric mixer at low speed to combine butter & cream cheese. Add vanilla and confectioner's sugar. Add milk to reach desired consistency. Frost cake and grate lime over frosting for tropical effect.

LADIES CLUB CAKE

2 sticks butter
2 C flour
8 oz. soft cream cheese
1 C powdered sugar
1 (10 oz.) Cool Whip (save some for top)
3 C milk
2 small pkgs. instant pudding mix (any flavor)
Chopped nuts (optional)

CRUST:
Mix the butter & flour. Pat into a 9x13 pan and bake at 350° for 15 minutes. Cool.

CAKE:
Beat cream cheese and powdered sugar. Add the Cool Whip. Pour in the crust.

TOPPING:
Mix together the milk and the pudding packages. Pour over Cool Whip mixture. Spread top with more Cool Whip (you may need two tubs), and cover with chopped nuts. Top can be decorated with cherries or anything you like if you want to get fancy.

LEMON LAYER CAKE

1 box lemon cake
1 lg. cream cheese
1 sm. cream cheese
3 C milk
2 boxes instant lemon pudding
2 boxes Dream Whip*

Bake a box lemon cake in a jelly roll pan according to the directions. Cool well.

Soften the cream cheese with part of the milk. Add the boxes of lemon pudding. Add the rest of the milk. Whip in the mixture until thick. Spread on cake. Next spread the packages of Dream Whip on the pudding. Chill at least an hour before serving.

* If you can't find Dream Whip, you can use Cool Whip.

MANDARIN ORANGE CAKE

CAKE:
- 1 Duncan Hines yellow cake mix
- 4 eggs
- ½ C oil
- 1 (16 oz.) can mandarin oranges

Do not drain the oranges. Mix ingredients together and beat until combined. Use medium speed on the mixer. Pour into two 8-inch greased pans. Bake at 350° for 25-30 minutes. Cool an cut each layer in half.

ICING:
- 1 (9 oz.) container whipped topping, thawed
- 1 (12 oz.) can crushed pineapple, undrained
- 1 sm. box instant vanilla pudding

Mix all ingredients together on slow speed. Frost between cake layers and top cake with icing.

MAPLE CHEESECAKE w/ROASTED PEARS

COOKIE CRUST:
- 12 graham crackers OR
- 46 vanilla wafers OR
- 30 chocolate wafers
- 3 T sugar
- ¼ tsp. salt
- 5 T butter

Choose which cookies or wafers to use. Process cookies and add remaining ingredients. Bake at 375° for about 12 minutes.

CAKE:
- 2 (8 oz.) cream cheese, room temp.
- ¾ C pure maple syrup
- 1 C cold heavy cream
- 2 C confectioner's sugar
- Nonstick cooking spray
- 2 pears – Bosc or Bartlett: sliced lengthwise 1/8 inch thick

Preheat oven to 450°.

Beat cream cheese on high until fluffy (about 3 minutes). Add ½ cup maple syrup and beat until smooth. In a medium bowl, beat the cream and sugar on high until soft peaks form (about 3 minutes). With a spatula, stir about 1/3 of the whipped cream into the cream cheese mixture, then fold in remainder. Pour into crust and refrigerate until firm (about 3 hours, or up to 1 day). Coat parchment-lined rimmed baking sheet with cooking spray. Arrange pear slices in a single layer and brush with 2 tablespoons maple syrup. Roast pears until soft (about 30 minutes). Remove from oven. Heat broiler. Brush pears with 2 tablespoons maple syrup and broil until browned in spots (about 3-4 minutes), rotating sheet frequently. Let cool. Arrange pears overlapping slightly on cheesecake.

MERK'S COFFEE CAKE

½ C shortening
¾ C sugar
1 tsp. vanilla
3 eggs
2 C flour
1 tsp. baking powder
1 tsp. baking soda
½ pint sour cream
6 T butter, softened
1 C brown sugar
2 tsp. cinnamon
1 C chopped nuts

Cream shortening sugar and vanilla thoroughly. Add eggs one at a time, beating well after each one. Sift flour, baking powder and baking soda together. Add to creamed mixture, alternately with sour cream, blending after each addition. Spread half of the batter in a 10-inch tube pan that has been greased and lined on the bottom with waxed paper.

Cream butter, brown sugar and cinnamon together. Add nuts and mix well. Sprinkle one half of the nut mixture evenly over the batter in pan. Cover with remaining batter, sprinkle on remaining sugar mixture. Bake at 350° for about 50 minutes or until done. Yield one tall coffee cake!

NEIMAN MARCUS CAKE

1 chocolate cake mix
1 stick melted butter
2 eggs
4 oz. chopped nuts

Mix together (it's thick) and press into a 9x13 glass pan.

1 lb. powdered sugar
8 oz. softened cream cheese
2 eggs
1 tsp. vanilla

Mix these ingredients together. Pour into crust. Bake at 350° for 30 minutes or so until top is golden brown.

NOODLE CHEESE CAKE

1 lb. noodles (medium), boil for minutes
1 lb. cottage cheese
1 pint sour cream
1 lb. can crushed pineapple with juice
1 ½ C sugar

2 sticks butter, melted
4 beaten eggs
1 tsp. vanilla
1 tsp. salt

Cream cheese & sugar together. Add eggs, butter, pineapple and juice and cooked noodles. Add vanilla and salt. Fold in sour cream. Mix thoroughly and place in a 9x13 pan. Bake at 350° for 1 ½ hours.

ORANGE COCONUT CAKE

CAKE:

1 box yellow cake mix
1 pkg. instant coconut pudding
   (1 large or 2 small)

¾ C salad oil
¾ C water
4 eggs

Combine all ingredients and mix for 5 minutes. Bake at 350° for 30-40 minutes.

GLAZE:

2 C powdered sugar
½ C orange juice

2 T butter

Bring to boil all ingredients. Punch holes in cake. Pour glaze over cake. Put cake back in oven for 10-15 minutes with oven off.

ORANGE CREAM CAKE

1 pkg. (18 ¼ oz.) lemon cake mix
1 envelope unsweetened orange drink mix (Kool Aid)
3 eggs
1 C water
1/3 C vegetable oil
2 Pkgs. (3 oz. each) orange gelatin (divided)
1 C boiling water
1 C cold water
1 C cold milk
1 tsp. vanilla extract
1 pkg. (3.4 oz.) instant vanilla pudding mix
1 (8 oz.) frozen Cool Whip (thawed)

In a mixing bowl, combine cake and drink mixes, eggs, water and oil. Beat on medium speed for 2 minutes. Pour into an ungreased 9x13 baking pan. Bake at 350° for 25-30 minutes, or until a toothpick inserted near the center comes out clean. Using a meat fork, poke holes in cake and cool on a wire rack for 30 minutes.

Meanwhile, in a bowl, dissolve one package of gelatin in boiling water. Stir in cold water. Pour over cooled cake. Cover and refrigerate for 2 hours.

In a mixing bowl, combine milk, vanilla, pudding mix and remaining gelatin. Beat on low for 2 minutes. Let stand for 5 minutes; fold in whipped topping and frost cake.

Serves 12-15. Refrigerate leftovers.

I suggest making it a day in advance – set out a few hours to warm before serving.

OVERNIGHT COFFEE CAKE

This is a good cake to make for Sunday Brunch and can be made overnight (for Mother's Day).

CAKE:

    1/3 C butter   ½ tsp. baking powder
    ½ C sugar   ¼ tsp. baking soda
    ¼ C brown sugar   ½ tsp. cinnamon
    1 C flour   ½ C buttermilk

Cream butter and sugars. Add eggs and mix well. Combine flour, baking powder, baking soda and cinnamon; add to creamed mixture alternately with buttermilk. Beat well. Spread into a greased 8-inch square baking dish.

TOPPING:

    ¼ C brown sugar   ¼ tsp. cinnamon
    ¼ C finely chopped pecans   1/8 tsp. nutmeg (optional)

Combine all ingredients. Sprinkle over batter. Cover and refrigerate overnight.

Bake uncovered at 350° for 40-45 minutes or until done. Serves 6-8.

PINEAPPLE UPSIDE DOWN CAKE

This was my Dad's favorite cake, so I always made it with love.

    2/3 C butter   ¾ C brown sugar

Place the butter and brown sugar in a frying pan and melt until it boils or bubbles. A cast iron pan works well because it's heavy and will be less likely to scorch.

    1 can pineapple slices
    Maraschino cherries (enough to fill centers of pineapples)

Place pineapple rings in the butter and sugar mixture. Put cherries in the center of the pineapples. Cut slices of pineapple into halves and line the sides of the frying pan with them (standing up on edge).

Prepare a box of yellow cake mix, following the directions on the box to mix the batter (do not bake in a separate pan). Pour the batter over the pineapple and cherries. Bake at 350°.

When the cake is done, loosen the edges with a butter knife. Remove from heat and allow to sit for five minutes, and then turn it upside down on a serving dish.

Optional: instead of using a cake mix, you can prepare the batter from scratch using the recipe below, or any recipe for yellow cake.

YELLOW CAKE FROM SCRATCH:
    1 2/3 C flour   2 eggs
    1 tsp. baking powder   2/3 C sugar
    ¼ tsp. baking soda   ¼ C milk
    ½ tsp. salt   ¼ C melted butter

Combine ingredients and beat 1 minute. Pour batter over pineapples and cherries as above. Bake at 350° and follow same steps as above.

EASY CARAMEL CAKE

CAKE:

½ C buttermilk, room temp
4 eggs, room temp
2 tsp. vanilla
2 ¼ C flour
1 ½ C sugar

1 ½ tsp. baking powder
½ tsp. baking soda
¾ tsp. salt
2 sticks butter, cubed & softened

Preheat oven to 350°. Adjust oven rack to middle position. Grease and flour two 9-inch round cake pans.

Whisk buttermilk, egg and vanilla. Whisk flour, sugar, baking powder, baking soda & salt. With an electric mixer, beat in butter 1 piece at a time until butter is pea-sized. Pour in ½ of the buttermilk mixture and beat until light and fluffy. Slowly add remaining buttermilk mixture to the bowl and beat until incorporated.

Divide batter evenly between the two pans. Bake 20-25 minutes or until golden. Cool in pan for 10 minutes, then invert onto racks. Let cool completely for at least 1 hour.

ICING:

12 T butter, cubed & softened
2 C brown sugar
½ tsp. salt

½ C heavy cream
1 tsp. vanilla
2 ½ C icing sugar, softened

Heat 8 tablespoons of the butter, brown sugar & salt until bubbles appear around the sides of the pan. Whisk in cream and cook until a ring of bubbles reappear; remove from heat & whisk in vanilla.

Transfer mixture to a bowl & with an electric mixer, gradually mix in the icing sugar until combined. Increase speed and beat until pale brown & just warm. Add remaining 4 tablespoons of butter, 1 piece at a time, and beat until light & fluffy.

ASSEMBLY: Place 1 cake round on a platter. Spread ¾ icing over cake, then top with 2nd layer. Spread remaining frosting over top & sides.

TRES LECHES CAKE

My daughter Melissa lives in Seattle, Washington. Some friends of hers, Marlene & Jesse, were going to visit Florida, & Melissa told them, "You must visit my parents while you are in Florida." They came and brought a "Tres Leches Cake", Spanish for "Three Milks Cake". Jesse is Mexican, so I learned to make the cake. I also found a recipe for Dulce de Leche Cheesecake, which translates to "sweet milk cheesecake" which is on the next page.

    1 box yellow cake mix (with pudding) baked as directed in 9x13 pan
        (I like Pillsbury White Cake better)

Poke holes in the cake with a fork all over.

TOPPING:
- 1 can evaporated milk
- 1 can sweetened condensed milk
- 1 pint heavy whipping cream
- ½ C rum (or to taste)
- (most do not use rum)

Pour topping mixture over cake. Let mixture absorb completely in refrigerator. Cover with whipped cream or Cool Whip and sprinkle sweetened coconut over top of cake.

OPTIONAL: Add macadamia nuts, cherries and/or pineapple.

DULCE DE LECHE CHEESECAKE

Butter a 9-10 inch springform pan and set aside. Adjust the oven rack to the lower third of the oven and preheat to 350°.

CRUST:
- 1 ½ C finely ground Maria cookies, vanilla wafers or graham crackers
- 6 T unsalted butter, melted

In a large bowl, combine the ground cookies and melted butter until thoroughly mixed. Turn the cookie mixture into the springform pan. With your fingers, pat it evenly around the bottom of the pan, gently pushing it up the sides to make a crust ½ to 1-inch tall. Refrigerate while you make the cream cheese filling and dulce de leche topping.

FILLING:
- 1 lb. cream cheese, room temp
- 3 large eggs, room temp
- 1 (14 oz.) can La Lechera sweetened condensed milk

Place the cream cheese in the bowl of an electric mixer and beat at medium speed until smooth and light, 3-4 minutes. Add the sweetened condensed milk and continue beating until well mixed, scraping down the bowl as needed. Add the eggs one at a time, again scraping down the bowl as needed, and continue beating until the mixture is well blended and smooth. Set aside.

TOPPING:
- 1 ½ C sour cream
- 1 C chopped pecans
- 1 (14 oz.) can La Lechera dulce de leche

In a medium bowl, mix the sour cream with the dulce de leche until combined.

Remove the springform pan from the refrigerator. Gently spread the cream cheese filling evenly, trying not to distress the crust. Place the cheesecake in the oven and bake for 35 minutes at 350°, or until it is set and the top is lightly browned. Remove from the oven and let cool for at least 10 minutes before you add the dulce de leche topping. Spoon the dulce de leche topping over the cream cheese filling. Add the pecans all around the edge, and place the pan back in the oven for 10 more minutes. Remove from the oven and let the cheesecake cool to room temp. Cover & refrigerate for at least 4 hours before serving. It tastes even better if it chills overnight. Before serving, run the tip of a wet knife around the edge of the pan to release the cheesecake. Remove the ring, then slice and serve the cake.

BOSTON CREAM PIE

From little up, my son Richard has loved Boston cream pie. From scratch, it can be a lot of work, but for Richard – anything. Or learn my secret. Fast & easy and just as good. First, here's the recipe from scratch:

Make the cream first and refrigerate while making the cake.

CAKE:
- 1 ¼ C flour
- 2 tsp. baking powder
- ½ tsp. salt
- 1 C sugar
- 1/3 C butter
- ¾ C milk
- 1 egg
- 1 tsp. vanilla

CREAM FILLING:
- 2 eggs
- 1 ½ C milk
- 1/3 C sugar
- 2 T cornstarch
- 1/8 tsp. salt
- 2 tsp. vanilla

GANACHE:
- 12 oz. bittersweet or semisweet chocolate
- 1 C heavy cream
- Flavoring – liqueurs, etc.

CAKE: Preheat oven to 350°. Grease & flour two 9-inch round cake pans. Mix flour, baking powder & salt in a bowl. Set aside. Cream butter & sugar together, add milk, egg & vanilla. Beat on medium speed for 2 minutes. Add flour mixture all at once. Beat for 2 minutes until smooth. Divide into two pans. Bake 25-30 minutes. Remove from pan – let cool.

FILLING (pastry cream): Pour milk into a 2 quart saucepan & combine with half of the sugar. Bring to a boil, stirring constantly to keep the bottom from burning. In a separate bowl, mix together the rest of the sugar, 2 tablespoons cornstarch & the 2 eggs. (Sift in the cornstarch so mixture has no lumps.) Slowly add the egg mixture into the saucepan while stirring. Bring to a full boil until it starts to come together. Quickly remove from heat. Add vanilla & any other flavoring you want, such as liqueurs. Stir in butter until melted. Cool cream – cover top with plastic wrap. Cool at least 2 hours.

BOSTON CREAM PIE, Continued

This is a good pastry cream. It can be used for many desserts, cream pies, cream puffs, etc.

GANACHE: Bring the cream to a boil. Pour over a bowl of chopped chocolate. Let stand a minute to soften chocolate. Whisk until smooth. Let cool.

TO ASSEMBLE THE CAKE:
Split the cooled cake in half to make two thin layers.* Fill the layers with the cream. Spread the ganache over top layer. Let it drip down sides.

* You can use both layers of cake for a larger cake.

****

Now for my fast & easy & just as good

Boston Cream Pie:

1. Use a yellow box cake mix.
2. Use vanilla pudding & pie filling.
3. Melt 6 oz. chocolate chips with 3 T butter. Add to 1 C powdered sugar, ½ tsp. vanilla & enough water to make a glaze.

Boston cream pie is not really a pie, and the cake is not too important. So if you make the good pastry cream and the ganache – any yellow box cake will do. Make it in 2 pans & split one layer to make the Boston cream pie.** Use the other layer for cake, or freeze it for future use.

** My secret for splitting a cake layer: Use a piece of sewing thread long enough for you to hold both ends, and pull it through the cake from the back of the cake toward you.

DIRT CAKE

1 (16 oz.) pkg. Oreo cookies
12 oz. cream cheese, room temp
6 T butter, room temp
4 pkg. (3.9 oz. each) instant chocolate pudding
4 ¾ C milk
1 (16 oz.) Cool Whip
Candy, for decoration

If using a flowerpot with a drainage hole, reserve 1 cookie to place over the hole. Place remaining cookies in a food processor. Process until mixture resembles dirt. Set aside.

In a large bowl, combine cream cheese & butter & stir until creamy. Set aside.

In another large bowl, whisk together instant pudding mixes & milk; stir until well blended. Using a spatula, fold pudding mixture into cream cheese mixture. Fold in Cool Whip.

In a flower pot or toy bucket, alternate layers of cookie "dirt" & pudding mixture, starting & ending with cookie "dirt". Chill at least 4 hours or overnight before serving. Garnish with gummy worms & flowers. Cover stems of flowers with plastic.

To sterilize a terra-cotta pot, place in a 350° oven for 2 hours. Flowers can also be made from gum drop candies.

MOM'S DATE & NUT CAKE

    2 C chopped dates   2 tsp. baking soda
    2 C boiling water

Pour the boiling water over the dates and baking soda. Set aside to cool.

    ½ C butter   2 eggs
    2 C sugar   2 tsp. vanilla

Cream all 4 ingredients in a separate bowl.

Dry ingredients:
    3 C flour   ½ tsp. ground cloves
    1 tsp. cinnamon

Combine in a third bowl.

Separate bowl: 1 cup chopped nuts, dusted with flour (any kind of nuts).

Add the dry ingredients and the date mixture to the cream mixture, alternating the wet with the dry. Blend. Fold in nuts.

Grease & flour angel food cake pan, or the equivalent in bread pans.

Bake at 350° for about 1 hour in an angel food pan. Less time if baking smaller loaves in bread pans. Check by touch or use a toothpick for doneness.

****

My sister Rosemary's changes: I have turned this into a bread by reducing the sugar, 3 rounded cups of flour, and one egg white. Mix as above. Pour into approximately 5 small greased and floured bread pans. Test for doneness.

BEST VANILLA FROSTING

5 T flour
1 C milk
1 tsp. vanilla

1 C butter
1 C granulated sugar

In a saucepan, whisk flour into milk & heat, stirring constantly, until it thickens. It should be very thick. Remove from heat & let it cool to room temperature. It must be completely cool before the next step. Stir in vanilla. While the mixture is cooling, cream butter & sugar together until light & fluffy. Then add the completely cooled milk, flour & vanilla mixture until it all combines & resembles whipped cream. If it looks separated, just keep beating.*

* For chocolate frosting, add some melted chocolate chips (or bittersweet chocolate) in the final mixing stage.

CHOCOLATE BUTTERCREAM

This is a good chocolate icing for any cake.

8 oz. semisweet chocolate, chopped
2 oz. unsweetened chocolate, chopped
1 lb. softened butter

5 egg whites
1 C sugar

Melt chocolate in a double boiler or microwave. Whip butter in mixer until smooth. Whip egg whites. Add mix until glossy & stiff peaks form.

Mix butter and chocolate until smooth. Fold butter and chocolate mixture into egg whites.

Refrigerate.

COOKIES

Note from the typist:

Large Nut Rolls are first because they are the best cookies I've ever eaten in my life. I've had other people's nut rolls, and they don't hold a candle to Amy's!

LARGE NUT ROLLS

DOUGH:

    8 C flour
    4 T sugar
    1 tsp. salt
    4 egg yolks, beaten

    2 pkg. active dry yeast
    1 (12 oz.) can evaporated milk
    1 lb. butter

Scald milk. Cool to lukewarm, add sugar & yeast. Set aside & let yeast work (15-20 min.). Cut butter into flour & salt. Add beaten egg yolks to yeast mixture & add to dry ingredients. Work until dough does not stick to hands. Refrigerate 6 hours or overnight. Divide dough into 7 or 8 balls. Roll out dough on a little flour like jelly roll, about 1/8 inch thick. Spread on nut filling.* Roll from the bottom up. Place seam side down on greased or parchment lined baking sheet. Brush with egg wash = 1 or 2 eggs beaten with 1 tsp. water per egg.

FILLING:

    3 ½ - 4 lbs. ground walnuts (should look like sawdust)
    3 C sugar
    ½ C melted butter
    1 ¾ -2 C light cream, Half &
        Half, or canned milk

    2 tsp. vanilla
    4 egg whites, beaten until frothy
    1-2 T honey, optional

Mix all ingredients. (Amount of milk depends on how fine you grind the nuts. The finer the grind, the more milk (2 cups). Coarser nuts need less milk.)**

Heat the milk to a boil, add sugar, salt & butter. Remove from heat. Let cool. Add vanilla & pour into nuts. Mix well. Fold in stiff egg whites. Stir until mixture is about the consistency of peanut butter.

Bake at 350° for 35-45 minutes on a greased baking sheet.

* I found the nut filling spreads easier if I brush a little melted butter on the dough before I try and spread the filling.

** I start with 1 ½ C milk; you can add more if the nuts are too thick.

KOLACKY – ROZKY
Slovak names for SMALL NUT ROLLS

Dick's mother, my mother in law, called them "cold dough cakes". Most people roll the dough into a circle, cut like a pie slice, add filling & roll up. Dick's mother made hers like small logs. That is the way I roll mine. I too call them small nut rolls, or cold dough cakes. This is Dick's mother's recipe.

SMALL NUT ROLLS / COLD DOUGH CAKES

DOUGH:

- 4 C flour
- 3 sticks butter
- 1 can evaporated milk
- 2 pkg. dry yeast
- 2 T sugar
- 3 egg yolks, beaten

Mix flour & butter like pie crust. Scald milk – cool to lukewarm. Add yeast & sugar. Allow yeast to work 15-20 minutes. Add egg yolks to milk & yeast. (Good idea to temper yolks by adding a little of the milk & yeast mixture before adding the yolks to all of the milk & yeast.) Pour over flour. Work until dough does not stick to hands. Refrigerate overnight.

FILLING:

- 1 lb. nuts, ground
- 2 C sugar*
- 3 egg whites, beaten to soft peaks
- 2 tsp. vanilla

Combine all ingredients.

Roll out dough thin – cut into 3-inch squares. ** Fill & roll in a mixture of ½ flour & ½ sugar. Place on greased cookie sheet, seam side down. Bake at 350° for 15-20 minutes. ***

* I find 2 cups sugar is too much – 1 ½ cups sugar is fine in the filling.
** If you cut the dough a little longer, not a perfect square, they roll easier.
*** I bake them at 375° for 15 min.

AMY'S TRADITIONAL ITALIAN ALMOND BISCOTTI

3 C whole almonds, rough chopped & toasted for 10-12 min.
1 C white sugar
1 C light brown sugar
½ tsp. ground cinnamon
2 tsp. baking powder
2 ½ C all purpose flour
3 large eggs
1 stick butter, melted & cooled
1 tsp. vanilla extract
Zest of 1 lg. orange (about 2 tsp.)
1 egg lightly beaten for glaze

Preheat oven to 350°.

In a large bowl, hand mix toasted almonds, sugar, cinnamon, baking powder & flour.

In a small bowl, whisk the 3 eggs, vanilla, orange zest & cooled melted butter. Whisk until well blended. Add to flour mixture. Work both together with floured hands. Mixture will be sticky, but keep on going! Keep squeezing the batter with your hands until a dough starts to form, adding a little flour if needed.

Once the dough is firm, form a ball. Divide the ball into 4 equal pieces. On a lightly floured surface, place 1 of the 4 pieces. Roll into a log shape about 8" long, 2" wide, & ¾" high. Repeat using the 3 pieces of dough. Place 2 logs on a parchment lined baking sheet. Pat the tops lightly to flatten. Brush top with beaten egg.

Bake at 350° for 40 minutes. Cool on a rack about 20 minutes before slicing. Use a serrated knife , slice cookies ¾" thick on the diagonal. Depending on how hard you want these biscotti, they are fine right after slicing, or you could put them back in the oven to toast, laying them on their sides.

You can toast them with the oven turned off, with just the heat from the hot oven. Or you could toast them for a few minutes at 350°. But it's important to know, the longer you toast them, the harder they become. And they can become very hard. You can only eat them by dipping them.

MOM'S BISCOTTI – JENNIE LANDI

1 C Crisco
2 C sugar
7 eggs
1 C nuts, almonds or walnuts, toasted & coarsely chopped
6 C flour & flour to work in dough

1 orange, juice & rind
2 tsp. baking powder
2 tsp. anise

Mix Crisco & sugar and beat until fluffy. Add eggs, beating well. Alternate wet & dry ingredients. Use extra flour to work dough on board. Makes 6 rolls. Bake at 350° for 25-30 minutes. Slice and toast at 350° for about 15 minutes.

ALMOND BISCOTTI – AUNT MADDY'S

2 ½ C sugar
2 C cake flour
1 ¾ plus 3 T all purpose flour
1/8 tsp. baking soda
1/8 tsp. salt
4 large eggs

2 tsp. unsalted butter, room temp
1 tsp. vanilla extract
¼ tsp. almond extract
1 ½ C whole almonds, lightly toasted (about 5 oz.)

Preheat oven to 300°. Grease & flour 2 large cookie sheets. Combine first 5 ingredients in large bowl of electric mixer. Add eggs, butter, vanilla & almond extract. Mix just until combined. Stir in almonds. Transfer dough to well-floured surface. Using well-floured hands, form into 5 or 6 1x6 inch logs. Space logs 2 ½ inches apart on prepared sheets. Bake until light golden brown (about 1 hour). Logs will spread and flatten.

Cool slightly. Cut with serrated knife on the diagonal, ½" wide. Place cut side down and toast about 30 minutes. Can be made 5 days ahead. Store in airtight container.

Makes about 5 dozen very hard cookies.

BISCOTTI – MARY GUERCIONE

6 eggs
1 1/3 C sugar
1 C oil
1 tsp. anise oil
5 C flour plus 1 extra C as needed
4 tsp. baking powder

Work dough. Make 3 rolls & place on greased cookie sheet. Flatten out a little. Bake at 375° for 15 minutes. Cool. Slice and bake at 400° for about 7 minutes on each side.

BISCOTTI ai CEREALI
Italian Snowflake Cookies

2 ½ C flour
1 tsp. baking powder
¼ tsp. salt
1 ¼ C sugar
10 T butter, softened
3 eggs
6 C cornflakes cereal (2 C lightly crushed; 4 C whole)
1 C semisweet chocolate chips
Confectioner's sugar for garnish

Preheat oven to 350°. Whisk flour, baking powder & salt in a bowl. In a mixer, cream sugar & butter until fluffy. Add eggs, one at a time, beating well after each addition. Add dry ingredients; mix well until dough forms. Fold in crushed cornflakes & chocolate chips. Divide dough into about 28 balls; roll in whole cornflakes. Space 1" apart on parchment paper-lined cookie sheet. Bake until golden & crisp, 20-22 minutes. Cool. Dust with confectioner's sugar. They freeze well. I double this recipe.

MOCHA CAPPUCCINO BUTTERSCOTCH BISCOTTI

DOUGH:
- 2 ¾ C flour
- ½ tsp. baking powder
- ¼ tsp. salt
- ¼ C Crisco
- ¼ C butter, softened
- 2/3 C sugar
- ½ C Jiff Mocha Cappuccino Hazelnut Spread
- 2 tsp. vanilla
- 3 eggs
- ½ C butterscotch chips or white chips

Preheat oven to 350°. Line baking sheet with parchment paper. Combine flour, baking powder & salt. Beat Crisco, butter, sugar, Jiff spread & vanilla in electric mixer. Beat in eggs, one at a time. Add flour mixture. Beat until smooth. Stir in butterscotch chips.

Place dough on lightly floured surface. Divide in half. Shape each ball into a 9 x 3 inch log. Place 4 inches apart on baking sheet.

Bake for 25-30 minutes. Cool on wire rack for 10 minutes. Cut on diagonal in ½ inch slices. Place on baking sheet. REDUCE oven to 300°. Bake for 15 minutes. Turn over. Bake 10-15 minutes more. Cool completely. (May have to do in 2 batches.)

GLAZE:
- ¼ C Jiff Mocha Cappuccino Hazelnut Spread
- 2 T white baking chips

Melt spread and white chips in small microwave bowl for 30 seconds. Stir until smooth. Drizzle glaze over cooled Biscotti. Chill 30 minutes or until glaze is set.

APRICOT HORNS

CRUST:

    ½ C butter
    3 C flour
    3 egg yolks, beaten
    1 cake of yeast

    1 T sugar
    8 T cream or top of milk
    1/8 tsp. vanilla

Mix flour & butter and add beaten eggs. Mix well. Add yeast which has raised in warm milk & sugar. Add vanilla. Knead well. Roll out thin & cut the rolled dough into squares. Fill each square with apricot filling and roll. Roll in a bowl of 3 T sugar & 1 T flour mixture to coat. Set on a cookie sheet, seam side down. Cover with a kitchen towel & let them raise for 20 minutes. Bake at 350° for 20-25 minutes.

FILLING:*

    6 oz. dried apricots
    1 ½ C water

    1 T lemon juice
    ½- ¾ C sugar**

Pour the water on the apricots & let them stand for an hour or 2 to soften. Add sugar and simmer on low heat for 20 minutes, being careful not to let it burn. At this point add the lemon juice and taste it. Add sugar if you want. Let it cool a little Put it in a food processor, pulsing it several times until you reach desired consistency.

* You can always use apricot preserves, or jarred apricot filling that you purchase at the supermarket.

** If you like it sweeter, you can add more sugar.

BEER COOKIES

Makes three 9x13 pans.

CRUST:
- 6 C flour
- 1 lb. Crisco
- 5 tsp. baking powder
- 1 tsp. salt
- 3 eggs
- 12 oz. bottle beer

TOPPING:
- 2 lbs. pineapple preserves for each pan
- Ground nuts to taste & to cover preserves.

Put all ingredients for crust in a bowl and mix by hand with your fingers. Roll out the dough. Layer as follows: pineapple, ground nuts, dough, pineapple, nuts, etc., to form 5 layers. Brush top with beaten egg white. Bake at 350° for 35-40 minutes.

PINEAPPLE FILLED LEMON COOKIES

- 1 dozen eggs
- 1 lb. melted oleo or butter*
- 2 ½ C sugar
- 8 tsp. baking powder
- 1 lg. can of canned milk
- 1 sm. bottle lemon flavor
- 8 C flour (about)
- Pineapple preserves

Make a well in flour and add butter. Add all other ingredients. Mix with hand. Roll into the size of large nut. Bake on lightly greased cookie sheet at 350° until golden (12-15 minutes). Cool. Cut off tops. Scoop out.** Fill with pineapple preserves. Replace tops. Ice with powdered sugar icing tinted pink from maraschino cherries. Cut cherries in eighths for top.

* This is an old recipe. I use butter not oleo.
** This recipe makes a lot of cookies, so you will have a lot of the scooped out cookie. I put it in a bowl with some instant pudding and it makes a good, fast dessert.

CARAMEL MARSHMALLOW BALL COOKIES

Sharon, my daughter-in-law, and I were setting up food as it came in for Baba Lednak's funeral. A lady brought in a large foil roaster with these cookies. We both laughed because they looked like softballs. We put out everything but those big round balls! The lady came in the kitchen and asked why her cookies were not put out. We told her that was the next tray that would come out. But before we did, laughingly we both ate one, and to our surprise, they were big & ugly, but delicious. Better for a fun party than a funeral!

2 bags marshmallows
2 bags caramels
1 lg. box Rice Krispies
1 can Eagle brand milk
2 sticks butter

Melt butter, caramel & milk in double boiler. Dip marshmallows quickly. Tap to remove excess caramel. Roll in Rice Krispies. Place on waxed paper. Chill and put in plastic bags. Keep in fridge until served.

EASY FILLED DROP COOKIES

1 C shortening
2 C brown sugar
2 eggs
½ C water, sour milk or buttermilk
1 tsp. vanilla
1 tsp. baking soda
1 tsp. salt
1/8 tsp. cinnamon
3 ½ C flour

Cream shortening & sugar. Add eggs & blend well. Stir in liquid and vanilla. Sift the dry ingredients, add to creamed mixture. Drop by teaspoonfuls on ungreased cookie sheet. Place ½ teaspoon filling on dough. Cover with ½ tsp. dough.

FILLING: Cook until thickened and cool.
2 C raisins or dates
1 T cornstarch
¾ C sugar
¾ C water
½ C chopped nuts

Bake at 375° for 10-12 minutes.

KNOT COOKIES*

DOUGH:
- ½ lb. butter, softened
- 1 ½ C sugar
- 6 eggs
- 2 T milk
- 1 tsp. anise extract
- 1 tsp. vanilla extract
- 8 C sifted flour
- 6 tsp. baking powder
- 1 tsp. salt

BUTTER ICING:
- ¾ box powdered sugar
- 1 stick butter
- 1 tsp. anise extract
- Food coloring
- Milk

Cream butter and sugar for cookies. Add eggs, milk, anise & vanilla. Combine sifted flour, baking powder & salt. Add slowly to the wet mixture. Grease cookie sheets. Roll dough into ½ inch logs & form knots. Bake at 400° for 8 minutes. Dunk in icing and let dry.

To make butter icing, combine powdered sugar & butter. Add anise. Slowly add milk to desired consistency. Add food coloring of your choice.

* They make beautiful pastel Easter cookies.

TORTA SECCA COOKIES

An Italian cookie, when translated means "Dry Cake" or "Hard Cake". It is a very good cookie. To make them, you need to flour your hands and with your thumb and first two fingers, pick up the dough and roll it between your hands to form a ball. "Pinch" tops of balls when putting them into a greased 9x13 pan, making sure they touch each other. Cut into bars or whatever shape you care to, while cookies are hot. The recipe calls for nuts, but sometimes I also add chopped dates and/or figs.

- 1 lb. butter
- 1 ½ C sugar
- 2 eggs, well beaten
- 5 C flour
- 1 tsp. baking powder
- 2 tsp. lemon extract
- 2 C walnuts, chopped

Blend butter & sugar together until creamy. Add well beaten eggs. Add flour & baking powder in small amounts at a time. Then add extract & walnuts. Bake at 350° for 30 minutes.

STRUFFOLI – HONEY BALLS

3 large eggs
1 T butter, softened
1 tsp. plus ½ C sugar

2 C sifted flour
½ tsp. baking powder

1 C honey
Flour for dusting

Vegetable oil for deep frying
Colored sprinkles (balls)

In a bowl, whisk together egg, butter & the 1 teaspoon sugar until foamy. Sift the flour with the baking powder & stir into the egg mixture. With your hands, work the mixture into a soft dough. Divide the dough into 4 pieces. On a floured surface, roll each piece into a rope about the width of your index finger & 12" long. Cut the rope into 1" pieces. Toss the pieces with enough flour to dust them lightly and shake off excess flour.

In a deep fryer, heat the oil to 375°. Fry the struffoli a few handfuls at a time, until puffed up & golden brown. Transfer with a slotted spoon onto paper towels to drain.

In a large saucepan, combine the honey & ½ cup sugar and heat over low heat, stirring until the sugar dissolves. Keep warm over low heat. Add the fried balls a few at a time, turning with a wooden spoon to coat all sides. Transfer the balls to a large plate & mound them into a pyramid, shaping with wet hands.

Sprinkle with the little colored candy balls & let stand for an hour or so. Break off pieces & eat. At Christmas time, we shaped the struffoli into a wreath & added a few red & green candied cherries.

MACAROONS

My Mother, Jennie Landi loved Macaroons. She also loved Chinese food, and at the end of a Chinese buffet, you can always find Macaroons. That was her sweet treat. In honor of my Mother, two Macaroon recipes I hope you also like.

VERY LIGHT COCONUT MACAROONS

8 oz. shredded or flaked sweetened coconut
1 C light brown sugar, packed
8 T flour
½ tsp. salt
Grated rind of orange, lemon, lime of your choice – This is optional

¼ C butter
4 egg yolks
½ tsp. vanilla

Preheat oven to 350°. Grease a sheet pan. Place all ingredients in a mixing bowl & blend thoroughly. With your hands, form into 1" balls. Place about 2" apart on the sheet. Bake 20-30 minutes or until golden brown. Remove from sheet to cooling rack.

TOASTED COCONUT MACAROONS

Preheat oven to 350°. Spread 2 (14 oz.) bags shredded, sweetened coconut evenly across 2 parchment-lined baking sheets. Toast until golden brown, 20-25 minutes, stirring 2 or 3 times to prevent burning. Let cool.

Meanwhile, beat 3 large egg whites with an electric mixer until stiff peaks form. Combine toasted coconut, 1 (14 oz.) can sweetened condensed milk & 1 tsp. vanilla in a bowl. Fold egg whites into coconut mixture. Wet hands & form into about 30 golf ball-sized mounds. Place on 2 parchment-lined baking sheets. Bake until browned & crisp-edged, about 20 minutes. Cool on a rack.

Keep refrigerated in a sealed container up to 3 days.

RICOTTA COOKIES

These cookies are moist & delicious & simple to assemble.

>2 ¼ C all-purpose flour
>1 tsp. baking powder
>Pinch of salt
>1 C granulated sugar
>½ C unsalted butter, room temp
>2 large eggs
>8 oz. fresh ricotta, drained
>½ tsp. vanilla extract
>2 tsp. lemon zest, plus ¼ C lemon juice
>2 C confectioner's sugar, sifted

Preheat oven to 325°. Sift together flour, baking powder & salt into a bowl. Set aside. Line two baking sheets with parchment paper.

Cream the sugar & butter in a mixer fitted with the paddle attachment on high speed until light & fluffy, about 2 minutes. Reduce the speed to medium and add the eggs one at a time, beating well between each addition. Plop in the ricotta, vanilla & lemon zest, and beat to combine. Add the flour mix and beat on low until just combined, but do not overmix.

Drop the dough in heaping tablespoons onto the baking sheets. Place in oven and bake, rotating pans halfway through the baking time, until the cookies are puffed, golden, and cooked all the way through, about 20-22 minutes. Remove from oven and cool on wire racks.

When the cookies are completely cool, make the glaze. In a bowl, whisk together the confectioner's sugar & lemon juice to make a smooth glaze. Adjust the consistency with a little water or more confectioner's sugar to make the glaze thick enough to stick to the cookies when dipped. Hold each cookie with two fingers, then dip the top of the cookies in the glaze and let dry on racks until all are done. Let dry for 2 hours before storing.

SESAME COOKIES

1 C butter
¾ C sugar
1 egg, room temp
2 tsp. anise extract
2 ½ C all-purpose flour

¼ tsp. baking powder
1/8 tsp. salt
½ C milk, or as needed
1 C sesame seeds

Preheat the oven to 350°.

In a large bowl, cream together the butter & sugar until smooth. Beat in the egg and anise extract until well blended. Sift together the flour, baking powder & salt; stir into the butter mixture until well incorporated. If you are using a stand mixer, let the dough mix for another minute to add lightness to the dough. The dough will be soft, but will hand roll easily.

Pinch off pieces of dough slightly smaller than a walnut, and roll them into small logs. Dip in milk, then roll in sesame seeds. Place cookies one inch apart on a cookie sheet. Cookies will not spread very much.

Bake for 17-20 minutes in the preheated oven, or until bottom and sides of cookies are lightly toasted. Remove from cookie sheets to cool on wire racks. Store in an airtight container at room temperature.

PINWHEEL COOKIES

FILLING:

    1 lb. dates   1 C water
    1 C sugar   1 C chopped nuts

Boil together dates, sugar & water for 10 minutes and mash while cooking. Cool. Add nuts.

DOUGH:

    1 C Crisco   4 C flour
    2 C brown sugar   ½ tsp. salt
    3 eggs, well beaten   ½ tsp. baking soda

Cream together Crisco & brown sugar. Add the eggs. Sift together the flour, salt & baking soda. Add flour mixture to the creamed mixture.

Work on the table with a little flour. Separate into thirds. Wrap dough in waxed paper and chill for an hour or 2.* Roll out each piece. Spread with one third of the filling on each piece & roll it like a jelly roll. Wrap the roll in waxed paper and chill overnight.

When ready to bake, remove from fridge and slice with sharp knife about ¼ inch thick. Place on lightly greased cookie sheet. Bake at 350° for 10 minutes.

* Note: This dough is difficult to handle. Make sure it is well chilled.

FLORENTINE LACE COOKIES

    2 C slivered almonds

Process in food processor until almonds look like "sand". Do not over process and make a paste. Set aside.

    ¾ C heavy cream   4 T butter
    ½ C sugar

Boil about 7 minutes until you see bubbles around edge of pan. Stir another minute.

    3 T flour   ¼ C orange marmalade
    1 tsp. vanilla   ¼ tsp. orange zest
    ¼ tsp. salt

To the creamed mixture, add almonds and the above ingredients. Mix all together. On 2 parchment-lined cookie sheets, drop 1 T batter: 6 cookies per sheet, about 3 ½ inches apart. With wet finger tips, flatten out batter by patting down to about 2 ½ inch circle. Bake at 350° for 15-17 minutes.

Everything can be mixed in the pan the cream was boiled in. Use a wooden spoon to mix. Rotate tray in oven halfway through the baking. Transfer cookies, still on parchment, to a wire rack to cool.

    4 oz. bittersweet chocolate, chopped fine

Microwave 3 oz. chocolate for about 1 or 2 minutes, until about two-thirds melted. Remove from microwave & stir in remaining 1 oz. chocolate. Stir until melted. Microwave a few seconds if necessary. Place chocolate in small ziplock plastic bag & snip off corner, making hole no larger than 1/16".

Pipe zigzag of chocolate over each cookie. Refrigerate until chocolate is set, about 30 minutes.

BERNADINE

1 lb. butter
2 ½ C brown sugar
2 ½ C white sugar
4 eggs
5 1/3 C flour

3 T honey
1 tsp. almond extract
1 tsp. baking soda
1 tsp. baking powder

Cream butter. Add dry ingredients, then add slightly beaten eggs, then honey and almond extract. Refrigerate overnight. Roll into balls the size of walnuts. Dip tops into milk then into sugar. Bake at 350° until brown, about 12 minutes.

DATE BALLS

8 oz. chopped dates
1 ½ stick butter
1 C sugar

¾ C pecans (3 oz.)
2 C Rice Krispies

In a pan put dates, butter & sugar. Cook 3 minutes. Remove from stove. Add nuts & Rice Krispies. Form into balls and roll in powdered sugar. Put in coffee can and refrigerate. Makes about 50 balls.

DOUBLE CHOCOLATE COOKIES

2 beaten eggs
½ C milk
1/3 C oil

2 C Bisquick
2 (4 oz.) pkgs. instant chocolate pudding
6 oz. pkg. chocolate chips

Mix eggs, milk, oil, pudding and 1 cup Bisquick. Then with wooden spoon, add the rest of the Bisquick. Add chips. Bake at 350° for 10-12 minutes.

Makes about 4 ½ dozen cookies.

DEATH BY CHOCOLATE COOKIE

2 pkgs. (16 oz.) Baker's semisweet chocolate, divided
¾ C packed brown sugar
¼ C butter
2 eggs
1 tsp. vanilla
½ C flour
¼ tsp. baking powder
2 C chopped nuts, optional

Preheat oven to 350°. Coarsely chop 8 squares of the chocolate and set aside. Microwave remaining 8 squares on high for 1-2 minutes. Stir until chocolate is melted & smooth. Stir in sugar, butter, eggs & vanilla. Stir in flour & baking powder. Stir in reserved chopped chocolate & nuts.

Drop by ¼ cup onto ungreased cookie sheet. Bake for 12-13 minutes or until cookies are puffed and set to the touch. Cool on sheet for 1 minute. Transfer to rack to cool completely.

Makes about 1 ½ dozen. Prep time 15 minutes.

DREAMSICLE COOKIES

½ C Tang
¾ C sugar
1 ½ C vanilla chips
1 ¾ C flour
½ tsp. baking soda
½ tsp. baking powder
½ stick butter, very soft
1 egg, slightly beaten
1 tsp. vanilla

Mix flour, baking soda & baking powder well. Add remaining ingredients. Mix until completely blended; will need to finish mixing with hands. Shape into balls the size of a walnut. Place 2 inches apart on sprayed cookie sheet. Bake at 375° for 12-14 minutes, until tops are very lightly browned. Cool 5 minutes on baking sheet. Remove cookies to rack to finish cooling.

FRUIT LAYER SQUARES

    4 C flour (may need more)   2 pkgs. active dry yeast
    ¾ lb. butter   1 C milk, warm
    4 egg yolks   ½ tsp. salt

Work butter & salt into flour by rubbing, or cut in like a pie crust. Beat egg yolks. Soak & dissolve yeast in milk. Add yolks to yeast & milk mixture. Then add flour mixture. Mix until flour forms a ball in bowl. Divide dough into 4 sections. Roll first section to fit 17x11 or 15x13 pan that has been greased. Cover with nut filling. Roll out second dough, place on top of nut filling, and cover with pineapple filling. Roll third layer and cover with apricots. Cover top with last layer of dough.

Bake at 350° for 35 minutes. When cold, spread with glaze.

GLAZE: 2 C powdered sugar, 2 T butter, rind & juice of lemon or orange

NUT FILLING: 1 lb. nuts ground, 1 C milk, 1 C sugar, ¾ tsp. vanilla. Mix and bring to slow boil. Cool.

PINEAPPLE: 2 (10 oz.) jars Bakers

APRICOTS: 1 (10 oz.) jars Bakers

FLOURLESS PEANUT BUTTER COOKIES

    2 C peanut butter   2 eggs
    2 C sugar   1 tsp. vanilla

Mix all of the ingredients together and roll a spoonful into a ball. Flatten with back of fork. Bake at 350° for 15-20 minutes.

You can add any chips, nuts and/or coconut. This recipe can be cut in half as it makes a lot.

FUDGE FILLED PEANUT BUTTER BARS

DOUGH:
    1 pkg. yellow cake mix   1 C peanut butter
    ½ C butter, melted   2 eggs

In large bowl, combine all ingredients. By hand, stir until dough folds together. Press 2/3 of the dough into bottom of ungreased 9x13 pan. Reserve remaining dough for topping.

FILLING:
    1 C semisweet chocolate bits
    1 pkg. Pillsbury coconut pecan or coconut almond frosting mix
    1 (14 oz.) can sweetened condensed milk (1 1/3 cup)

Mix filling well. Spread over dough. Cover filling with remaining dough. Bake at 350° for 20-25 minutes. Cool. Cut into 36 squares.

PRALINE TOFFEE THINS

    24 graham crackers   ½ lb. butter, no substitute
    ½ - 1 C pecans, chopped   ½ C sugar

Spread aluminum foil over cookie sheet. Spray with Pam or grease well. Cut graham crackers into small strips and arrange on cookie sheet. Melt butter, add sugar and bring to a boil. Boil for 3 minutes. Add nuts and pour over crackers. Bake at 350° for 11 minutes. Cool a short time before removing from pan.

HUNGARIAN PEACH BARS

2/3 C milk
1 pkg. dry yeast
1 tsp. sugar
3 C all-purpose flour
½ lb. butter
6 egg yolks, beaten

1 jar (2 lbs.) peach preserves
1 lb. nuts, ground (12 oz. pkg.)
¾ C sugar
6 egg whites
¾ C sugar

Dissolve yeast and sugar in lukewarm milk. Mix flour and butter together as for pie dough. Combine beaten yolks with yeast mixture and all the flour mixture; mix well. Shape into 3 balls. Roll out one ball to fit on an 11x18 ungreased tart pan. Spread with ½ of the preserves.

Combine nuts with ¾ cup sugar. Sprinkle 1/3 of this mixture over the preserves. Roll out a second ball of dough and place over nuts. Spread remaining half of the preserves and another 1/3 of the nut mixture. Cover with remaining dough. Let rise 1 hour.

Bake in preheated oven at 350° for 30 minutes.

Beat egg whites until stiff. Gradually add ¾ cup sugar. Remove cookies from oven. Top with remaining nut mixture. Return to oven for 15 minutes more until lightly browned.

PINE NUT COOKIES

2 ½ C flour
¼ tsp. salt
1 C (2 sticks) unsalted butter, room temp
½ C sugar

3 large egg yolks
1 ½ tsp. pure vanilla extract
1 tsp. grated lemon zest
1 C pine nuts or slivered almonds
1 large egg white, lightly beaten

Preheat oven to 350°. Line several baking sheets with parchment paper. In medium bowl, whisk flour & salt.

Using mixer, beat butter & sugar until fluffy. Add egg yolks, vanilla & lemon zest. Beat to combine. With mixer on low, gradually add the flour mixture, mixing just until incorporated.

Place the pine nuts or almonds in a small bowl, and the egg white in a second small bowl. Roll dough into 1 inch balls (about 1 tablespoon each). Dip the top and sides of each ball first in egg white, then into nuts, pressing gently.

Place cookies, nut side up, 2 inches apart. Bake until nuts are golden brown and cookies are lightly golden around edges (16-18 minutes). Let cookies cool 5 minutes, then transfer to wire rack to cool completely. Makes 38 cookies.

SNOWBALLS

1 ½ C shortening
¼ tsp. salt
2 T vanilla

1 ½ C nuts
3 ½ C flour
¾ C powdered sugar

Combine all ingredients <u>except</u> powdered sugar & mix at low speed. Roll into 1" balls & place on ungreased cookie sheet. Bake at 325° for 18-25 minutes (depending on oven), until very lightly browned. Cool 5 minutes. Roll in sifted powdered sugar while warm, and again when cool.

WITH A LITTLE HELP FROM MY FRIENDS

These recipes are in alphabetical order by last name of contributor.

M.J. AMODEO

MJ is a friend from Lowell Burrell, PA, who after many years, we met again in The Villages, FL – It's a small world.

OYSTER STEW

12 oz. of oysters
½ medium onion, chopped
2 T garlic, chopped
4 T butter
3 C milk
3 C Half & Half
1 T parsley, chopped
½ C white wine

Lightly sauté onion & garlic in 1 tablespoon of butter. Add wine, milk, and Half & Half. When this is hot and not quite boiling, add the oysters. Turn off when the oysters begin to curl. Add the remaining butter, parsley, and salt & pepper to taste.

SCALLOPED POTATOES

8 potatoes (peeled, sliced & partially boiled)
1 can cream of chicken soup
1 (12 oz.) pkg. shredded sharp cheese
½ C butter
1 pint sour cream
Bread crumbs

Melt together: chicken soup, sharp cheese & the butter. Add to the potatoes. Add the sour cream and mix well. Spray 9x13 pan with Pam. Top with bread crumbs and bake.

****

CAROL BASSO

Every once in a while as you go through life, you meet someone that just wows you. Such is my friend Carol Basso – An artist extraordinaire, a wonderful cook, and a good friend that I love to spend time with. These are her recipes:

GERMAN MEAT BALLS

2 lb. ground meat
1 C bread crumbs
3 eggs
1 pkg. dry onion soup mix

Mix ingredients and shape into walnut sized balls. Place in a 9x13 pan. Cover with sauce.

SAUCE:

1 C brown sugar
1 can whole cranberries
1 sm. can sauerkraut (12-14 oz.)
1 bottle chili sauce (12 oz.)
then refill bottle with water

Combine and pour over meat balls. Bake at 350° for 2 hours.

CUCUMBER SANDWICHES

Loaf of dark party bread
2 (8 oz.) cream cheese, softened
2 pkgs. ranch dressing
Sliced cucumbers

Mix cream cheese & ranch dressing with a small amount of milk. Spread on party bread. Top with a thin slice of cucumber. You can sprinkle a small amount of lemon pepper – Good to go.

CAROL'S SHRIMP DIP

Combine the following in a small bowl and chill:
- 1 (8 oz.) can shrimp
- 1 pt. sour cream
- ½ C chili sauce
- 4 tsp. lemon juice
- Salt & pepper
- 2 tsp. horseradish
- 7 dashes Tabasco

Serve with potato chips.

CAROL'S POTATOES

- 8 potatoes, cooked & dried, cut into chunks
- 1 lb. American cheese, slices, tear into 1/3" strips
- 1 C Hellmann's mayo
- ½ C chopped onion
- Salt & pepper to taste
- 1 lb. bacon, partially fried
- ¼ C sliced stuffed green olives

Combine first 4 ingredients & place in buttered 9x13 pan. Sprinkle with salt & pepper. Top with bacon & green olives. Bake at 325° for 1 hour.
You can use shredded American Cheese in a bag.

NANTUCKET CRANBERRY PIE

In a 10" pan, combine: 2 C raw cranberries, ½ C nuts, ½ C sugar
Mix together and pour over the cranberry mixture:
- ¾ C margarine, melted
- 1 C sugar
- 1 C flour
- 1 tsp. almond extract
- 2 eggs, beaten

Bake at 325-350° for 35-40 minutes – watch!

(Buy berries in the fall when available and freeze for later use.)

****

JOANNE BATEMAN

There are baked beans & there are baked beans – but Joanne's are the tops!

OHIO BEAN CASSEROLE

1 can baked beans
1 can wax beans
1 can green beans
1 can baby lima beans
1 can kidney beans
8 oz. can tomato sauce
1 can tomato soup

1 C brown sugar
1 C chopped celery
1 lb. pork sausage
2 med. onions, chopped
2 T prepared mustard
½ tsp. chili powder

Brown & drain sausage, onions and celery. Drain beans: mix with sugar, mustard, chili powder, tomato soup and tomato sauce. Add sausage, onions & celery. Put in large casserole dish and bake for 1 hour at 350°. Or I like to put in crock pot on low for 4 hours.

****

GAIL BENOIT

...

Gail's comment on her Apple Spice Cake: This is a wonderful cake to make in the fall of the year. The spices remind me of apple pie but it's easier than pie. My children loved to come home after school and have a large piece of cake with some vanilla bean ice cream. Gail is a new friend that I met in Art Class. Come to find out that every time I mention her name to anyone, it is followed by "Isn't she a nice person." And she really is.

GAIL'S APPLE SPICE CAKE

2 1/3 C flour
3 C sugar
2 tsp. baking soda
¾ tsp. cinnamon
¼ tsp. cloves

¼ tsp. nutmeg
4 C chopped, peeled apples
   (you can use a variety of apples)
½ C soft shortening
2 eggs

Combine flour, sugar, baking soda, salt & spices in large mixing bowl. Mix until well blended, 2 to 4 minutes.

Add the apples, shortening, nuts and eggs. Beat at medium speed until well blended and pour into a greased and floured 9x13 pan. Bake in a preheated oven at 325° for 45 minutes or until a toothpick comes out clean. Cool on a wire rack then place on cake plate. Frost with Caramel Frosting.

CARAMEL FROSTING

1/3 C butter
½ C brown sugar (packed firmly)
3 T milk

1 ½ C confectioner's sugar
   (sifted)
1 tsp. real vanilla

Melt butter in saucepan and add brown sugar and a dash of salt. Stir over medium heat until sugar melts, then add milk and bring to a boil. Pour the mixture into a mixing bowl and allow cooling for 10 minutes, then add the confectioner's sugar and vanilla. Beat together until the consistency is of a spreading consistency. Add additional confectioner's sugar if too watery. Drizzle over cake, allowing drizzle to flow down sides of cake. Enjoy.

****

"LADY JEAN" - JEAN BLOME

A candy maker from the Old School who came up with a new twist on fudge – cheese!

VELVEETA FUDGE

¾ lb. Velveeta, cut into ½ inch cubes
1 C butter or margarine
1 ½ pkg. (4 oz. each) Baker's unsweetened chocolate, broken into pieces
2 T light corn syrup
2 pkgs. (16 oz. each) powdered sugar (about 8 cups)
1 ½ C chopped pecans
1 tsp. vanilla

Microwave Velveeta, butter, chocolate and corn syrup in microwaveable bowl on high for 3 min. or until blended. Add chocolate mixture, in batches, to sugar in large bowl, beating with mixer on medium speed until blended after each addition. Stir in nuts and vanilla. Pour into 9x13 pan sprayed with cooking spray. Smooth top with spatula. Refrigerate several hours or until firm before cutting into 1-inch squares.

Substitute:
- 1 C creamy peanut butter in place of chocolate for peanut butter fudge
- ½ C crushed peppermint candies for the chopped pecans

Make ahead: For longer storage, wrap tightly and freeze up to 2 months. Thaw in refrigerator overnight before serving.

****

NOREEN CHERRY & GENETTE HEINZ

Noreen and Genette are my neighbors in The Villages, FL. Best neighbors anyone can have. Generous, and always ready with a helping hand.

This recipe was given to Noreen by Grandma Kit Cherry, 2/17/91.

Grandma Nora Regan's Irish Soda Bread

- 4 C self-rising flour
- ¾ tsp. baking soda
- 3 tsp. baking powder
- ½ stick butter, cut with knife
- ½ tsp. salt
- Caraway seeds, if desired
- 1 C raisins
- ½ C sugar
- ½ tsp. nutmeg, if desired
- 1 C buttermilk
- 2 eggs, beaten

If using whole wheat flour: double the butter to 1 stick; add additional ½ cup buttermilk.

Mix dry ingredients. Cut in butter. Add eggs and milk. Make a cross on the top. Bake 40 minutes at 350°.

Best if made in a cast iron skillet!

****

LINDA DeGOOD

A classy lady I am happy to call friend. She makes beef jerky & sends it home to her family every Christmas & Easter.

BEEF JERKY

    2 – 2 ½ lbs. London Broil

Freeze, then put in refrigerator about 8 hours to thaw slightly. Cut into thin slices – it is easiest to cut when still mostly frozen (only the top has some softness). Cut about the thickness of regular bacon.

Combine and mix well:

3 C soy sauce	1 ½ tsp. salt
5 T Worcestershire sauce	½ tsp. garlic powder
5 tsp. Liquid Smoke seasoning	½ tsp. onion powder
¾ tsp. pepper	4 T light brown sugar

Pour the marinade over the meat slices. (I put them in an 11x13 glass baking pan and put a piece of saran wrap right on top of the meat to hold the marinade on the meat.)

Marinate for 12 hours or more … then pour off the marinade and put mea slices on racks of a dehydrator. Dry slices, checking bottom layer after 1 ½ - 2 hours. The pieces should be pretty hard … not too "chewy".

It will take about 8 hours (maybe a little more) to dry, depending on the thickness of the slices and the amount to dry. Usually 4 hours for 1 ½ lb. and 8 hours for 2-2 ½ lbs. piece of London Broil. Rotate slices up to next layer as the racks empty.

A dehydrator can be bought at WalMart for about $35.

****

MARY DODSWORTH

My niece Nancy Caffo was married at her home in Webster, NY. Her sister Mary Dodsworth had these wonderful dips at the wedding and was nice enough to send me her 4 dip recipes.

CLAMS CASINO DIP

3 cans chopped clams, drained (save juice)
½ C finely chopped onion
½ C finely chopped green pepper
¼ C pimento
¼ lb. melted butter
1 C Italian flavored bread crumbs
Dash of garlic salt
1 tsp. Tabasco sauce

Bake at 400° for 30 minutes. If desired … put bacon bits on top … real bacon makes it greasy. Serve with crackers.

MUSHROOM DIP

1/3 C Parmesan cheese
1 C shredded cheddar cheese
1 env. Italian dressing mix
8 oz. mushrooms, chopped
¾ C mayo (I use light)
1 tsp. cayenne pepper

Mix all together and bake at 350° for 20 minutes in 8 x 8 dish. Serve with crackers or tortilla chips.

HOT ARTICHOKE & SPINACH DIP

1 (8 oz.) cream cheese, softened (I use light)
¼ C mayo
¼ C Parmesan cheese
¼ C Romano cheese
1 clove garlic, minced
½ tsp. dried basil
¼ tsp. garlic salt
1 (14 oz.) can artichokes, drained, chopped
½ C frozen chopped spinach, drained
¼ C Mozzarella cheese

Preheat oven to 350°. Grease small baking dish. Mix together cream cheese, mayo, Parmesan, Romano cheese, and garlic salt. Gently stir in artichokes and spinach. Transfer to baking dish, top with Mozzarella, bake for 25 minutes.

CHICKEN WING DIP

3-5 chicken breasts (skinless/boneless)
1 bottle Frank's hot sauce
1 pkg. cream cheese
Blue cheese salad dressing
Mozzarella cheese

Put chicken in small dish (9-inch pan). Pour Frank's hot sauce all over. Cover. Cook at 350° for 30 minutes.

Cut up chicken / shred with fork. Spread softened cream cheese in chicken. Pour thin layer of blue cheese salad dressing over. Sprinkle with Mozzarella cheese. Cook 15 more minutes or until cheese melts. Serve with hearty crackers and I also cut up celery sticks.

****

JENNA DODSWORTH

Jenna is my beautiful niece from Canandaigua, NY. My sister Rosemary, her grandmother, taught her to make this her favorite salad.

JENNA'S CUCUMBER SALAD

Wash and peel 3 or 4 large cucumbers. Leave a few strips of green. Slice about ¼ inch thick. Salt and set aside.

This part is to taste; really not a recipe.

Mix: White or apple cider vinegar with rice vinegar. (Enough to cover the cucumbers.)
Add a natural sweetener (Truvia) and McCormick "It's a Dilly" or plain dill weed.

Taste: You can add onion powder, garlic powder, celery salt, or sliced sweet onion. Any combination of your favorite spices until you get the flavor and tartness you like. You can add a little water to cut the tartness.

Rinse cucumbers. Add to the brine. Cover and refrigerate. Great as a snack. Especially good with fresh local cucumbers.

A classy mother & daughter at the top of their class, Mary and Jenna Dodsworth.

****

EMILY EMIGH
(Sounds like Amy)

Emily, President of the Three River Pittsburgh Club. A leader amongst leaders, athletic & energetic, and she cooks too. This recipe was from her mother. It can be an Appetizer or a side with pork or chicken.

RED CANDY CINNAMON APPLE SLICES

Bag or box of cinnamon candy (the best is Red Hots). Peel & slice 8 apples. Put candy and apples in boiling water. Lower heat – Simmer until apples are tender. Remove from heat. Cool in pan. Put in container with lid. Refrigerate. You may need to add water while simmering.

I have seen it made with cucumber spears instead of apples.

****

ROB EMIGH

Artistic, friendly, a wonderful person to spend time with, an excellent golfer, and he also makes the best Long Island Iced Tea. He always brings a big pitcher when my daughter Melissa visits Florida.

LONG ISLAND ICED TEA

1 C vodka   2 C orange juice
1 C gin   4 C Coke (2 cans)
1 C rum   1 lemon
1 C tequila

Rob, Brian, & Emily Emigh

****

MARY ANN FISHER

This is my sister-in-law's recipe. She always brings one when she comes to visit. Thanks, Mary Ann.

DREAM CHEESECAKE

- 1 (9 oz.) cream cheese
- 1 pt. sour cream
- 1 tsp. cream of tartar
- 6 eggs, separated
- 3 T flour
- ½ tsp. salt
- 1 tsp. vanilla
- 1 ½ C sugar
- 1 C graham crackers
- 4 T oleo/butter

Melt oleo/butter. Add crumbs. Line buttered spring form pan. Save ¼ cup crumbs for topping. Save rest for crust. Make foil collar to go around the pan as cheese cake will rise a little.

Take 6 egg whites with 1 tsp. cream of tartar and beat until foaming. Add 3 T sugar until white peaks set up. Set aside.

Mix cream cheese until creamy and add sugar. Mix well. Add flour, salt, then add egg yolks. Mix well. Add sour cream & vanilla and mix. Fold in the egg whites with a spatula. Pour into the pan and bake at 325° for 1 to 1 ½ hours or until center is dry.

****

DOE PINFOLD

My friend, along with her husband, Peter, have lived all over the world. She is a good cook & a wonderful dinner guest. Peter and I are learning all there is to know about wine as he serenades us with songs about "Charlie & his Missus."

FREEZER PASTRY

- 1 egg
- 1 T white vinegar
- 6 C flour
- 1 tsp. salt
- 2 sticks Crisco

Mix egg & vinegar in a cup & fill with water to 1 cup measure. Mix flour, salt & Crisco. Blend together like pie crust. This crust can be used when you make it. Or freeze it and bring to room temperature & roll.

****

KAREN GUARIN

#1 Pittsburgh Steelers Fan, #1 Pittsburgh Pirate Fan, #1 Pittsburgh Penguin Fan, she loves them all!

BEEF BAR-B-Q

1- 6 lb. chuck roast
1 stalk celery
1 green pepper, chopped
1 onion, chopped
1 (14 oz.) ketchup
1 T vinegar
1 tsp. Bar-B-Q sauce
2 tsp. salt
1 ½ C water
1 tsp. pepper

Cook in crock pot on low for 8 hours. Pull apart with forks & bile on buns.

****

KELLEY KAUFMAN

A dear friend, a jazz lover, a lover of life who came to the aid of my daughter, Jeannine, when Jeannine was diagnosed with cancer. Kelley made my daughter hats and sent loads of information our way.

Kelley and me at my house.

The following are some Jewish recipes from Kelley.

HONEYED CARROTS

Mostly served at New Year – Rosh Hashanah

- 1 lb. carrots
- ¼ C butter
- ¼ C pecan halves
- 3 T honey
- 2 T golden raisins
- ¼ tsp. grated orange rind
- Salt & pepper to taste

Cut carrots into 1-inch rounds. Cook carrots in salted boiling water, covered, until tender. Drain. Stir in remaining ingredients and bring to a boil. Cook until liquid is absorbed and carrots are glazed (approx. 10-15 minutes).

HOT FRUIT CASSEROLE

- 1 C brown sugar
- ¾ C cognac
- 1 lg. jar applesauce
- 1 lg. can apricots
- 1 med. can chunky pineapple
- 1 lg. can peaches
- 1 med. can plums
- 1 med. can cherries

Make sure all fruit is pitted. Mix cognac with brown sugar. Layer bottom of a 9x13 Pyrex dish with applesauce. Follow with fruits listed, and after each layer add a bit of the cognac and sugar mixture. Bake for 3 hours at 250°.

APPLE GLAZED RIB LAMB CHOPS

- 4 lamb loin or 8 rib chops, cut 1 inch thick
- ½ C apple juice
- ¼ tsp. ground cloves
- Salt & pepper
- ½ C brown sugar
- ¼ tsp. dry mustard

Place lamb chops on broiler rack. Sprinkle both sides with salt & pepper. In small saucepan, combine remaining ingredients. Cook over medium heat until sugar dissolves. Broil lamb chops 3-4 inches from source of heat, about 6 minutes per side, or until desired degree of doneness, brushing frequently with apple glaze.

****

DIANNE KNIGHT

Without her encouragement, I would never again have picked up a paint brush. She keeps me going, and we laugh a lot together. Thanks, Dianne.

BALTIMORE CRAB CAKES

1 lb. crab meat
1 egg, beaten
½ tsp. prepared yellow mustard
2 tsp. parsley flakes
2 tsp. Old Bay seasoning
2 T mayo

Toss all together. Shape into patties. Broil 10 min.

CRAN-ORANGE RELISH

1 bag cranberries
1 naval orange
¾ C sugar

Mix all in food processor. Consistency of slaw. Can be made 5 days ahead.

MILLION DOLLAR POUND CAKE

1 lb. butter, softened-room temp
3 C sugar
6 lg. eggs
4 C all-purpose flour
¾ C milk
1 tsp. almond extract
1 tsp. vanilla extract

Mix batter until creamy, 1-7 minutes. Gradually add sugar. Beat at medium speed until fluffy. Add eggs, one at a time, beating until yolk disappears. Add flour to creamed mixture with milk. Beat at low speed (get rid of lumps with mixer). Add extracts. Pour into greased 10" tube pan. Bake 1 hour 40 min. at 300° until toothpick comes out clean. Cool 8-10 min. Remove from pan and cool completely.

****

KATHY LYLE

This is a recipe from my neighbor Kathy Lyle. Kathy lives across the street from me. Like her recipe, Kathy is sweet.

PINEAPPLE CASSEROLE

1 can crushed pineapple & juice
¾ C sugar
3 eggs, beaten
2 T cornstarch
Pinch of cinnamon

Mix all ingredients. Pour into 2 quart casserole dish. Sprinkle small amount of cinnamon on top. Bake at 350° for about 45 minutes.

****

RITA MAPPIN

A good friend & my Pittsburgh connection. We never miss a chance to go for fried fish together. Over the years I have traded many recipes with Rita, a good friend and a good cook. This is her recipe.

OVEN BAKED PECAN-CRUSTED CHICKEN FINGERS

2 lbs. boneless, skinless chicken breasts, cut lengthwise into strips
1 C pecan pieces
½ C bread crumbs
1 T plus 2 tsp. Essence, recipe follows
2 large eggs
¼ C olive oil
Chopped parsley, garnish
Honey Mustard Dipping Sauce, recipe follows

Preheat oven to 375°. Lightly grease a large baking sheet.

RECIPE CONTINUES ON NEXT PAGE.

OVEN BAKED PECAN-CRUSTED CHICKEN FINGERS, Continued

In the bowl of a food processor, combine the pecan pieces, bread crumbs, and 1 tablespoon Essence. Pulse for 1 minute to combine. Pour into a shallow dish. In a bowl, beat together the eggs, olive oil and remaining 2 teaspoons of Essence. One at a time, dip the chicken into the egg mixture, then dredge in the pecan mixture, shaking to remove any excess. Transfer to the baking sheet and bake, turning once, until the chicken is cooked through and the crust is golden, 15 to 20 minutes.

Remove the chicken from the oven and transfer to 4 plates. Garnish with parsley and serve with the Honey Mustard Dipping Sauce on the side.

ESSENCE (Creole Seasoning):

- 2 ½ T paprika
- 2 T salt
- 2 T garlic powder
- 1 T black pepper
- 1 T onion powder
- 1 T cayenne pepper
- 1 T dried leaf oregano
- 1 T dried thyme

Combine all ingredients thoroughly and store in an airtight jar or container. Yield: about 2/3 cup.

HONEY MUSTARD DIPPING SAUCE:

- ½ C mayo
- 2 T honey
- 2 T Creole mustard, or other hot whole-grain mustard
- Pinch of salt
- Pinch of cayenne, or to taste

In a small bowl, combine all the ingredients and stir well to combine. Cover tightly with plastic wrap and refrigerate until ready to use. (Will keep refrigerated in a covered non-reactive container for two weeks.)
Yield: approx. ¾ cup

****

SHEILA MYDOCK

A wonderful cook, who taught me how to make pirogi. This is a new version of her old recipe, but just as good. Her husband, Don, is my good fishing buddy.

DOUGH:
- 3 eggs
- 5 C flour
- 2 tsp. salt
- 1 pt. sour cream

Mix and add flour a little at a time if needed to roll out.

FILLING:

Boil potatoes. While potatoes are boiling, sauté onions in margarine. I usually use a whole onion. Mash potatoes with 8 oz. sharp cheese and above onion mixture ... no liquid. (I like my potatoes to be a nice orange color.) You may also fill them with sauerkraut also mixed with the onions. Make sure you precook sauerkraut and squeeze very dry.

Roll dough in sections and cut with a biscuit cutter or glass. Put a spoon on potatoes in center of circle and fold and crimp edges to seal the dough. (This will be in a half moon shape.) It takes practice but the results are delicious.

Boil the pirogues and cool in ice water. They may be frozen, pan fried slowly or baked in the oven with butter. Serve with buttered onions, and some like them with sour cream.

This dough recipe is so light.

****

DR. HOWARD NADER

This recipe was given to me by my good friend and my dentist for 50 years, Dr. Howard Nader. Doc Nader is not only a great dentist, but cooks with great passion. And if he were not a dentist, he would be a renowned chef. I travel from Florida to Pennsylvania just to have him clean my teeth. And I would go twice as far for one of his meals. He is retiring from dentistry, but he will never stop cooking. This dish is a favorite of his and loved by his grandchildren.

YAKNI

- 6-8 med. onions, cut lengthwise
- ½ lb. butter
- 1 chicken or cut up chicken parts, both white & dark meat
- 2 (12-16 oz.) cans of stewed tomatoes

Broil your chicken until tender. When it's cool, skin & debone. Set aside.

Sauté onions in butter until they become transparent. Add chicken to onion mixture, salt & pepper to taste. Simmer together 5-10 minutes. Drain stewed tomatoes and add to the chicken mixture, reserving juice. Let it simmer for 5 minutes. Add as much juice as needed to reach the consistency you like. Should be a little soupy. Serve over Syrian rice.

SYRIAN RICE

- 1 C Orzo
- 1 C regular long grain rice
- 1/3 C melted butter
- 1 (10 oz.) can of chicken broth, hot or use the broth from the boiled chicken
- 1 tsp. salt
- Pinch of turmeric

Brown Orzo in butter over medium heat. When golden brown, add rice and sauté a few minutes. Transfer to a microwaveable bowl and add the rest of the ingredients, plus half a cup of water. Cover and microwave at medium temperature for about 15 minutes. At the end of the time, if the rice is too dry, add a little more water, and cook a minute or two longer.

LYNN NEETER

Lynn and her husband, Phil, know how to throw a party. They do so much for so many, and it is always a good time. Thanks for all the golf outings, thanks for the progressive dinners, and thanks for the New Year's Eve parties.

BETTER THAN COOKIES CHOCOLATE BARK

Saltine crackers
2 sticks of butter
1 C sugar
1 bag of chocolate chips, any flavor

Line cookie sheet with foil and cover the foil with crackers lined up side-by-side. Melt butter and sugar on low heat and pour over crackers. Bake at 350° for 12 minutes. Spread the chocolate chips on the hot crackers and let melt a little. Then smooth them out a bit. When they are cool, break apart like bark.

PASTA TO-GO

Prepare your favorite pasta until it is almost done the way you like it. Drain the pasta and spray it with olive oil Pam. Let cool and pack in individual freezer bags of the proper serving size (1, 2, or 4 servings), and then freeze. To use, just thaw and use like fresh pasta. Our favorite is elbows with olive oil, lemon and garlic. Microwave for 1-2 minutes.

Lynn at one of the great parties.

****

LINDA PAOLILLO

My dear friend Linda not only gave me a great recipe, but she has also written a beautiful prayer, "Precious Blood", for all those who may need it.

Precious Blood

Lord, send me down your Precious Blood,
So I'll be covered with your love,
When I'm upset or all a-fright,
I know your blood will make things right,
These words were sent from you above.
When I asked to be covered by your blood.
So thank you Holy Spirit, too –
For He knows how much, Lord, I love you.
I asked my Holy Spirit to guide me,
I know He is always beside me.
With my Guardian Angel by my side,
There is no place I'd want to hide.
So, if I remember to call on you,
Your Precious Blood will see me through.

By Linda Paolillo

CHOCOLATE BITTERSWEETS

½ C butter
½ C powdered sugar
¼ tsp. salt
1 tsp. vanilla
1-1 ¼ C flour

Cream well butter, powdered sugar, salt & vanilla. Add flour. Shape 1 tsp. of dough into balls, put on ungreased cookie sheet. Press hole in center of each ball. Bake at 350° for 12-15 minutes.

CREAMY NUT FILLING:

3 oz. cream cheese, softened
1 C powdered sugar
2 T flour
1 tsp. vanilla
1 C chopped nuts
½ C coconut

Blend cream cheese, powdered sugar, flour & vanilla. Cream well. Stir in nuts & coconut.

CHOCOLATE FROSTING:

¼ C chocolate chips, melted
1 T butter
1 T water
¼ C powdered sugar

Melt chips, butter & water. Add powdered sugar.

Put creamy nut filling in holes of baked cookies. Top with chocolate frosting. Small cookie, but delicious!

Recipe freezes well – Recipe can be doubled.

****

JACQUIE RALPH

A beautiful petite lady, a gracious hostess, my eating-out buddy, and a professional photographer who makes us all look as good as her.

BRISKET

- 5 lb. brisket
- 1 lg. onion
- 2-3 cloves garlic
- Salt & pepper
- 2 bottles Heinz chili sauce
- 4 bay leaves
- 1 tsp. ground ginger
- 2 heaping T Kitchen Bouquet
- Garlic powder

Insert slivers of garlic into a cut made into the brisket. Salt & pepper brisket. Slice large onion over top of brisket. Place brisket in a roasting pan. Sear to seal in juices. Mix 2 bottles of Heinz chili sauce with remaining ingredients: bay leaves, ground ginger, Kitchen Bouquet & garlic powder. Pour mixture over browned seared meat.

Roast meat on high at 400° for about 15 min. Cover. Reduce heat to 325° for 3½ to 4 hours. Add a half cup of water.

Let cool and rest. Cut against grain to serve. Pan dripping makes a wonderful sauce. Leftovers can be frozen in slices to defrost for a great sandwich.

****

GORDON AND "TOBY" RALPH

This recipe has been shared with hundreds of people, both in words and in Mason jars at Thanksgiving and Christmas, often made in a half dozen batches by Gordon and Jacquie to share, continuing a tradition after Dad died at age 94. His memory lives on with the recipe and this poem in his personal bible.

REMIND ME GOD
Dear God when I am lonely and perhaps I feel despair
Let not my ailing heart forget that you hear every prayer.
Remind me that no matter what I do or fail to do
There still is hope for me as long as I have faith in you.
Let not my eyes be blinded by some folly I commit
But help me to regret my wrong and to make up *for it.*
Inspire me to put my fears upon a hidden shelf
And in the future **never** to be sorry for myself.
Give me the restful sleep I need before another dawn.
And bless me in the morning with the **courage** to go on. Amen

CRANBERY RELISH SPECIAL

1# Cranberries
1 small can pineapple chunks, drained, reserve juice
Orange juice
1 cup chopped nut of your choice
1.5 cups of sugar
1 cup raisins
½ t ground cinnamon
¼ t allspice
½ t ground ginger
Dash of salt

Put cranberries in saucepan and pour over combination of reserved pineapple juice and enough orange juice to make 1.5 cups.

Add all other ingredients except pineapple and nuts and cook until cranberries pop. Remove from heat and cool. Stir in pineapple and nuts. Great with fowl. Relish can be frozen.

****

JILL HOLLAND RUSTICI

Jill's recipe for dates is a real crowd pleaser, but I love her Oriental Noodles.

DATES WRAPPED IN BACON
Appetizer

Toothpicks soaked in water for 15-20 minutes.
Pitted dates
Bacon slices cut in halves

Preheat oven to 400°. Take baking sheet, cover in aluminum foil and lightly spray with peanut oil. Take bacon piece, wrap around pitted date and secure with toothpick. Place on baking sheet. When all the dates have been wrapped, place baking sheet in oven and bake for 15 min. Check for doneness, and when brown, rotate pieces to ensure even color. When fully baked, remove from oven & allow to stand a minimum of 10 min. as they will be extremely hot. Dates may be served warm or at room temperature. They will disappear as if by magic!

ORIENTAL NOODLES

One pound of pasta (I prefer a fine pasta such as angel hair. You may use any type or shape.)

    3 T toasted sesame seed oil, or more to taste
    2 T tamari or Japanese soy sauce, or more to taste
    3 or 4 scallions, sliced

Cook pasta al dente. Drain well. Coat with sesame seed oil and toss well. Add tamari and stir, mixing well again. Taste and add more of either liquid until you are pleased with flavor. Add scallions, stir, and allow to stand at least a half hour before serving. It is best served at room temperature, but may be served cold, if you prefer.

****

VERA SWIERGOL

My oldest & dearest friend, Vera Swiergol, claims she only has a kitchen because it came with the house, and in a heart beat she could turn it into a library. This is her recipe and I have made it on many occasions.

LASAGNA SANDWICH

MEAT FILLING:

1 lb. ground beef
¾ C chopped onion
1 clove garlic
1 T parsley flakes
½ tsp. basil
½ tsp. oregano
½ tsp. salt & dash of pepper
1 (6 oz.) can tomato paste

In a skillet, brown meat in olive oil. Drain. Add remaining ingredients. Simmer uncovered 10 minutes.

CHEESE FILLING:

1 C ricotta, 1 egg, ¼ C grated cheese - Mix.

CRUST:

2 cans Pillsbury Crescent Rolls
2 slices Mozzarella cheese
Milk
Sesame seeds

Unroll and cover bottom of ungreased cookie sheet with crescent rolls. Place ½ meat down the center of dough, leaving an inch at top & bottom. Top meat with cheese mixture. Add remaining meat. Place cheese slices on top and fold over ends of dough and seal. Brush with milk & sprinkle with sesame seeds. Bake at 375° for 20-25 minutes. (If you make it ahead, do not put milk & seeds on until ready to bake. To hold unbaked roll, cover with saran wrap & refrigerate.)

My Oldest & Dearest Friend

****

MARY ANN SWIERGOL

My life-long, beautiful friend & the world's best cookie maker. The story goes that this recipe has ended friendships. But now that the secret is out, we can share. Thanks, Mary Ann.

SERBIAN TORTE CAKE

½ lb. butter
2 C sugar
6 egg yolks
1 lb. graham crackers, ground
1 lb. nuts, ground

2 ¼ C milk
3 tsp. baking powder
1 ½ tsp. vanilla
6 egg whites, beaten until stiff

Mix ingredients in order listed, folding egg whites into mixture last. Grease & flour pan well. Bake at 350° for 25 minutes. Bake as 2 cake, or 4 rounds, and still bake for 25 minutes.

ICING FOR SERBIAN TORTE:

1 C milk, regular
4 T flour
½ C butter

½ C Crisco
1 C granulated sugar
2 tsp. vanilla

Mix small amount of milk into flour, add balance. Cook until thickened. Remove icing to a bowl to cool at room temperature. Cream together Crisco and butter, add sugar and continue beating in mixer. Combine with milk. Beat until fluffy. Flavor with vanilla and spread on cool cake. This icing should be kept in a cool place for ideal keeping.

****

ED WRIGHT

Ed is by far the best male cook I know. He will invite you to dinner, make a new recipe with everyone watching, and it always turns out great.

TRINIDADIAN-STYLE CHICKEN

AMISE MARINADE:
- 6 cloves garlic, chopped
- ½ C vegetable oil
- 2 shallots, coarsely chopped
- 1 bunch green onion, trimmed & chopped
- 1 bunch fresh flat leaf parsley, leaves & stems coarsely chopped

Place the garlic, shallots, green onions, parsley & vegetable oil in a food processor (blender will work) and puree. Transfer the garlic mixture to a container and set aside.

CHICKEN:
- 1 chicken (~ 3 lbs.) cut into pieces (less back part)
- 1 C sugar
- ¼ C vegetable oil
- ½ white onion, small diced
- 1 green chile, seeded & cut into strips or diced (optional)
- 1 unripe plantain, halved lengthwise & chopped
- 4 plum tomatoes, chopped
- ¼ C Worcestershire sauce
- ½ C chicken stock
- Kosher salt
- 1 C fresh cilantro leaves

After cleaning, cut each piece in the middle all the way to the bone and add to a big bowl. Take half of the Amise Marinade and pour over the chicken. Work marinade into the chicken well and then cover. Put in refrigerator for 3 hours (up to 24 hours).

In a wide based pan, heat the sugar and vegetable oil over medium high heat. Swirl the glaze until the sugar caramelizes and browns, approx. 7-10 minutes. As soon as the sugar caramelizes, add the chicken pieces in one layer, skin down, and brown the chicken on all sides, about 5 minutes.

RECIPE CONTINUES ON NEXT PAGE

TRINIDADIAN-STYLE CHICKEN, Continued

Add the onion, plantain, tomatoes, and Worcestershire sauce to the pan and stir. Pour in the chicken stock and bring the ingredients to a boil. Add the reserved marinade and reduce heat to medium. Cook for 30-40 minutes and season the dish with salt to taste. Turn off the heat.

Transfer the chicken to a serving plate and garnish with cilantro leaves just before serving.

OPTION: Add additional chicken stock to chicken pieces and let sauce be loose. Cook some rice and pour sauce over the rice.

Ed and his Trinadadian Chicken

PICKLED TOPPING

½ C white wine vinegar
¼ C water
½ cinnamon stick
1 shallot, cut into ¼" thick slices

2 jalapeños, seeded & cut into ¼" slices
1 T sugar
Kosher salt

In a small pot, bring the white wine vinegar, water & cinnamon stick to a boil. Add in the shallot, jalapeños & sugar, and then remove the pot from the heat. Adjust the seasoning with salt (if desired) and let the mixture set for 10 minutes.

Discard the cinnamon stick and strain the liquid, reserving the pickled shallots and jalapeños for the Plantain Gratin. (Note: the pickling is so good, the next time I make it I will triple the recipe.)

****

PLANTAIN GRATIN

4 ripe plantains, peeled & halved lengthwise
1 tsp. vegetable oil (see note below)
Kosher salt
1 C grated white cheddar cheese
3 green onions, trimmed & chopped
¼ C fresh cilantro leaves

Preheat the broiler. Place plantains in a baking dish and drizzle them with the vegetable oil (NOTE: I put oil in a cup and brush the oil on each plantain half) and salt to taste. Broil the plantains for 5-7 minutes or until slightly caramelized. Sprinkle the cheese and green onion over the plantains and continue to broil for 3-4 minutes or until the cheese melts.

Transfer the plantains to a serving dish and garnish with the Pickled Topping and fresh cilantro leaves.

SALSA COUSCOUS CHICKEN

3 C hot couscous or rice (cooked as directed on package)
1 T olive or vegetable oil
¼ C coarsely chopped almonds
2 garlic cloves, minced
8 chicken thighs (skinless), also de-bone if you like
1 C Old El Paso Garden Pepper or Thick'n Chunky Salsa
¼ C water
2 T dried currants or raisins
1 tsp. honey
1 ¾ tsp. cumin
½ tsp. cinnamon

While couscous or rice is cooking, heat oil in large skillet over medium-high heat until hot. Add almonds; cook 1-2 minutes or until golden brown. Remove almonds from skillet with slotted spoon; set aside.

Add garlic to skillet; cook and stir 30 seconds. Add chicken; cook 4-5 minutes or until brown, turning once.

In medium bowl, combine salsa and all remaining ingredients; mix well. Add to chicken. Reduce heat to medium; cover and cook, stirring occasionally for 20 minutes or until chicken is fork tender and juices run clear. Stir in almonds. Serve chicken mixture over couscous.

CABBAGE SALAD

1 med. head cabbage
2 sweet onions (red or yellow)
¾ C sugar

Slice onions thin, then shred or chop cabbage. Place in alternate layers in a large bowl (cabbage first the layer of onion – end with cabbage). Pour sugar over top – Do Not Mix. Cover while making sauce.

SAUCE:

1 C vinegar
1 tsp. celery seed
1 tsp. dry mustard
1 T sugar
1 C cooking oil
1 T salt
1 tsp. pepper

Combine all ingredients except oil. Bring to a boil in a small saucepan. Add oil and bring back to a boil. Pour over cabbage & onion immediately – Do Not Mix. Refrigerate overnight. Do Not Mix until ready to serve. Keep refrigerated.

****

M.J. WRIGHT

Ed Wright's sister-in-law and a great game player.

MANDARIN ORANGE DESSERT

For those watching their calories and sugar … this is a delicious tasting dessert that doesn't break the calorie or sugar bank! Enjoy.

2 C low fat crushed vanilla wafers
¼ C light butter, melted
2 cans (15 oz.) sugar free mandarin oranges, reserve the juice
¼ C sugar substitute (Splenda, Truvia)
3 (8 oz.) fat free sour cream
2 pkgs. sugar free instant vanilla pudding
1 fat free whipped topping

Place the vanilla wafers and light butter (stirred) in the bottom of a 9x13 baking pan. I prefer glass. Stir the reserved juice, sugar substitute, sour cream & pudding mix. Fold in oranges. Pour the orange mixture over the vanilla wafers, spreading evenly. Top with whipped topping. Chill for at least 1 hour.

BEVERAGES

This section is one page ... and a little bit of fun from:

The Supper Club Holiday / Party Cooking Class

December 1, 2013

ARGENTINEAN MARGARITA

2 parts Silver Tequila
1 part orange liqueur (Triple Sec, Cointreau, Grand Marnier)
3 parts Simply LimeAid

Shake & pour into glass or pitcher. Upon service, top with splash of Malbec.

SUPPER CLUB BLOODY MARY MIX

1 carton tomato juice
Worcestershire sauce
Horseradish

Salt / pepper
Hot sauce to taste
Fresh juice of 1 lemon & 1 lime

Bloody Mary bar add ins:

SPICES
Celery salt
Garlic salt
Montreal steak seasoning
Crushed red pepper flakes
Old Bay
Wasabi
Cayenne / Chili powder
BBQ / Mesquite

TOPPINGS
Bacon
Salami
Salad shrimp
Pickles
Olives
Giardiniera vegetables
Pepper rings
Lemon / Lime wedges

PEACH BELLINI PUNCH

GARNISH:
Slice lemons, limes, oranges. Place individual on a plate or baking sheet. Sprinkle with sugar substitute. Place in freezer for 3 hours.

PUNCH:
Fill glass or pitcher with ice. Fill the glass or pitcher half full with equal parts Peach Schnapps, Pineapple Juice & Orange Juice. Shake or stir and top with Champagne. Add garnish upon serving.

www.ingramcontent.com/pod-product-compliance
Lightning Source LLC
Chambersburg PA
CBHW082105230426
43671CB00015B/2611